HOW TO **PRUNE**

HOW TO **PRUNE**

techniques and tips for every plant and season

John Cushnie

Kyle Cathie Limited

To Simon, who slowly but surely
is becoming a gardener

First published in Great Britain in 2007 by
Kyle Cathie Limited
122 Arlington Road
London NW1 7HP
general.enquiries@kyle-cathie.com
www.kylecathie.com

ISBN 978-1-85626-738-0

10 9 8 7 6 5 4 3 2 1

Edited by Caroline Taggart
Designed by Isobel Gillan
Copy editor Jane Struthers
Picture research and editorial assistance Vicki Murrell
Index by Sarah Ereira
Production by Sha Huxtable and Alice Holloway

John Cushnie is hereby identified as the author of this work in accordance
with Section 77 of the Copyright, Designs and Patents Act 1988.

A Cataloguing in Publication record for this title is available from
the British Library.

Printed in Singapore through Tien Wah Press

OPPOSITE TITLE PAGE *Loropetalum chinese;* THIS PAGE *Cordyline australis*

Contents

Introduction

Pruning is one of the few aspects of gardening where nature doesn't lend a helping hand, and I suppose that is natural. The jungle landscapes have survived for thousands of years without human interference, but using a machete to beat a path to the patio is not my idea of gardening. A 'wild' garden with flowering meadow and food for wildlife is, perhaps, what nature would like us to have, but even that needs a certain amount of maintenance, including pruning and rejuvenating.

What every good gardener knows – and those new to gardening quickly find out – is that most permanent plants, when left to their own devices, become overgrown, untidy messes that produce less flower and fruit. Most of my gardening friends wouldn't dream of going into the garden without a pair of secateurs and a folding knife. But there is more to pruning than cutting off the odd branch, and neither snipping nor slashing is the answer.

Throughout this book I will remind you that pruning promotes growth. Fortunately, plants differ from humans in that when a limb is removed several more will grow to replace it. This is useful when you are building up a framework of branches on a new shrub or tree but works against the gardener who is trying to curtail the size of a plant.

The other important message to convey is that the correct time to prune often depends on the time of year when the plant flowers. Without that knowledge you may well cut off the very branches that would have justified the plant's existence. In the following chapters all the pruning techniques that are governed by a particular time of year are covered.

Pruning is not a difficult operation. I will dispel the mystery and show you, step by step, the right way to treat your plants. You will have the satisfaction of doing the job well, so the plants and your garden benefit.

◁ *This wisteria has a long-established framework that will carry a thousand flowers.*

▷ *A useful crop of juicy pears from a confined vertical space.*

Why prune?

As I have already pointed out (and will point out a number of times in the following pages), pruning promotes growth. When you want more branches, as in the case of a climbing rose, then pruning will encourage more new flowering shoots to form. But there are other reasons for pruning.

△ *Prune out old stems of euphorbia to leave room for new basal shoots.*

▽ *Prune Cornus alba each spring to ensure strong, new, brightly coloured stems.*

- Very old branches will produce fewer flowers. With a fruiting tree, fewer flowers mean less fruit. Removing any branches that grow towards the centre and shaping the tree to allow maximum light to the crop will result in better quality fruit.

- For plants with attractively coloured bark, annual pruning will ensure a plentiful supply of brightly coloured stems. With willows this applies only to the young bark, while the bark of birch trees improves as the trees age. If the trunk itself is coloured, any unwanted,

low side shoots should be removed when small to avoid leaving scars on the bark. The dogwoods are exceptional for their winter bark colour, which is brightest on the young stems. Prune the plant in spring to encourage new growths, cutting the stems back to within 5–10cm of ground level. The new growths will sprout from the base and by autumn will be all set to provide another winter spectacular.

- The shape of a plant is important. It only takes a single branch growing in the wrong direction to spoil the otherwise elegantly domed head of a mature tree. A compact shrub is so much more attractive than an untidy, straggly, overgrown plant. If you are into bonsai or topiary then much of your life

will be spent shaping and curtailing the growth of the plants, with the help of a pair of secateurs.

- It is crucial that diseased branches, such as those infected with canker, are removed before the spores spread to other parts of the tree or neighbouring plants. Prune the cankered portion by cutting well below the visual damage, then collect and burn the prunings.

- Some large, overgrown shrubs such as rhododendrons and escallonia may be rejuvenated by a severe pruning, leaving only the stumps of the thickest branches. With watering and feeding, new shoots will push out from the remaining parts of the shrub and the plant will have a new lease of life.

△ *Keep the centre of Cercis open, removing thin, spindly shoots.*

△ *Strong new growths arising from the stump of a rejuvenated camellia.*

Equipment

As with all aspects of gardening, always buy the best tools you can afford. Cheap equipment will be in continual need of sharpening, giving it a shorter useful life. An essential part of the kit is a sharpening stone to keep your tools sharp. Use it frequently, and don't use tools for jobs for which they weren't intended.

△ *Clean, sharp secateurs are an essential pruning tool. This bypass type is my preference.*

Those same friends who never go into the garden without a pair of secateurs equally wouldn't dream of using them to cut string, because of its blunting effect. Blunt blades are a nuisance, causing damage to the plant and wasting valuable time.

Check that the tools are comfortable to use and feel good when handled. A knife with a folding blade or blades is an essential piece of pruning equipment. Keep this knife clean and sharp. It is ideal for paring smooth the rough bark edges of wounds made with a saw. If you are buying your first pruning knife, pay as much as you can afford but don't be seduced into splashing out on a fancy wooden, bone or plastic handle. Such a handle is much less important than a straight blade of good quality steel that will be easy to sharpen and will hold its edge.

A useful tip for a small tool, which can easily be lost, is to tie a brightly coloured piece of string or tape to the handle. When you set it down in the garden and forget where you left it the colour will make it easier to find.

Secateurs are the other essential. Buy the most expensive pair that you can afford. Cheap secateurs will let you down. They will break or the blades will be incapable of holding a good edge. There are two types. Those where the cutting blade comes to rest on a steel block are known as anvil secateurs. Those where a thin blade and a thicker one bypass each other in a scissor action are called bypass secateurs. I prefer the latter as there is no risk of a soft stem being bruised, as it can be when flattened against the anvil. To avoid leaving a small stump that could become infected with disease spores you should always cut with the thin blade closest to the bud or main stem.

Loppers are really long-armed secateurs. The handles are either 60–90cm long or are telescopic, allowing you to reach above your head or into the centre of a clump of branches. Usually, loppers have a wider throat between the two blades than secateurs and their long handles provide the necessary leverage when cutting thick branches by hand.

A hand-held saw with a curved blade will help you to tackle larger branches. I dislike those with double-edged blades where the top side can damage nearby stems or branches that you want to retain. The type that folds so the blade edge is secure in a groove in the handle is safe, light and easy to use.

Hand-held hedge clippers, used by an expert, will leave a neat, straight, clipped hedge. You can use hand shears to clip over the soft growth of lavender and the dead flower stems of heather.

Motorised hedge clippers go hand in hand with ear defenders, gloves and safety goggles. All electrically powered cutters should be cabled through a RCD (residual current device), commonly referred to as a circuit breaker. This will instantly shut off the power if you accidentally cut through the electric cable.

This is not a book about tree surgery. While many professional gardeners and quite a few keen amateurs own and use a chainsaw, I would encourage you to employ a qualified, professional tree surgeon to carry out any work involving machinery and tree climbing. Many trees are protected by law and you need to check with your local authority before embarking on anything major.

Hygiene is very important when pruning. Many plants are toxic or have sap that is an irritant. When pruning such plants it is good practice to wear gloves. Clean the blades of your equipment on a daily basis using a disinfectant. Sap left on the cutting blade can result in diseases being transferred from one plant to the freshly made cuts on another. When pruning fruit trees with a lot of canker, clean the blades after pruning each plant, to prevent the disease being passed to an uninfected tree. Before storing hand-held tools, rub the blades and moving parts with an oily rag: a film of oil will protect the steel and prevent it rusting.

▽ *A folding pruning saw works well if you have to deal with a cluster of thick branches.*

Nutrients and pruning

Remember the connection between pruning and growth. In simple terms, the plant's roots draw up water and nutrients to feed the plant, so the roots grow and expand at a rate to supply the leafy top growth. If you suddenly remove a lot of the branches the roots will continue to supply food, resulting in a crop of inferior, weak, spindly shoots usually close to where the branch was cut off.

Pruning less drastically – i.e. removing only a few branches at a time – allows the plant to produce new, sturdy growths that will in time make healthy replacement branches.

The principal nutrients required by plants are nitrogen (N), phosphate (P) and potash (K). Together they are frequently referred to as NPK. Nitrogen encourages fast growth and is useful if you want plants to grow quickly to screen or hide an eyesore, or you want to encourage new growth on an old shrub or conifer that has been recently pruned. Too much nitrogen will encourage thin, weak growths towards the top of the plant. It should be applied early in the summer, as a late application will encourage soft growth that is prone to winter frost damage.

Phosphate helps to establish a good root system that holds the plant firmly in the ground and collects water and food. Where roots have been damaged prior to planting or have been pruned to prepare the plant for transplanting then an application of phosphate will help the plant to produce replacement fibrous roots.

Potash aids the production of flowers and fruit, and when applied in autumn it will firm up growth produced late in the summer to make it more resistant to freezing winter temperatures. With the trend towards warmer summers there is even more risk of a sudden cold spell of weather damaging late growth.

A balanced fertiliser contains all three elements. Smaller quantities of other elements, such as magnesium (Mg) and iron (Fe), are called trace elements. Although they are beneficial to the health and well being of the plant, they are normally already in the soil (particularly heavy clay soils) and available to the plant's roots.

Type of soil will affect the way a plant absorbs nutrients. In sandy, free-draining soils, they will quickly leach down out of reach of the roots. Heavy clay retains nutrients better, but tends to become waterlogged in winter.

△ Pyracantha *'Mohave'* responds well to training as an espalier.

◁ Prunus *'Accolade'*: a balanced fertiliser will result in plentiful growth and flower like this.

Pest and disease control

Plants are prone to damage from pests and diseases. In some cases an attack may be crippling, resulting in the death of the plant. Other troubles only cause short-term marking of foliage or minor stem damage.

△ *Rabbits can cause enormous damage, chewing the bark off a wide range of plants. Serious loss of bark will kill plants such as this hamamelis.*

Prevention is better than cure, so only purchase healthy plants from a reputable nursery, store or garden centre. Examine the whole plant – roots as well as stems and leaves. Avoid plants with dead or damaged roots, dead twigs or discoloured patches of bark.

If discovered early, the infected parts may be pruned off to slow down or stop a pest or disease attack and prevent the problem spreading to other plants. Check your plants regularly by simply wandering around the garden with secateurs and a plastic bag in which to place any infected material you remove. Never compost diseased prunings. Burn the material and use the wood ash as a beneficial potash mulch around other plants.

I have made no attempt to cover the range of pests and diseases that attack plants and have only mentioned those where pruning can help in the battle for survival.

PESTS

There are some pests, such as slugs, snails, cutter bees and leaf miners, that may do a bit of chewing, marking or making holes in the foliage but, apart from disfiguring a few leaves, they do no lasting damage and are not worth losing sleep over.

Other pests, such as the cherry black fly, may be eliminated by pruning. The leaves at the tips of branches of fruiting cherries and the ornamental flowering *Prunus avium* and *P. padus* are attacked in late spring by dense colonies of black aphids. The leaves curl up and by midsummer they will have turned brown and died. Nipping out and burning the affected tips of large ornamental trees is a simple alternative to applying insecticides.

Big-bud mites attack the buds of hazel, blackcurrant and yew, which makes them swell. The buds then fail to open. On blackcurrants the mites cause a virus-reversion disease that affects the yield of fruit. Prune out infected branches in early spring and burn the prunings.

The caterpillars of some moths, and especially the brown-tip moth, can completely defoliate plants such as hawthorn, apples and roses. Colonies of grey-black, hairy caterpillars hide and feed under a dense silken web. Prune out and burn the silk nests in late autumn after leaf-fall. Wear gloves and eye protection as the hairs of the caterpillar can cause a skin rash.

Wildlife can do enormous damage to plants. Squirrels, rabbits, hares and deer all chew bark and, even where small amounts are removed, the plant suffers. Disease spores such as canker enter the wounds, causing additional problems. When the damaged bark completely girdles the trunk, water and nutrients are prevented from moving through the tree and it will die.

Pruning to remove the damaged bark, which leaves a small, smooth wound, may allow the tree to recover, but the best remedy is to prevent attack by fencing off the area or protecting the individual plants with wire mesh.

Birds, especially the finches, love the fat, winter fruit buds of apples and plums. They can significantly reduce the crop yield. Where branches are stripped of buds a spring pruning will encourage more shoots that will produce more buds, but unless you protect the tree with a net the birds will return to continue the destruction.

DISEASES

With many diseases, pruning to remove the affected part is the only method of saving the plant. There is no control for some diseases, such as Dutch elm disease and honey fungus, and the shrub or tree will quickly die. In the case of Dutch elm disease there may soon be new cultivars of elm that are resistant to the beetle that transports the disease. If you have lost a plant to honey fungus

there is no chemical control. It may help to dig a trench 30cm deep around the recently killed plant, throwing the excavated soil to the inside of the trench. Erect a vertical wall of 1000-gauge polythene sheeting in the trench with the top 5cm protruding. Backfill the trench. This may prevent the mycelium of the fungus from spreading. Dig up the plant

▽ *The grey-white dead stems on this acer are caused by dieback. Prune out by cutting back to healthy wood.*

△ *Prune out apple canker as soon as it appears to prevent it spreading to healthy stems.*

with as much root as possible and burn it where it is. Keep the sheeting in the trench to quarantine the infected soil for as long as possible.

The spread of silver leaf disease through plum and cherry trees can be slowed down by removing diseased branches as soon as the disease shows. Cut the infected branch at least 15cm below the point where brown staining of the wound is evident. The disease spores are less active in summer, so prune then and paint the wound with a proprietary sealant to reduce the risk of a further attack through the cut. Occasionally, if action is taken early, the tree will survive.

Cankers, especially those attacking the bark of apple, pear and ash trees, appear as sunken areas of bark, usually discoloured, with the bark cracked and flaking. Where the canker has girdled the branch, cut it off at least 15cm below the diseased area. Where the point of entry of the fungus spore is through a small wound or a bud, and only a small area is affected, then it is worth cutting out that portion and painting the wound with a sealant. Badly affected trees with damage to all the young and older branches may not be worth treating and should be removed by the root to prevent the disease spreading.

Bacterial canker is another killer of plum, cherry and peach trees and is often first noticed as sunken areas of bark that ooze amber-coloured, resin-like gum. Prune as for other cankers.

Fire-blight disease is a killer of hawthorn and pyracantha. The flowers wilt and wither before dying, followed in late summer by the death of the leaves and stems. Pruning may slow down fire-blight's spread through a mature plant but even so you should make the cuts at least 60cm below where the damage shows. Young plants should be removed and burned.

Fungi are also the cause of dieback and black spot diseases. Early pruning to remove the infected stems will reduce the risk but is unlikely to be a complete cure.

Coral spot fungal disease is easily recognised. The dead portions of woody stems are covered in small, raised, bright orange or red pustules. Magnolia, flowering currant and maple are particularly prone to attack. The control is to cut out all dead twigs and branches and burn the prunings.

HEALTH AND SAFETY

If you are doing lots of pruning at the same time then it is essential to dress comfortably in protective clothing that allows you to work easily. Gloves should not be so bulky as to make hand and finger movement clumsy.

Constant bending to prune new roses is murder on the back muscles so use a light and easily transported kneeling stool. Try not to prune above your head for more than a few cuts. Craning to look at high branches may cause shoulder and neck ache.

If you are pruning trees, use a ladder or pruning table and make sure that it is steady and secured to the tree with a rope. Don't be tempted to climb the tree. You may damage the bark or break small branches with your weight. It is difficult to hold yourself in position with only one hand while the other is wielding a saw or secateurs.

Clematis wilt disease gets a bad press. It gets the blame every time a plant withers and dies. In fact, most of the time the wilting is caused by slugs chewing the stem at ground level. Wilt disease is rarely a problem with species clematis, although it does attack *Clematis armandii* and clematis varieties. It is caused by a soil-borne fungus entering through a wound at soil level and preventing the plant from drawing up water. The first sign is the total collapse of the stem or the whole plant. Cut an affected plant back to healthy stems or to below soil level. That may save the plant, allowing new shoots to grow from dormant buds.

Peach leaf curl disease makes a mess of new, young foliage. It distorts and blisters the unfurling leaves, turning them red or purple. Cutting off the infected leaves before spores form will reduce the risk of it spreading. Burn the leaves.

'Witches' brooms' is the imaginative name for the masses of twiggy growths, resembling birds' nests, that appear in trees such as birch. The growths are caused by mites or various fungi. Personally I like to see them but if you feel that they are spoiling the shape of the tree you should cut them out along with the branch on which they are growing.

Mechanical damage, where branches are broken by storms, youthful enthusiasm or the weight of a crop of fruit, should be dealt with as soon as possible by removing the branch back to a main limb or the trunk. The freshly made pruning cut should be left smooth to reduce the risk of fungal disease spores landing on the rough surface and infecting the plant. Use a sharp knife or coarse sandpaper to smooth ragged bark left by a saw cut. Wherever possible, remove heavy falls of snow from plants to prevent similar damage.

Frost or biting, cold winds can kill young soft wood. Prevention is, again, better than cure, so apply potash fertiliser in early autumn to harden up the growth. If the damage is already done, prune in late spring or when all risk of frost is past to remove the affected parts.

Good hygiene is crucial to success when tackling pest and disease problems so always burn rather than shred or compost diseased prunings. Every time you use tools to remove diseased material you must clean them in disinfectant to prevent spreading that disease to healthy plants.

▽ *Early-flowering shrubs such as this magnolia are prone to frost damage on flowers in morning sun. Camellias are also particularly vulnerable. Don't prune the affected parts until all risk of frost has passed; otherwise you will promote weak new growth that may suffer the same fate.*

Pruning basics

As with a child or dog, early training will determine the eventual shape of the plant. Prune to direct new shoots the way you want them to go and provide flowers, berries or fruit year after year. Knowing how your plant grows is essential to choosing the right time and method of pruning.

△ *Deciduous birch will survive in the wild without pruning.*

WHEN TO PRUNE – DECIDUOUS AND EVERGREEN

Trees, conifers and shrubs are either deciduous or evergreen and, because of the difference in the way they grow, the two groups need to be pruned at different times.

Deciduous plants lose their leaves in autumn and become dormant in early winter, with no sap flowing for some months thereafter. That means that if you prune during this time, there is no risk of the plant bleeding through the cut ends of branches.

Birch trees are notorious for losing water if pruned in spring – a wound will drip for days, forming wet puddles on the ground directly below the cut branches. Excessive bleeding of sap in late spring will weaken the tree. In Scotland there has been for centuries a flourishing business for home-brewers making an aromatic wine from the birch sap, but then they do have a lot of birch trees in Scotland. I am informed that after a couple of glasses of the stuff you would be in no fit state to use any sharp implement!

▷ *Apart from removing double leaders that form a narrow angle, there should be no need to prune the evergreen* Ilex aquifolium *'Ferox Argentea'.*

It is, of course, easy to see the framework of a deciduous plant in winter. You can spot branches that are diseased or rubbing together and it is no problem to get close enough to remove them.

Exceptions to this rule are trees of the *Prunus* family, such as plum, damson and fruiting and ornamental cherry. They need to be pruned in summer when in full leaf to avoid fungal diseases. Fortunately by that time the flow of sap is greatly reduced. Summer pruning is also essential for trained fruit trees. The excess growth is removed to retain the shape of the tree and build up the fruiting wood (see page 154–157).

Evergreens retain their leaves and as a result are never dormant. There is less activity in winter but sap continues to flow and plants produce some growth. Pruning is more difficult as the leaf cover makes it harder to choose the right branch and select the position where the cut should be made. With mature evergreen trees and conifers, try to get inside the canopy of the tree so you can see where to make the cuts. It is also very uncomfortable pruning evergreens when it is raining.

▷ *Prune* Hydrangea macrophylla *in spring, removing old stems at ground level. New shoots will appear at the base of the plant.*

▷▷ Sambucus nigra *f.* porphyrophylla *'Guincho Purple' is grown for its dark purple foliage. It responds well to hard pruning, producing lots of new, young growths. Always prune immediately above a side shoot or dormant bud.*

WHEN TO PRUNE – HABIT OF GROWTH

In the introduction I emphasised the importance of timing when it comes to pruning. It is therefore vital to know the plant's habit of growth. Does it produce lots of stems? If so, it may need to be regularly thinned by removing some of the oldest branches from the centre of the plant. Is it quick- or slow-growing, at what time of the year does it flower, and are the flowers produced mainly on the new growths, those one year old or on older wood? Some plants are tolerant of a hard pruning in which some of the oldest branches are removed close to the base. Other shrubs and conifers that have been neglected and are in need of rejuvenation may be severely pruned, leaving stumps that will produce strong new growths.

Plants that produce berries or fruit shouldn't be pruned until the crop is harvested or the display of berries is finished. Once you have this information you will be able to decide how to prune a particular plant. For more information, see the Shrubs section that starts on page 36 and individual entries in the directory that starts on page 174. Among the ornamental garden plants clematis and roses are more complicated than most, so they have special sections of their own (see pages 102–109 and 110–133).

WHAT TO PRUNE

The three Ds – dead, diseased and damaged branches – should always be removed first. Prune out all the unwanted material, cutting back to above a suitable (healthy) bud, side shoot or main branch.

Emergency pruning

1 Accidents happen, and broken branches should be pruned back to undamaged wood…

2 …just above a bud or side shoot.

3 The finished job: a clean cut close to a healthy side shoot.

△ *Shorten side shoots back to a bud that is pointing in the direction in which you want the shoot to grow.*

Always inspect the plant for signs of disease before commencing pruning. It would be a mistake to remove a branch because it is too close to a neighbouring limb only to find that the branch you have chosen to leave has canker and must be removed. If in doubt as to the extent of the spread of a disease such as canker or dieback, cut at least 15cm below where symptoms are apparent.

Where there are lots of small, diseased branches to be removed from fruit trees it is a good idea to lay a sheet of plastic beneath the tree. That way all the diseased cuttings can be collected and burnt. Small pieces of stem that are overlooked and left lying on the ground or in long grass will continue to produce spores and spread the disease to other plants.

▷ *Hornbeam has a hard wood that is seldom infected by disease spores.*

Crossing branches should be the next to go. Try to keep the centre of the plant open to encourage air movement and allow light into the heart of the plant. With some fast-growing shrubs a year's neglect will allow branches to cross from one side of the bush to the other. They may cause congestion in the centre of the plant or cause damage by rubbing against other permanent branches. Usually they can be easily removed before they do much damage. Either remove the entire branch or shorten it back to a side shoot that is heading in the correct direction. With trees it is important that these crossing branches are removed when young before they thicken up; otherwise they will leave large wounds when they are removed.

SHAPING

Always consider the shape of the plant and, before removing or trimming a branch, imagine how it will look after pruning. Unless it is absolutely necessary, such as when you are cutting out a diseased branch, avoid any pruning that will result in gaps or leave the plant looking one-sided or unbalanced.

A basic piece of information that will stand you in good stead while pruning is that a bud will form a shoot growing in the direction in which it is pointing. So if the bud on the stem is pointing outwards, pruning above it will result in the shoot from that bud growing outwards. If you prune above a sideways-pointing bud the shoot will grow towards that side. This can be used to good effect when pruning roses or fruit trees, where you want to create a framework of branches with the centre of the plant free of growth. Prune to buds that are pointing in the direction of any gaps in the framework of branches and avoid cutting above those buds pointing towards the centre of the bush.

It is worth remembering that the bud which is highest up (the one furthest from the roots of the plant) will produce the strongest and most vigorous shoot. The lower down the stem the bud is positioned, the weaker the shoot will be.

WOUNDING

A wound is a wound and, as in our bodies, disease may just as easily enter a small cut as one where a large branch has been removed. Wounds are the inevitable result of pruning, so it is important to minimise the amount of damage you inflict on a plant when cutting it back.

Avoid making pruning cuts to young shoots during periods of severe cold. The sap flowing from the cut might freeze and shatter the end of the shoot. Some plants, such as birch trees and vines, 'bleed' profusely in spring when the sap is rising and should therefore be pruned in late winter, before they burst into life.

Always make a clean cut using well-sharpened equipment. Blunt tools will result in torn bark or wounds with ragged edges. If using a saw, smooth the surface of the wound and the rim of the bark with a sharp knife or coarse-grade sandpaper. This will speed up the healing

process, with a callus quickly covering the cut to reduce the risk of disease spores of coral spot or dieback becoming attached to the cut surface (see page 16). Slope the cut to allow water to run off. If the cut is above a bud, slope it away from the bud rather than towards it.

If you leave a long piece of stem above a bud it will die and may become infected with a fungal disease. Cutting exactly level with the bud may cause it to dry out or the pruning implement might damage it. Ideally, you should make the sloping cut 2–3 mm above the bud.

Most young branches will have visible buds appearing as small bumps on the side of the stem. Old wood will have dormant buds that are not noticeable. Cutting large branches to a suitable height for rejuvenation will, with many shrubs, trigger the dormant buds to produce shoots. Once the shoots appear the stump should be shortened back with a sloping cut to just above where the new growths appear. If the stump is left it may die back, with the loss of the newly acquired shoots.

Young branches up to 2.5cm thick can be cut using a pair of sturdy secateurs. A knife blade may be used to remove stems thinner than pencil thickness and to smooth the surface of larger wounds. The folding saw and extension loppers are invaluable for thicker branches and when cuts have to be made close to the base of the plant where the branches are congested. The smaller the wound, the quicker it will be healed over by a callus.

Making the cut

Knowing how and where to cut is crucial to ensuring that the pruned plant grows in the direction you want. Even when pruning out diseased stems (left) you need to make the cut the right way.

1 **Wrong**. The cut is too high above the bud, encouraging disease to enter the stump.

2 **Wrong**. The sloping cut is in the direction of the bud.

3 **Wrong**. The cut is too close to the bud.

4 **Right**. The cut is above the bud, sloping away from it.

REMOVING LARGE BRANCHES

When removing large main or side branches of trees or shrubs you should make the cut just above a healthy, lower side branch that is growing in the required direction. With the cut in this position the plant will produce lots of growth cells to seal the wound quickly. If you leave stumps that refuse to produce new growths they will decay and might become diseased.

Great care must be taken when removing large side branches. Simply sawing through the branch will allow it to drop before the cut is finished. As it falls, the cut end will tear away from the trunk, leaving a large bark wound.

To prevent this happening, make the first cut anywhere along the stem but at least 60cm beyond the side shoot or main branch where the finished cut will be made. Removing that portion of the unwanted branch will reduce the weight, leaving a small, light length of branch to be pruned. Clear the debris from the area to give yourself a comfortable working space for the final, all-important cut.

Now examine the branch where it comes away from the main trunk. There will probably be a collar visible where the bark is slightly ridged on the upper side of the branch with a raised collar on the underside, usually at an angle to the vertical trunk. Make the cut on the branch in a line that joins the upper ridge and the lower collar.

If you can saw with one hand while supporting the shortened branch with the other hand, you will stop it tearing down the bark where it joins the main branch or trunk. Alternatively, another person can support the branch stump while the final cut is made. Smooth the wound with a sharp knife, removing any ragged edges to the bark.

NARROW-ANGLED FORKS

With many trees such as birch, maple and beech, a narrow angle between two branches is an accident waiting to happen. It can occur at any time but often happens in the early stages of a tree's life, when two stems vie to become the leader. If both are allowed to grow then there will be a weakness where they come together, due to the double layer of bark that grows in the small space between them. Unlike timber, a mass of bark has no strength. High winds or a storm will cause one of the branches to split away, spoiling the head of the tree and possibly causing serious damage where it falls.

Check young plants for these forks. Where there are two main branches or trunks, select the weaker or the one growing at a slight angle from the vertical and remove it, using secateurs, close to the base of the remaining branch and without damaging it. Where the two branches are thin and the angle is very narrow, leave 2cm of stump until the remaining branch thickens. You can then cut back the stump flush with the tree.

If the remaining leader is at an angle, use a bamboo cane to support the stem and train it to grow in an upright direction.

Pruning out a narrow angle

Early removal of the weaker of two branches that form a narrow angle will improve the shape of the tree and eliminate a potential weakness in the structure.

1 A narrow angle formed between closely spaced branches.

2 Where to cut.

3 The weakest limb removed.

4 A neat, flush cut.

5 Paring the cut surface with a sharp knife to leave a smooth surface makes it difficult for disease spores to survive.

RING-BARKING

Ring-barking is a peculiar form of pruning in which a strip of bark is removed to slow down the flow of water and nutrients to the head of the plant. This will reduce the vigour of the plant and is a particularly useful method of keeping a tree within bounds in a small garden. Reducing excess vigour in trees such as apples and pears will also encourage flowers and fruit to form.

Using a sharp knife, carefully remove a strip of bark 5mm wide in a band halfway round the main trunk 30–45cm above ground level. Remove an identical band on the opposite side of the trunk halfway round and at least 5–7cm higher up. The sap has to flow through the gaps between the half-rings, which reduces its volume and slows it down. Do not make a continuous band around the trunk or the sap will be cut off altogether and the tree will die. Other forms of bark removal will help to shape a young tree. See nicking and notching on pages 150–153.

◁◁◁ *Regular pruning of crab apples (see pages 134–157) will result in a profusion of flowers and apples.*

◁◁ *Ring-barking an apple or pear tree will reduce growth and encourage flower and fruit.*

◁ *Making two half rings will allow some water and nutrients to rise from the roots.*

Nipping, snipping and pulling

Some plants, such as herbaceous perennials, die down in the winter, so pruning is a simple operation of removing, by cutting or pulling off, all the dead stems at ground level. You can do this in early winter to tidy the bed; alternatively, you can leave attractive, dead seed heads and leaves to cheer up the garden until early spring. If you do not remove them at that stage, however, the new growths will be forced to compete with them for space and there is more risk of fungal disease.

△ and ▷▷ Pinching out a chrysanthemum is an important job but one of the easiest ways of pruning, with no equipment needed! The result will be a profusion of glorious flowers like the one shown opposite.

As I said earlier, most gardeners never head out into the garden without a knife and a pair of secateurs. You may intend to dig a drain, scarify the lawn or even relax with a cup of coffee but you will always see some plant that will benefit from pruning.

▷ With dahlias, remove only the growing tip.

I put this operation under the heading of fussy pruning — the totally unnecessary action of removing little pieces of plants. Perhaps the end of a leaf is ragged or has been chewed by a kamikaze pest, a tiny twig is broken or the tip of a shoot is a few centimetres higher than its neighbours. They all have to be snipped off. This sort of pruning is harmless and may well be therapeutic for the gardener if not the plant. However, there are other small bits of pruning that are essential to the continued good growth of plants.

Using your fingers to nip or pinch out the growing tip of a shoot will encourage it to produce side shoots. The soft, young growth of chrysanthemums can be removed by pinching the tip with your fingernails. On plants where you don't want side shoots, like tomatoes, rub them out when they are still small. If they are missed and become larger than 7–10cm in length, you must snap them off at the axil where the leaf stalk joins the stem.

Disbudding is carried out on dahlias and chrysanthemums by reducing the number of buds on each stem. When the tiny buds are only a few millimetres in diameter, you carefully rub them out with your finger. All the plant's energy is then concentrated in the remaining buds, thus increasing the size of the flowers. When visiting flower shows it is a common sight to see individual flowers on display that are bigger than dinner plates.

Deadheading is the term used to describe the removal of the spent flower before all of the plant's energy is devoted to producing seed. Deadheading will speed up the appearance of the next flush of flowers. With some plants, such as sweet peas, leaving old flowers to become seed pods will dramatically slow down the plant's flower production until eventually it ceases completely.

△ *Deadheading: remove lily flowers before they set seed.*

▷ *Fading sweet peas should also be removed before they set seed. Producing seed pods diverts the plant's energy away from the important business of flowering again and again.*

Most pruning of herbaceous perennials comes under the umbrella of deadheading. With many plants, such as delphiniums and lupins, removing the old flower stalk will encourage side shoots to flower later in the season. It is possible to have too much of a good thing, so deadheading will prevent thousands of seedling mullein (*Verbascum*) or foxglove (*Digitalis*) becoming weeds in the garden.

Removing the dead flowers from bush roses improves the look of the plants, although some shrub roses have such fantastic rosehips that I allow them to remain. If you want to try this effect in your garden, I recommend *Rosa moyesii* 'Geranium', whose cherry-red flowers are followed by beautiful orange-red, flagon-shaped hips. The 'old rose' *R. rugosa* makes a superb hedge with carmine-red flowers and tomato-shaped, orange or orange-red hips.

When deadheading use a pair of secateurs, cutting the flower stem 3 or 4 leaves below the old flower. This will encourage new flowering shoots to appear further down the stem.

Reversion is a curse of variegated cultivars. For no reason that we can explain, nature will sometimes allow a plant to produce a completely different leaf, such as a variegation – gold or silver leaf margins or splashes of colour on green leaves. This variation from the norm is known as a sport, and if removed and propagated it can produce very attractive plants. However, the fact that it was able to become a sport means that, if left to herself, nature will let the sport revert to the original (usually all-green) plant. This is different from plants growing in deep shade where the lack of sunlight produces pale or yellow leaves.

While the reverted growths won't kill the plant, the green leaves will produce more chlorophyll and plant food, allowing them to grow strongly at the expense of the variegation. Eventually this excess growth will smother the plant you originally planted.

Assuming this is not what you want, prune out green shoots as soon as they appear. To prevent them growing back, cut them off as close to the main stem as possible, removing the shoot without leaving a stump. I love the evergreen shrub *Elaeagnus pungens* 'Maculata', whose leaves are supposed to be deep yellow with a glossy dark green border, but it is the bane of my gardening life.

Parts of the plant continually revert to produce stems with all-green leaves, which I then remove. The trouble is that they keep appearing and life is too short to spend my time snipping. Invariably the plant loses the variegation and I have yet another lovely, large, all-green elaeagnus, so I plant another *E. pungens* 'Maculata'.

The same problem occurs with plants such as *Fagus* var. *heterophylla* 'Aspleniifolia', grown for their ferny foliage or deeply cut leaves. Keep a careful watch for branches with plain leaves and prune out all the reverted growth. If reverted branches appear high up on a tree, use extension pruners to remove them.

△ *This variegated holly* Ilex × altaclerensis *'Lawsoniana' is a variegated 'sport' of the all-green* Ilex × altaclerensis *'Hendersonii'. Left to grow, this reverted shoot will be more vigorous than the sport and gradually become dominant.*

▷ *and* ▷▷ *Whole branches of* Elaeagnus pungens *'Maculata' are prone to reverting to all-green leaves (right). Remove as soon as they are seen to allow the less vigorous variegated shoots to regrow (opposite).*

Pruning shrubs

Most popular garden shrubs are dealt with individually in the plant directory which begins on page 174, but it is worth pointing out that many of them, including magnolia, exochorda and pieris, may never need to be pruned once they are planted out in the garden – unless they have been planted in the wrong position or have outgrown their allotted space.

△ *Remove dead flower stems of lavenders such as this* Lavandula angustifolia *in autumn.*

Where neither edible nor attractive fruit, berries or seed heads follow the flowers, deadheading to remove the old flowers will leave the plant looking tidy. Long shoots that are spoiling the overall shape of the plant may be shortened back in spring to the same length as the majority. And that is pretty much all you will ever need to do – these are low-maintenance shrubs that are a real boon when gardening time is precious.

Other shrubs will deteriorate quickly if they are not pruned at least once a year. Given some simple pruning, some short-lived shrubs such as lavender and cistus that tend to build up woody stems will continue to produce flowers for a few years longer than expected. In spring or after flowering (see individual entries in the directory) shorten all the one-year-old shoots back to within 2–4cm of the old hard wood. The older wood will not produce new shoots, so the new growths have to come from the younger stumps.

With some other shrubs the older wood will continue to send out new shoots, and plants such as dogwood (*Cornus*) can be cut back hard in spring, leaving stumps with two buds.

With many deciduous shrubs the best approach is to completely remove a few of the oldest branches at the base each year in late spring. Strong, new, flowering shoots are then produced from ground level rather than from halfway up the old branches and the clutter of congested branches is thinned out. Where lots of new shoots appear at the base of a shrub, it will be necessary to thin out the weakest and those growing into the centre of the bush.

If you have shrubs with low-hanging branches close to the ground, don't rush to remove these. Many of the most popular garden shrubs – including rhododendron, magnolia, hamamelis and camellia – can be propagated by layering the shoots where they touch the soil. Some, such as dogwood, will root everywhere a branch rests on the ground and, if not thinned out, will become a thicket of branches.

Pruning a hardy fuchsia

1 Hardy outdoor fuchsias tend to become leggy, with bare stems.

2 Fuchsias benefit from the removal of the oldest branches close to soil level.

3 The finished job. The new growths will reach 1m and will flower by summer.

Spring pruning bold, vigorous shrubs

Some shrubs that flower in summer on this year's growth are pruned in spring, before the new growth really gets started. Many of them make enormous amounts of growth in the few weeks between pruning and flowering.

1 *Buddleja davidii* is one shrub that easily gets out of control. It flowers on the current growth, so prune in spring...

2 ... cutting all the previous year's growth back to within 5cm of the old wood

3 It will soon recover with 2m-long flowering shoots.

Spring pruning bushy shrubs

The technique here is similar to that for buddleias, but it is used for smaller plants that require gentler handling and less powerful tools. *Hydrangea paniculata* is interesting in that it is treated differently from other hydrangeas (see directory).

1 *Hydrangea paniculata* flowers on growth made in spring and early summer.

2 In late spring shorten the previous year's growth to within 2–5cm of the older wood.

Pruning to produce a spur system

Pruning bougainvillea is a bit like pruning a fruit tree, only in this case you are aiming to produce a spur system that will promote flowering without fruit.

1 Thin out weak and spindly shoots in early spring, either before or just as growth commences.

2 Cut all the laterals back to 3 or 4 buds to produce flowering spurs.

3 Prune established plants by shortening the long growths by three quarters of their length. Prune badly placed shoots to within 3 or 4 buds of the main framework.

Pruning after flowering

With spring-flowering shrubs such as forsythia, which produce most of their flowers on the young growths made the previous summer or autumn, pruning should be carried out after flowering. Prune the stems that flowered, cutting each one immediately above a strong side shoot or healthy bud.

1 A forsythia in spring, ready to be pruned after flowering.

2 Cut out the oldest stems close to ground level.

3 Once the old flowering stems have been removed, young growths are produced at the base of the plant.

4 The younger shoots shown here, which also produced flowers, have been pruned back to strong side shoots.

Late-spring pruning

Some imported shrubs survive in climates less favourable than that of their native country. At one time I had a collection of over 70 species and varieties of hebe enjoying life in Northern Ireland. Then we had a prolonged period of late frost and most of them were wiped out. That's gardening for you.

1 The secret of success tender shrubs such as hebe is to leave pruning until late spring when all risk of frost is over. Pruning encourages new shoots to grow, and these are the most prone to frost damage. This plant has a mass of shoots that need to be pruned back.

2 Shorten the previous year's growth to strong side shoots. At the same time, cut back any damaged growths to healthy side shoots or buds.

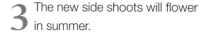

3 The new side shoots will flower in summer.

Summer pruning

Some shrubs such as weigela that flower in summer and early autumn on stems produced that year should be pruned when flowering is finished. If you live in an area that is prone to late spring frosts, you can delay pruning until spring. Pruning in late winter encourages early growths that may be damaged by frosts.

1 Prune weigela immediately after flowering has finished.

2 Remove the flowering branches back to a strong side shoot. Cut old branches as close to the base as possible.

3 These older stems can then be shredded and used as a mulch.

Hard pruning

A large number of shrubs, including escallonia (shown here), rhododendrons and laurels, can withstand severe pruning. Big, old, overgrown plants with all their growth and flowers at the top of the plant and out of sight above your head can be rejuvenated by cutting all the main branches to knee height.

△ *Escallonia rubra 'Crimson Spire' will flower into autumn but essential pruning should be carried out earlier in the season.*

Do this work over a two- or three-year period by removing one third of the oldest branches from different areas of the plant in late winter or early spring each year. Make a sloping cut without trying to find a bud. Dormant buds will produce shoots directly from the trunk. With tender, loving care, including watering and feeding, the shrubs will make a full recovery, producing strong, new growths from the base of the cut branches.

1 A large, overgrown escallonia shrub with any flowers appearing at the tips of the branches.

2 Escallonia is tolerant of hard pruning and all these bare branches may be cut to leave stumps.

3 For thicker stems, a pruning saw is the answer.

4 These stumps will soon produce strong new growths but will benefit in summer from regular watering and high-potash liquid feeds.

5 By early summer the strong new shoots are beginning to emerge.

Climbing shrubs

Where shrubs and climbers are grown as wall plants it may be necessary to curtail their growth to keep them within their allocated space. Vigorous plants such as wisteria may require annual pruning after flowering is finished or when the berries have fallen or been eaten by birds.

△ Wisteria needs to be pruned regularly to prevent it covering a building.

Old, bare or non-flowering stems need to be cut out at ground level to reduce congestion and encourage strong new shoots from the base of the plant. Where the stems of climbers are a tangled mass then prune them to thin out the congested mass, leaving the leaves to wither. At that stage the cut stem can be clearly identified and cut into sections that can be removed piece by piece.

Other wall-trained plants may need to be pruned to within 2–4 buds of the permanent framework of branches. All the side shoots produced during the summer should be shortened in late winter or early spring each year. This treatment encourages the plant to build up a spur system of flower buds close to the main stems, which is where you want them to be.

1 Shorten new growth in winter to encourage spurs.

2 The spurs will flower the following year on fat flower buds. Prune the lower branches to encourage growth that will keep the plant's 'legs' covered.

3 In summer, shorten side shoots to 3 or 4 leaves.

4 The result is lots of flowers low down on the plant, hiding bare branches.

Hedges

A hedge is simply a collection of plants that are planted sufficiently close together to form a solid line. They can all be the same cultivar or different plants that are compatible. Not every plant makes a good hedge. In a mixed planting they must all tolerate the same degree of pruning.

△ *A well-clipped hedge like this traditional box specimen is a work of art.*

▷ *Yew is slow growing and evergreen, so purchase and plant yew hedging plants as early in the spring as possible.*

Deciduous trees, such as rowan and crab apple, are less tolerant of regular clipping than hawthorn and beech, so mixing rowan and beech, for example, is not a good idea. The plants also have to grow together in a satisfactory manner while in close competition with neighbouring plants for nutrients and water. Either select those species that are tried and tested and visible in the local hedgerows or include an occasional new species to see how it performs when pruned.

Hedge pruning starts immediately after the hedge has been planted. Bare-rooted plants will settle more quickly if you shorten the stems back by one third or half their height. This will encourage side shoots to form, thickening the plants at the base and reducing the likelihood of unsightly bare stems. Don't cut the main stem (leader) of large-leafed evergreens until the plants reach the desired hedge height. Shorten side shoots in early summer to thicken the plant.

SIX PLANTS FOR FORMAL HEDGES

These are the urban hedges that visitors to England fall in love with – perfectly clipped with not a leaf out of place. A formal hedge requires regular clipping throughout the growing season to achieve a neat and tidy appearance.

Broadleaf **(Griselinia littoralis)** Am evergreen with glossy, bright apple-green or variegated leaves and inconspicuous, greenish-yellow flowers in spring. New growths are prone to frost damage in cold areas.

Beech **(Fagus sylvatica)** A deciduous tree with glossy, dark green leaves. When grown as a hedge it retains its mid-brown, dead leaves throughout winter.

Hornbeam **(Carpinus betulus)** A compact tree with mid-green leaves turning orange in autumn, and greenish-yellow female catkins in spring.

Laurel **(Prunus laurocerasus)** An evergreen shrub with long, glossy, dark green leaves, paler on the underside. Upright racemes of fragrant, white flowers in spring.

Privet **(Ligustrum ovalifolium)** An evergreen or semi-evergreen shrub with dark green leaves and panicles of white flowers in summer.

Yew **(Taxus baccata)** An evergreen conifer with small, linear, dark green leaves. Inconspicuous male, yellow cones in spring.

FOUR PLANTS FOR DECIDUOUS HEDGES

To maintain their shape, deciduous hedges should be pruned in winter or early spring during the plants' dormant period. Where necessary, you can give the hedge a further tidy-up by clipping it during the summer.

Blackthorn (Prunus spinosa) A spiny, bushy shrub with deep green leaves and single white flowers in late winter or early spring.

Hawthorn (Crataegus monogyna) A thorny shrub or small tree with glossy, dark green leaves which are pale green on the underside. Clusters of fragrant, white flowers with pink anthers are produced in late spring and early summer.

Shadbush (Amelanchier canadensis) A compact shrub or small tree with mid-green leaves which turn yellow, orange and red in autumn. The arching racemes of small, white flowers appear in early spring.

Spindle (Euonymus alatus) A bushy shrub with corky, winged, four-angled stems and dark green leaves that turn bright red in autumn. The small, insignificant, green or white flowers appear in spring.

FIELD HEDGE

Field hedges can consist of as many as 12–15 different plants, some of which (such as ivy and bramble) have arrived without permission.

In rural areas where the garden borders a field it is desirable to 'fit in' with an existing mixed hedge, but under no circumstances allow a local, friendly farmer to cut your hedge on your behalf. His idea of hedge cutting and mine (and hopefully yours) would differ. Most farmers' hedges are given a short back and sides using a tractor flail on a long arm. The shoots, stems and branches are smashed rather than cut. The operation makes a mess of the hedge, with the operator seemingly determined to teach it a lesson rather than shape it.

With more personal control over the pruning equipment you can avoid cutting the wild rose until after it flowers and the birds will benefit from the hips. You can prune the wild honeysuckle in late winter, cutting out the oldest, twining stems close to the base. If they are a tangled mass of growth, simply cut and leave the stems to die in the hedge. Other gems such as spindle, holly, gorse and Guelder rose can be encouraged while the hawthorn is kept neat and tidy. Even brambles, although a weed in the garden, have a place in the field hedge. You can prune them separately in late autumn after the bramble jelly has been made.

FORMAL HEDGE

Hedges with large leaves, such as laurel (*Prunus laurocerasus*), benefit from clipping with secateurs. This is a boring job if you are dealing with a long length of hedge, but it is a lot more satisfactory than ripping, shredding and slicing the long, glossy, green leaves, leaving some to turn brown and die while they are still hanging in the hedge.

In cold areas that are subject to frost, evergreen conifer hedges should not be

▷ Lay down a sheet to make it easy to collect prunings.

Bareroot hedges

1 A newly planted mixed hedge with deciduous and evergreen species.

2 Shorten the growths by one third to one half to encourage side shoots. This makes the plants bushy, with no gaps at the base.

pruned during autumn and winter as the short back and sides allows the cold to penetrate to the normally protected centre of the tree, causing parts of the hedge to become bare with dead branches. Thuja, cypress and yew are excellent for dense, closely clipped, evergreen hedges.

Lay a sheet at the base of the hedge before starting to cut. The clippings can then be easily collected for composting or shredding.

SHAPING A HEDGE

This process starts in the second year after planting and continues throughout the hedge's life. Unfortunately, most gardeners who regularly prune their hedges clip them to form a box shape with vertical sides and cut them straight across at the top. This is not the ideal shape, particularly if you live in a cold area. Heavy falls of snow will lie on and weigh down the hedge, breaking branches and

FIVE PLANTS FOR EVERGREEN HEDGES

Evergreens are pruned in spring just before they are starting to come into growth. Spring-flowering shrubs grown as a hedge are clipped after flowering.

Berberis x stenophylla A strong-growing shrub with arching branches and spiny, dark green, linear leaves. The small racemes of deep yellow flowers appear in late spring.

Box (Buxus sempervirens 'Handsworthiensis') A vigorous, dense shrub with an upright habit of growth and masses of glossy, dark green leaves that are larger than the traditional box leaf.

Elaeagnus pungens 'Maculata' A dense shrub with occasionally some spines on the stems. The glossy, dark green leaves are splashed dark yellow in the centre. Pendant, silvery-white flowers are produced in autumn.

Holly (Ilex aquifolium 'JC Van Tol') A dense, bushy shrub or small tree with glossy, dark green leaves. It is lightly spiny on the lower leaves and without spines on the upper leaves. The small, female flowers are white, appearing in spring and early summer.

Kohuhu (Pittosporum tenuifolium) Bushy shrub or small tree with wavy-margined, glossy, mid-green leaves and small, honey-scented, deep red-black, bell-shaped flowers in late spring and early summer.

forcing it out of shape. As the hedge becomes taller and wider, a flat top is more difficult to reach across to cut.

Light is important for good growth and maximum leaf-cover at the base of the hedge. To this end, a hedge with sloping sides tapering towards the top allows light to penetrate to the sides and has the advantage of making it easier to cut the top of a wide hedge. Never shape a hedge with the sides sloping in towards the base. If you do, the resulting lack of light will cause leaf-drop and bare patches lower down, close to the ground.

Make a frame to help you shape a hedge with sloping sides. Make two identical timber A-frames using roofing laths or two lengths of 5 × 3cm timber screwed together at the top and secured

◁ *A mature hedge that has been badly cut. The base of the hedge is shaded, causing it to lose its leaves.*

with a cross-bar close to the base. Set one at either end of the hedge and between them run horizontal strings 30cm apart along both sides. For long lengths, set another A-frame without the cross bar in the middle of the length of hedge. Trim the plants back to the cords.

The shape and size of the hedge is important. It has to serve the purpose it was designed for, whether that is privacy, shelter or screening. However, the taller it becomes the more difficult it is to manage. A hedge that can be cut while standing on the ground takes considerably less time and effort than when steps, a ladder or scaffolding is required. High hedges that are very wide are a nightmare when cutting across the top, requiring tools with extension arms.

Make sure that any staging is secure, and if you are using steps have someone on the ground holding them steady. Where the ground is soft, stand the legs on planks of timber to prevent them sinking and making the support unstable.

A pair of hedge clippers rather than powered clippers is the safest tool to use when you are off the ground. With electrically powered clippers, make sure that the lead is attached to and over your shoulder. Use a belt or looped cord to keep it in place. That way there is less chance of you cutting through it. Always fit a circuit breaker, sold as a residual current device or RCD.

▷ *A well pruned* Lonicera *hedge sloping in towards the top to allow daylight to reach all parts.*

Pruning a yew hedge

1 Yew hedges are tolerant of severe pruning and will re-grow from the bare branches and stumps.

2 Where the branches are too thick for secateurs they may be cut by a saw or long-armed loppers.

3 It is fairly safe to prune yew hedges hard but some tender, loving care will be of benefit afterwards.

4 A yew hedge, before and after splitting to reduce the width.

5 One year on after splitting one side of the yew hedge. The bare side is covering over nicely.

INFORMAL FLOWERING HEDGES

These are becoming more popular as perimeter hedges. They are excellent in an urban situation but they can, when in full flower, look garish in a rural setting. The two evergreen shrubs that are most often used are varieties of white-, pink-, cerise- and red-flowering escallonia, and berberis, especially *Berberis darwinii* (dark orange flowers) and *B.* × *stenophylla* (deep yellow flowers).

Of the deciduous flowering shrubs, *Forsythia* × *intermedia* 'Spectabilis' would be my favourite for hedging. Irrespective of weather conditions, it produces its bright yellow flowers early in the season and makes a dense hedge. For sheltered gardens I love the almost hardy *Fuchsia magellanica* with its summer and autumn flowers and orange-brown, peeling bark.

In a year when there has been good growth, a flowering hedge can start to look untidy by late summer. If necessary, trim it lightly, though the neatness will be at the expense of some of next year's flowers.

Many of the flowering shrubs used for hedging can be renovated by pruning hard and leaving the stumps to re-sprout. Check the pruning details for individual plants in the plant directory section.

FIVE SHRUBS FOR FLOWERING HEDGES

Hedges that are grown for their flowers are seldom formally clipped. They are kept tidy with secateurs and are pruned after the main flowering period is over.

Camellia A bushy, evergreen shrub with glossy, dark green leaves, paler green on the underside, and white, pink or red, single or double flowers in autumn or late winter and spring.

Escallonia 'Iveyi' An evergreen shrub with glossy, dark green leaves and panicles of small, white, fragrant flowers in mid-to-late summer.

Forsythia A deciduous shrub with mid-to-dark green leaves and bright yellow flowers in early spring usually before the leaves appear.

Gorse, whin (Ulex europaeus 'Flore Pleno') An evergreen shrub with spine-tipped shoots and spine-like leaves. The solitary, bright yellow flowers are fragrant, appearing at any time of the year but especially in spring.

Ramanas rose (Rosa rugosa) A deciduous shrub rose with spiny stems and leathery, wrinkled, dark green leaves. The single, carmine-red or red-purple flowers have prominent yellow stamens, are single and fragrant, and appear in summer and early autumn.

REJUVENATING OLD HEDGES

Some species of old, neglected hedges can be renovated by pruning hard and leaving the stumps to re-grow. Deciduous hawthorn, blackthorn and beech respond well to severe pruning in winter or early spring, producing new growth that year from the cut stumps. The evergreen conifer yew, even as an old plant, will re-grow after being cut down to 60–90cm stumps. If the width of a yew hedge has to be reduced you should do the work over two years, cutting one side each year in late spring or early summer, to avoid checking its growth completely.

With other conifers, including the ubiquitous Leyland cypress (× *Cupresso-cyparis leylandii*), it is important that only the outer 'shell' of green foliage is trimmed. This is needed to stop the hedge from spreading out sideways, but cutting into old wood and removing all of the green growth will result in bare patches, with most of the older wood refusing to produce new growths.

After severely pruning an old shrub you want the plant to respond by producing new growth. It will help if you feed it with a balanced fertiliser and keep the ground in the root area moist.

▽ *Remove the oldest branches of* Fuchsia magellanica, *cutting them as close to the ground as possible.*

Topiary

Topiary has been popular since Roman times. There is a certain appeal in pruning a plant to a particular shape and then maintaining that shape through regular clipping. The art, if art it is, used to be the domain of the gardener as opposed to the owner of the garden. Times have changed; few of us employ gardeners and now everyone who feels the urge can get out there and create an interesting, living, sculptured shape.

△ Yew is an obedient plant, ideal for topiary. Insert four canes of equal length into the ground the same distance apart and secure the four tips directly above the centre of the plant to make a perfect pyramid. With hand clippers or shears clip in line with the canes from the top down each side. The result will be a neatly trimmed pyramid-shaped tree.

▷ More commonly seen in formal hedges, privet adapts itself well to more frivolous shapes such as this ballerina.

It only looks easy. A lot of patience and free time is required and you need to have a fairly philosophical outlook in case you give your peacock a snip too many and turn it into a one-legged chicken or your eagle has its wings clipped in more ways than one.

Some plants are more suitable than others for topiary (see box overleaf). The plant has to be totally hardy as a severe late frost can destroy years of dedicated work. It also has to be slow-growing, naturally compact and bushy with small, preferably evergreen, leaves. And it has to be tolerant of repeated pruning and capable of producing new shoots from the older wood. Large-leafed shrubs such as laurel are unsatisfactory for topiary as the partially cut leaves look untidy.

As with other fashions, plant shapes seem to come and go. At present, smaller pieces of topiary are selling like hot cakes in the garden centres. A matching pair of balled or pyramidal holly or box plants makes a wonderful statement on either side of the front entrance. Balled bay trees formed on top of a 60–100cm bare stem are popular, as are spirals of golden conifers. Fully shaped animals are criminally expensive, making it well worth the effort of growing and shaping your own.

SHAPING YOUR OWN

The aim is to form a shape that is in keeping with its surroundings and is pleasing when viewed from every angle. It has to be said that big, bold, free-standing shapes are simpler to achieve than smaller, intricate ones where it is so easy to get the balance wrong. If you are trying to create animals and birds the details and proportions are important. If the swan's neck is too short, wait another year until the shoots grow to the right length or cut your losses and change the topiary into a duck.

It is important to start with a healthy, well-rooted plant with a balanced head of branches. In the early stages it is only

IDEAL TOPIARY PLANTS

Common box (Buxus sempervirens) has small, glossy, green leaves and grows to 4–5m. The dwarf cultivar *B. sempervirens* 'Suffruticosa' grows slowly to a height of no more than 1m. *B. sempervirens* 'Marginata' has yellow-margined, dark green leaves and grows to 2–3m. The small-leafed box (*B. microphylla*) forms a dense, rounded, evergreen shrub with small, dark green leaves that turn bronze in winter. It will grow slowly to 75–90cm.

Lonicera nitida forms a bushy, evergreen shrub with small, glossy, dark green leaves and pairs of tubular, creamy-white flowers in spring. It will grow to 3–4m in height. As a mature plant the branches tend to arch downwards. *L. nitida* 'Baggesen's Gold' is similar with bright, golden-yellow leaves that remain yellow-green towards the centre of the plant. It is vigorous, growing rapidly to a height of 1.5m.

English yew (Taxus baccata) is an evergreen conifer with small, linear, dark or light green leaves that are paler green on the underside. It will slowly grow to 10–15m in height with a spread of 8–10m. This was and still is the preferred choice for large, specimen topiary plants. With yew there is the opportunity to select a cultivar where the natural shape lends itself to what you have in mind. The Irish yew (*T. baccata* 'Fastigiata') is columnar and ideal for clipping into an obelisk. *T. × media* 'Brownii' is naturally spherical with a dense mass of shoots. It is easily converted into a ball or sphere up to 2m in diameter.

Privet (Ligustrum ovalifolium) is evergreen (except in cold, exposed areas) with rich, bright green leaves 5cm long. *L. ovalifolium* 'Aureum' has green leaves with bright yellow margins. The cultivar *L. ovalifolium* 'Argenteum' is similar but has creamy-white leaf edges. Privets have stiff, upright shoots that require constant clipping to maintain the topiary shape.

Other plants that tolerate constant pruning are holly (*Ilex* species), bay trees (*Laurus nobilis*), common myrtle (*Myrtus communis*), arborvitae (*Thuja* species), hemlock (*Tsuga* species) and the evergreen holm oak (*Quercus ilex*).

necessary to clip or prune the plant to encourage a bushy specimen with lots of shoots. Feeding with a balanced fertiliser will encourage steady growth. An excess of nitrogen or potash food will produce soft or sturdy growth respectively (see page 13).

Plants for container-grown topiary can be planted in the open ground for the first couple of years to take advantage of the better growing conditions with less need for watering. Then lift them in autumn and pot them up ready for detailed shaping the following spring. Always leave a 5–7cm gap between the top of the compost and the rim of the container. This allows for watering and liquid feeding, and an annual top up with a layer of fresh compost. Use a soil-based compost, preferably John Innes No 2, available in garden centres and DIY stores.

For specimen topiary planted in lawns, keep the immediate surrounding area as weed-free bare soil, preferably mulched with composted bark. Protection from rabbits, squirrels and deer is crucial to prevent serious damage to bark and stems.

For free-standing, large topiary plants, regular clipping will build up the basic shape. Clip as often as necessary to keep

◁ *A standard ball of box ready for another light trim. Maintain the shape by removing short lengths of stem with hand shears. If it looks untidy you have left it too long between clippings.*

growth under control – that may mean two or three times during the growing season. If you prune in late summer there is less likelihood that the plant will make significant growth before winter. To avoid damage to late growths in cold, exposed or frosty areas, the shoots should be hardened by applying a couple of high-potash, liquid feeds in early autumn.

▽ With intricate shapes, regular clipping by hand is the surest way to keep the plant looking smart. Power tools don't give you enough control.

If you have 'a good eye' and a steady hand, you should be able to make squares or rectangles freehand without guides. When clipping, stand back every few minutes to check that the correct shape is being maintained.

Curves for balls and crescents will need a pre-formed shape with a timber or rigid plastic frame to act as an outline. Pyramids can be shaped using four bamboo canes the same length, forming a square at the base and securely tied together at the top, with the 'join' positioned directly above the centre of the plant.

If you can't resist the temptation to develop topiary on top of a clipped, formal hedge, allow a strong shoot or a cluster of shoots to grow out of the hedge, making sure that they are well marked to prevent anyone removing them accidentally when clipping the rest of the hedge. Start to make the shape while the stem or stems are still flexible. Regular clipping will build up a bushy, compact head. Bear in mind that the larger the finished topiary the more resistance it will have to winds, thus putting pressure on the stems that carry the shape.

Thank goodness the expertise has been taken out of animal topiary. You can purchase wire frames in more or less any shape or size that you require. They are hinged for ease of access while clipping and to enable you to remove them when you have finished. Choose from birds, pigs, rabbits, cats, horses, elephants and even life-size humans.

Keeping topiary tidy

1 Young box growth ready for trimming. Put a sheet underneath to collect the clippings.

2 Using hedge clippers, shape the plant by removing young growth.

3 The finished job. The plant looks neat and tidy but will need the same treatment again within a few weeks.

Secure the frame to a timber stake driven into the ground or fix it to the container in which you are growing the young plant. As the plant grows up inside the frame, tie the outer shoots to the perimeter of the frame, using raffia or soft twine that will eventually rot. Clip the other shoots regularly to produce side shoots that will grow to fill the 'body' of the frame. For small body parts, such as beaks and ears, clip the stems whenever they have grown a few centimetres to build up bushy stems with lots of side shoots and leaves.

You can rejuvenate old, neglected topiary provided that the chosen plant will tolerate hard pruning (see pages 46–47 and 56–57). There is always a risk that the stems that have to be cut to stumps may not re-grow, and even if they do it will take time. A better decision may be to start again with a new plant.

Holes and gaps caused by bare or dead branches can be filled in by removing the old wood and cutting the surrounding stems to encourage side shoots. Then train these in and clip them to match the surrounding growth.

◁ A privet Pied Piper – this chap is obviously ready to blow his own trumpet.

▽ The simplicity of clipped box softens a paved area.

Knot gardens

As with topiary, the secret of a good knot garden lies in the selection of suitable hedging plants. Box (*Buxus sempervirens*) is the traditional choice; my favourite variety is *B. sempervirens* 'Suffruticosa', which is very compact and slow-growing. Varieties of *Euonymus fortunei* such as 'Emerald Gaiety' (white-margined green leaves) and 'Emerald 'n' Gold' (bright green leaves edged with yellow) also make good, thick, low hedges.

△ *When clipping the hedge, start with the sides, making sure that the surface is uniform and not waving in and out.*

Don't make the design too complicated. Draw it up on a piece of paper first. Remember that the lines you draw represent hedges that will be up to 30cm wide, so leave sufficient room for growth, especially at any tight curves and spirals. Knot gardens are meant to be viewed from above and if you make the compartments between the hedges too small, they will shrink as the hedging matures and the effect will be lost.

Choose young shrubs about 30cm high and plant them 22–25 cm apart; as they grow they will form a continuous hedge. At this spacing digging a single trench is easier than making individual planting holes. After planting, lightly clip both the sides and the top of the plants to encourage them to branch and become bushy at the base. Unpruned plants will grow tall with 'bare legs'.

If you want to plant up the compartments within the knot pattern, choose low-growing ground cover such as vinca, ajuga or sedum that won't smother

▷ *Cutting the hedges on a slope so that one appears to grow under another reinforces the 'knot' impression.*

the hedge. Alternatively, a selection of various colours, sizes and textures of gravel mulch is attractive and reduces the need to weed. Spread a sheet to collect the clippings when you cut the hedge or they will get mixed into the gravel.

With box you have to clip up to four times during the growing season. Unless there are miles of hedge I prefer to use hand shears, which give more control than powered clippers, and clip the sides when straddling the hedge with the shears pointing downwards. Cut the top when the sides are done. If you make the top of one line of hedge slope down when it is within 60–90 cm of the line of hedging crossing its path and back up again on the other side, it looks as if one hedge is growing through and under the other.

Use a soft, long-handled brush to clear any clippings off the hedge before they turn brown and encourage fungal diseases. Regular applications of a liquid fertiliser during summer will keep the hedge furnished with young growth.

Trees

Unlike fruit trees, fruit bushes and many shrubs, deciduous, ornamental trees are not in continual need of pruning. However, if you allow a tree to start life with a bent main stem and don't train it to an upright position then, generations later, its lean will be remarked on and it will have been your fault!

△ *A healthy* Acer palmatum dissectum *can survive for decades without ever being introduced to pruning equipment.*

Early formative shaping to remove branches that make narrow-angled forks and crossing branches should produce a healthy framework; the tree can then be left to its own devices for years and often until it reaches maturity, with only the three Ds (dead, diseased and damaged branches) to watch out for. Thereafter, there are several operations that may have to be performed on the head or crown of the tree.

Removal of the three Ds is known as crown-cleaning and should be carried out as and when necessary. After cleaning, some crown-thinning may be in order. This involves the removal of crossing branches and spindly growths. It opens up a crowded head and allows light to penetrate to all parts of the branch system and the ground below.

Crown-lifting involves removing low branches of the tree, either to allow more light through to underplanted carpeting plants or to facilitate cutting the grass below the tree canopy. Branches tend to become lower as they mature, with the weight of wood and foliage bending them down closer to the ground.

▷ *Coniferous trees and shrubs all have different pruning requirements, but most need to be cut back regularly to stop them growing too large for the average garden.*

Crown-reduction, which reduces the top and side branches, may be desirable on a mature tree for three reasons: to afford a better view, to keep the tree clear of power lines or because the tree has become too large for its surroundings. While it shouldn't have been planted in that position in the first place, you are still stuck with a big tree.

I don't like resorting to crown-reduction of a mature tree but it is often the only alternative to completely removing the tree. It looks sad for a few years until re-growth commences and it isn't always successful in the longer term. With some trees, notably lime and eucalyptus, the remaining stumps may suffer from dieback. Where the wound does form a callus you may, in the following years, be plagued by weak, spindly water shoots that are useless as permanent branches and give the tree a hedge-like appearance.

CONIFERS

Most conifers, if allowed to grow, will become too large for small or even medium-sized gardens. Fortunately if

they are pruned from an early age their height and spread may be contained for many years. The secret is to retain their overall shape by thinning the branches rather than shortening them. When selecting those to be pruned out, move around the tree, removing a branch here and there to prevent the tree becoming lop-sided. Some conifers tend to lose their shape as they become older and at that stage it will be necessary to shorten branches to keep the plant tidy.

Removing the top portion of a mature conifer can lead to serious problems. If there has been total cover and you have removed it then, in cold areas, frost will be able to penetrate to the inside of the tree.

Semi-prostrate conifers, such as some of the junipers and yews, may become widespread, smothering other dwarf plants and killing off lawn grass. Cutting the horizontal stems back to side shoots annually in spring will ensure that the plant remains compact. Thin out crossing branches to reduce the risk of the foliage of those below becoming brown.

With most upright conifers, such as pines and firs, there is one central leader with branches spreading out from a central trunk. If the leader is damaged for any reason, the next shoot down from the top will, of its own accord, tend to grow vertically to replace it. You can encourage this action by training the shoot upwards on a supporting bamboo cane. The main stem of the blue spruce is usually trained up a cane but it has a habit of producing upright side shoots that, if not shortened to half their length, will compete with the leading shoot.

The monkey puzzle (*Araucaria araucana*) has a habit of sending out a side shoot from the base. This will grow vertically and close to the main trunk, and should be removed as soon as it is noticed. The longer it is allowed to remain, the more difficult and dangerous it is to remove due to its extremely sharply pointed, evergreen leaves. If allowed to remain it will spoil the shape of the tree.

▽ *Being slow-growing, Thuja occidentalis 'Pyramidalis Aurea' is an exception among conifers in that it is unlikely ever to need to be clipped.*

Some cultivars of juniper and spruce have been propagated from young foliage, resulting in conifers with fine, neat foliage. These newly developed cultivars are prone to revert to the foliage of the original plant, and if this is allowed to grow it will smother the weaker shoots. Keep an eye out for this and prune out the coarser-leafed shoots as soon as you notice them. Prompt use of the secateurs to remove the unwanted growth while it is still small will prevent the more aggressive stems smothering the desired habit of growth.

Most conifers are reluctant to produce green shoots from old wood (though junipers and yews are exceptions to this general rule). It is therefore important that when maintaining the shape or curtailing the growth of conifers such as Leyland cypress (× *Cupressocyparis leylandii*) you don't prune back beyond the green leaves into the old, black, leafless part of the branch.

▽ Koelreuteria paniculata *needs pruning only to remove dead or broken branches.*

Pleaching

The word 'pleach' is from the French *plechier*, meaning to plait or braid. In some forms of pleaching the young stems are twisted or braided together. Alternatively, you can take a short cut and tie the stems to horizontal bamboo canes or wires, then train them along the canes from either side and past one another.

△ *Once established, pleached branches support each other and need no further help from you.*

In the northern hemisphere, rows of trees that are planted from east to west will have less balanced amounts of sunlight on either side than rows running north to south, resulting in poorer growth on the sunless north side. The three most common objectives of pleaching are:

• To form an arched walkway, with the branches of two parallel rows of trees trained over and twisted together to form a leafy, colourful and interesting passage.

• To form a wall of greenery, usually above 2m high, of clean, straight tree trunks that support the screen.

• To form a natural 'growing' roof with open sides.

The secret of success is to start pruning the trees from the point where you want branches to form. For example, if there is to be a 2m clear trunk below the head of the tree then you will eventually have to prune off all the lower branches. In the short term, allow small side shoots to remain as they will help the girth of the main trunk to thicken and expand. Shorten them each spring for two years in order to build up lots of leaves. When pruning them off, cut them flush with the trunk without leaving a stump that would re-grow or attract disease.

To encourage the horizontal branches, remove the top 10–15cm of the main stem (trunk). A new leader will grow, complete with side shoots. Train these shoots horizontally by tying them to wires or canes (see pages 76–77). Continue this operation over a 2–3 year period until the pleached tree has reached the required height and there are sufficient horizontal side shoots to achieve the desired effect. Remove any shoots that are growing out of the front or back of the tree rather than to the sides.

As the side shoots grow they will meet up with those from the neighbouring tree. Traditionally at this stage they can be twisted or braided together. If you feel the need to cheat, it may be easier to use ties to hold them together. Use soft green garden twine or raffia that will eventually decay rather than choke the expanding

stems. Once the formation is complete, annual pruning in late spring and again in late summer will be necessary to thin the growths and prevent overcrowding.

A roof of pleached branches will need a strong framework of wires or canes to support and hold the stems until they thicken and remain in place of their own accord. You can staple bamboo canes or lengths of galvanised bull-wire to timber poles or tall tree stakes. Eventually the framework is removed and you are left with an outdoor room to be proud of and which will be the envy of your friends.

The best trees for pleaching are those that produce long, strong, pliable stems. My favourite is the lime, especially the red-twigged lime (*Tilia platyphyllos* 'Rubra'). The London plane (*Platanus* × *hispanica*) has enormous leaves and is quick to grow.

Crab apples, especially *Malus hupehensis* 'John Downie', work well when pleached, although there is the risk of canker disease with so many pruning cuts. To counterbalance that, there is the advantage of pink buds opening to white blossom in spring followed by a crop of beautiful orange-red fruit in autumn.

△ *Clever use of pleaching, where side branches have been trained upwards to form an archway.*

Pleaching step-by-step

1 Pleached lime. Shorten new growths to build up lots of leaves. They will then be available to replace less productive spurs.

2 Twist branches together so that they overlap. This will double the amount of foliage on each branch.

3 Tie in the new lime growths to horizontal cane supports. Use a soft twine that won't cut into the bark of the tree.

4 Use sturdy canes firmly secured to a main frame. Once the plants are in leaf there will be a large area that has to withstand strong winds.

5 A well-pleached lime tree with lots of spurs. In leaf it will become a solid wall of green.

Coppicing

Coppicing is the act of cutting a plant close to the ground in winter or early spring, producing strong new growths for fencing hurdles, fence poles and firewood. In addition to this practical purpose, in the garden coppicing is a way of adding interest and colour from those trees and shrubs with brightly coloured young bark.

△ These hazel stumps will rise in spring like the phoenix.

▽ Coppiced hazel alongside a layered hazel hedge.

The technique has been practised for thousands of years and there are wooded areas in France where there has been continuous coppicing for over 500 years. The trees are cut to within 5–10cm of the ground in winter, using a sharp axe or billhook that slices through each stem with a single cut. Thinner stems may be pruned with loppers or secateurs. When too many new stems are formed you can use secateurs to thin them to the desired number. However, not every tree and shrub can withstand this sort of very hard pruning every year or every second year.

Ash, hazel and alder are excellent trees for coppicing. The stems of willow and dogwood, in particular, brighten up a dull winter's day. Coppicing *Eucalyptus gunnii* will provide you with a manageable-sized tree, growing to 2–3m high annually. There will be a continuous supply of the aromatic, beautiful, silvery, blue-green juvenile foliage that is loved by flower arrangers.

The empress tree (*Paulownia tomentosa*) has large, softly hairy leaves and foxglove-like, deep pink, fragrant flowers with yellow and purple blotches on the inside. When coppiced in early spring it will send up vigorous, thick, straight stems to 3m high, carrying exceptionally large, ornamental leaves.

Coppicing for strong new growth and colour

2 Cut every other year in winter, shortening the stems to within 5cm of the base.

1 A coppiced *Salix alba* var. *vitellina* 'Britzensis'. This process is the same as for the pollarded plant (see page 83), but is at ground level, eliminating the need for staking.

3 If each of these stumps produces two shoots there will be a thicket of stems.

Coppicing dogwood

1 With dogwoods (such as this *Cornus sericea* 'Flaviramea') it is the young stems that have the best bark colour. In this variety, older stems turn from yellow to greenish-yellow.

2 In spring, cut the stems close to ground level or close to the main framework of branches.

3 All the stems are cut, leaving stumps to produce the new, young, coloured shoots.

4 Prunings can propagated as hardwood cuttings.

Pollarding

Pollarding is similar to coppicing but the pruning is carried out higher up on the plant. I remember the first time I came across a pollarded willow. It was *Salix alba* var. *vitellina* 'Britzensis' but at the time I didn't know that.

△ *Pollarding* Paulownia tomentosa *in spring results in strong shoots with the large leaves that make this plant so desirable.*

∇ *Pollarded* Tilia platyphyllos *'Rubra' on 2m clear trunks. The bright red stems are dramatic in winter.*

From a distance it looked like an orange ball floating above the shrubs. As I drew closer I assumed something was on fire. It is hard to imagine how a cluster of orange-brown stems could be so deceiving. That was over 45 years ago, yet I can still clearly picture the tree and I'm sure that I always will.

Not all trees are suitable for pollarding. They must be able to withstand the regular heavy pruning and

show resistance to the diseases that could enter through the wounds. Willow and some species of lime, such as the red-twigged form (*Tilia platyphyllos* 'Rubra'), are ideal for this severe pruning.

Select a tree with a trunk as thick as your wrist. In winter or early spring, use a handsaw to cut the head of the tree immediately above a cluster of side shoots and about 2m above ground level. Prune the side shoots back to within 2–3cm of the main trunk. Pruning promotes growth so the stumps will produce more shoots. These young stems will have the best bark colour. Prune every second year, or prune 50 per cent each winter, to keep a supply of new growths.

Any growths that appear at the base or on the bare trunk should be cut off as close to the bark as possible. Eventually there will be too many stems cluttering up the head of the tree and you will have to prune them to thin out the excess.

Pollarded trees develop a 'lollipop' head and will require staking to prevent damage during storms. Run the timber stake up into the branches of the tree, using strap-ties to secure the head above and below the new growths.

1 Pollarded *Salix alba* var. *vitellina* 'Britzensis' produces its best bark colour on young growths.

2 Prune every other year in winter, cutting the growths back close to the main trunk.

3 The finished job with a hedgehog effect. The mass of new, brightly coloured growths may need to be thinned.

Root pruning

I am always amazed by the number of occasions when I prune the roots of trees, shrubs and even perennials. You expect to be continually working on the branches of plants for myriad reasons but you wouldn't expect to see much of the roots once the plant is in the ground.

△ *Prune off damaged roots using well-sharpened equipment.*

However, they are certainly on display when planting bare-rooted material such as hedging plants, roses or small trees.

It is difficult to lift plants out of the ground without damaging their roots. Commercial growers use mechanical lifters, so some damage is to be expected when you buy a bare-rooted plant from a nursery.

Examine the plants before planting them and, making a clean cut, trim off any broken or damaged pieces of root. Occasionally you will find a single root that is much longer than the others. Shorten it back to be in balance with the remainder. Roses often have all their roots pointing in one direction because the rootstocks have been machine-planted before the varieties are grafted on. Spread out the roots as much as possible, and if there is a tangled mass prune out the one root that is causing the most trouble. A well-rooted rose will be none the worse for losing one piece of root. Make sure that all the fine roots are retained.

Ash trees grown in light, sandy soil will have large, thick, fang-like roots with very few fibrous roots. If you purchase a bare-rooted plant then trim back the cut ends of the larger diameter roots using sharp secateurs. Use a fine, moisture-retentive soil to backfill around the roots without leaving air pockets. This will encourage fine hair roots to grow on the main roots.

Container-grown plants may also need their roots pruned. It is worth noting the difference between a containerised plant and one that is container-grown. The former is a bare-rooted plant that has been potted up at the start of the winter season. The roots will be starting to spread through the compost but you need to take great care when removing the plant from the pot. The compost is likely to fall off, leaving you with a bare-rooted plant, probably in leaf. At the very least the plant will wither and suffer, but the check to the plant will prevent it taking up water and is just as likely to kill it. You can avoid this by only buying a bare-rooted plant in its dormant season.

A container-grown plant will have been growing in a pot for at least one season and will have built up a good root system. When it is removed from the pot the roots will hold the compost in place in the shape of the container. If there has been vigorous root growth, or if the plant has not been re-potted into a larger pot, there may be a congested mass of fine roots. Tease these out, using your hands to pull the ball of roots apart, or lever them apart with the help of a hand-fork. If they are tightly packed you may have to cut down through the mass to separate them. It won't matter if some fine roots are broken or cut. When you have finished the roots should be loose and looking like 'a bad hair day'. Once the plant is re-potted or in the ground the roots will quickly spread in search of nutrients and water.

Remember that some plants can be propagated from root cuttings. This may be used to advantage when propagating plants such as *Paulownia tomentosa*, *Chaenomeles* species and phlox. The process works equally well for terrible perennial weeds such as bindweed (*Convolvulus*) and dock (*Rumex*), where one small piece of root soon becomes another weed on the rampage. Bear this in mind when root pruning. Gather up all the prunings as some of them are likely to become rooted and you may not want a collection of plants.

Another time when root pruning is essential is when you are planning to move a large tree, conifer or shrub. It

◁ *All plants, including this* Clematis *'Special Occasion', will benefit from a congested rootball being teased out and old dead roots cut off.*

may have become too big for the available space, it might be blocking the view or if it has sentimental value you may want to take it with you when you move house. (If this is the case, do get permission from the new owners of your house before digging up the garden that they have bought.) The large roots hold the plant securely in the ground and transport the water and nutrients collected by the thin, fibrous roots. The more of these small roots the plant has, the more quickly it will settle into its new position and start collecting water and nutrients.

If time allows, prepare the tree or shrub the year before it is to be transplanted. In late autumn dig a trench 30cm deep in a circle around the plant. For a tree, line up the trench with the outer reach of the canopy of branches. For large shrubs and mature conifers, make this trench at least 120cm in diameter.

Prune any thick roots that are exposed, making a clean cut on the inner side of the trench, closest to the trunk. Backfill the trench with a good quality, free-draining, moisture-retentive compost. By the following autumn lots of new, young roots will have grown into the compost. Lift the tree or shrub, retaining this mass of useful, fibrous roots, and replant with topsoil around the roots. Plant at the same depth as before, firming the soil with your feet. The transplanted tree may need support – to avoid damaging roots, insert the stake first, then position the tree. Arrange the soil in a saucer shape around it.

△ *When transplanting, examine the root system and prune off any broken roots, being sure to make a clean cut.*

▷ *To avoid damaging the roots, insert the stake before planting the tree.*

To support large trees, use four rope guys attached at one end to pegs driven into the ground and at the other end about one third to halfway up the tree trunk. Use a loose, fixed noose to prevent the rope tightening on the trunk and causing bark damage. If the bark is soft, slip the rope inside a length of rubber or plastic hosepipe before wrapping it around the tree. This will pad the rope. Stretch the ropes out to form angles of at least 50° between the rope and the tree trunk on opposite sides of the tree and securely tie to the pegs. Water in to settle the soil around the roots and bark-mulch the soil surface to help prevent the ground drying out. Depending on the size of the tree, you may have to keep the rope supports in place for 2–3 years or more.

Pruning the roots of a fruit tree is a useful way of reducing growth and encouraging more flowers and fruit. It will also work with other trees where there is excessive growth or where you want a lot of flowers, but it is time-consuming. With young trees the easiest way is to dig up the tree in early winter and shorten the strongest roots that are travelling sideways. Trim any broken or damaged roots. Shorten the tap root (the root heading straight down into the ground) by one half.

With mature trees, root pruning is carried out in the same way as for transplanting established plants (see above). After the exposed roots have been cut, backfill the trench with the topsoil that you dug out.

Thugs

Throughout this book I have mentioned that pruning promotes growth, and never is this knowledge more important than when you are pruning rampant border plants, which can often become more troublesome than weeds. Many spread by suckers or underground stolons.

△ *Rubus cockburnianus produces white-stemmed, spiny, arched shoots and spreads as quickly as any other bramble.*

▷ *The suckers of* Rhus typhina *will quickly form a thicket and can push up through tarmac.*

▽ *Lamium (deadnettle) is acceptable in small doses.*

Others crawl over the ground, rooting wherever the stems touch the soil. With some, the growth may be curtailed by hard annual pruning at the start of the growing season or you can remove the suckers by pulling the young growths from the plant roots. With others, pruning encourages them to spread by diverting their growth into side shoots or suckers.

The curse of all sensible gardeners is the white-stemmed bramble (*Rubus cockburnianus*), a thicket-forming, deciduous shrub with exceptionally thorny, arching branches that are covered in pure white bloom in winter. Pruning the vigorous canes will divert the growth into more shoots that spread at an alarming rate. The answer is to dig out the roots, making sure that any young suckers are also removed.

The stag's-horn sumach (*Rhus typhina*) spreads rapidly and quickly forms a thicket. Hard pruning will encourage branching and even more suckers than usual. Instead, pull each sucker off close the surface or dig down and chop them off at the root of the plant.

Unfortunately Irish ivy (*Hedera hibernica*) is as good at creeping over the ground as it is at climbing. The stems will root everywhere they touch the ground and, like rose of Sharon (*Hypericum calycinum*) and yellow archangel (*Lamium galeobdolon*) they will gallop over the garden if pruned. To thicken an area of these low-growing plants, a light topping with a strimmer or hedge clippers will encourage fresh foliage and new sideways growth.

Suckers

The suckers of some shrubs and trees can be an awful problem in the garden and the best advice is to spot them early and deal with them immediately. With other plants such as the Chilean fire bush (*Embothrium coccineum*), the suckers are highly desirable and are a useful means of propagation.

△ Embothrium coccineum *gives suckers a good name – only a sucker would uproot and dump them!*

When grown in a lawn, the suckers of trees such as poplar and cherry cease to be a problem. Regular cutting with the lawnmower makes sure that they never become established. *Populus nigra* is the least troublesome of the poplars in that it only sends up suckers from a root that has been damaged. Where the unwanted suckers are coming from the roots, you must dig down and pull off each sucker. Don't cut them, otherwise the remaining stumps, no matter how small, will produce more shoots. With roses the suckers can grow from the roots of the stock that the cultivar was grafted onto, from the stem just below the graft union or, in the case of standard roses, from the main stem below where the plant was grafted at the top of the stem. Trees such as stag's-horn sumach (*Rhus typhina*), robinia, gleditsia and ailanthus are notorious for sending up masses of suckers that can penetrate concrete and tarmac. Remove them as soon as you see them; pull them off at the stem or root rather than cutting them, which would leave a stump to re-grow. Avoid planting suckering plants close to hard surfaces.

▷ Robinia pseudoacacia *'Sunburst' is deservedly a much-loved tree that is unlikely to sucker until it is at least 15 years old.*

Removing
unwanted suckers

3 However, the stumps will undoubtedly produce new shoots which will need to be removed all over again.

1 This old plum tree is swamped by suckers that are removing energy from other growth.

2 Looking better already – all the suckers have been cut as close to the base as possible.

EPICORMIC GROWTHS

These shoots are produced from dormant buds that become active close to the wound where a large branch has been pruned. With some trees, such as apples, they are known as water shoots and are so vigorous and sappy that they are useless as replacement branches. With other plants, such as lime trees, the shoots will grow into replacement branches. Where there are several shoots, prune them off leaving one strong shoot that is trained in as a replacement for the missing branch. Trim all the other shoots flush with the bark of the branch and use a sharp knife to pare off any remaining stump.

There is one lime tree, *Tilia × europaea*, that continually produces masses of growths around the base and from swollen growths (burrs) on the trunk. Remove them as close as possible to the trunk when they are still small, using a sharp knife.

SURFACE ROOTS

Tree roots that rise to the surface of lawn grass are a nuisance. Those belonging to ornamental cherries may become large enough to damage a lawnmower. With mature specimen trees, removing one such root won't be a catastrophe. Chop out the offending length of exposed root, making clean, smooth cuts at either end. Repair the lawn by filling the dip or trench with topsoil and sow grass seed or lay turf.

◁ *Ornamental cherries are the worst offenders for surface roots in grass.*

Houseplants

Climbing houseplants, such as *Hoya carnosa*, *Jasminum officinale* and *Stephanotis floribunda*, are usually sold as young plants in flower, with their stems trained several times around a wire hoop or spiralling around a tripod of bamboo canes. It is this form of training that forces the young plant into flower.

As soon as such plants have finished flowering they need to be taken off their support and the shoots disentangled. Reduce the length of each stem by one third to one half, cutting above a leaf or pair of leaves. Re-pot into a larger pot using fresh compost. Train the new growth up a trellis, wire or bamboo supports. To encourage flowering side shoots, weave the stems around or across the supports rather than vertically. In warm conditions, vigorous climbers will quickly fill their allotted space and will need to be regularly pruned to check their growth. Old, non-flowering stems may be cut out at the base, removing two or three stems each year in late winter or early spring.

Many of our best-known houseplants, such as silky oak (*Grevillea robusta*), rubber tree (*Ficus decora*) and Norfolk Island pine (*Araucaria heterophylla*), are really trees in their native habitat. Invariably they grow embarrassingly large for their position in the house or conservatory. Reducing the height by pruning immediately above a leaf or pair of leaves will encourage side shoots to form. These in turn may be shortened, but in the fullness of time the plant will need a larger home.

Always prune your houseplants in late winter or early spring when they are still resting. However, climbing plants may need restrictive pruning during the growing season, according to their rate of growth and their allotted space.

△ *Shorten side shoots of* Jasminum officinalis *to keep it tidy.*

▽ *Monstera deliciosa makes a large, handsome foliage plant, so provide plenty of space. Don't prune the aerial roots.*

Pruning an indoor fuchsia

Fuchsias' ballerina-like pendulous flowers are produced on the new growths. Prune in early spring by nipping out the growing tips to encourage side shoots. Shorten older wood by two thirds to allow new growths to sprout from the base. Tender fuchsias such as this *F.* 'Swingtime' can be moved to a sheltered spot outside once all risk of frost is over.

1 Shorten thin, spindly shoots by two thirds.

2 Prune old shoots back to a healthy side shoot.

3 Hard pruned and ready to grow away from the base…

4 …the plant will produce lots of new growths that will carry the flowers throughout the summer.

Bonsai

Bonsai culture, where even the largest trees are grown as tiny specimens in small containers, originated in Japan. The plants become, over many years, gnarled and twisted, resembling mature trees looked at through the wrong end of a telescope

To prevent the trees growing at the normal rate, bonsai growers trim the roots of their miniature plants annually. Deciduous bonsai plants are pruned in early spring or in late autumn, evergreens in early spring or in late summer.

Regular shaping, training and pruning of the stems are also essential. Use soft wire such as copper to train the stems to the shape and in the direction you want. Don't use copper wire on cherry trees as it has an adverse reaction with *Prunus* species. The wire will hold the stems in position until they firm up. During spring or autumn use secateurs or a sharp knife to remove unwanted shoots and give the tree the characteristic 'old' bonsai look. Evergreens such as pine and cedar make wonderful bonsai specimens. Deciduous trees that are worth growing include beech, oak, birch and Japanese larch. Flowering and fruiting crab apples (*Malus*) are worth the meticulous pruning required for success.

△ Small but happy to flower – a bonsai azalea.

◁ Soft copper wire is used to shape the stems to the desired shape.

Bonsai
step-by-step

1 Carefully remove the plant from the container and cut the root ball open. Prune out the old roots in the centre of the ball and tease the younger roots out from the compost.

2 On average, one third of the total root system should be pruned every time the bonsai is re-potted. The fine, usually white, roots at the ends of the older roots are known as root hairs and are short-lived. Regular pruning will help to produce new, active roots.

3 Re-pot in the same pot using fresh compost. Pot on at the same depth as it was previously grown, pushing the compost through the roots with your fingers. Make sure there are no air pockets, then water gently to settle the compost around the root ball.

Palms

Some groups of plants, such as palms and bamboos, have peculiar habits of growth that do not lend themselves to normal pruning techniques. With palms, the same basic approach applies to all the species normally grown in gardens.

Palm trees such as *Phoenix canariensis* are described as broadleaf evergreens and if you have the right climate you can grow a wide range of them. They all have the same pruning requirements.

Palms grow from the tip of the stem, which is often enclosed in a rosette of leaves. This makes them difficult to shape because it prevents you from supervising the direction any branches will take. I would recommend removing side shoots. They are usually produced at the base of the plant, which spoils the shape and causes overcrowding of the leaves.

When a large, old trunk dies, cut it off at the base. Prune out dead flower shoots from the centre of the rosette or the main trunk. Dead leaves are brown and make the plant look untidy. Cut them off as soon as they die, pruning them to within a few centimetres of their base, making two cuts so that the stump is shaped like an inverted 'V'. The following year, pull the dead leaf stump away from the trunk.

Livistona australis *(top) and* Chamaerops humilis *(left) are two palms that don't need much pruning apart from the removal of dead leaves.*

Palms

1 Basal side shoots tend to spoil the shape of a palm.

2 Cut or pull them off while they are still small.

3 The leafless trunk of a palm is part of its beauty.

Bamboos

Bamboos are another large group of plants that all have the same pruning needs. Major pruning is needed only when plants are mature and have formed large clumps – that is, when they are about 4–5 years old.

△ Phyllostachys sulphurea *'Houzeau' is a striking, golden-stemmed variety.*

To allow space for new canes, thin them out at ground level in early summer , removing only those canes that are at least three years old and have begun to spread beyond their allotted space. Mature bamboo canes are hard on the blades of secateurs, so it is better to use a saw or machete. Avoid removing too much leaf cover as the plants' roots prefer to be cool and in shade.

Some bamboos are quick to spread. A useful way of containing them where they border a lawn is to run the lawnmower over the emerging shoots.

▷ Phyllostachys nigra *(black bamboo) can be a useful architectural plant in a modern garden, but even isolated clumps like this will still need to be thinned.*

Bamboos

1 This is *Phyllostachys nigra* before pruning. Although not as rampant as many other bamboos, it is still likely to spread beyond its allocated space.

2 During pruning, avoid removing too much leaf cover.

3 The finished job, with the canes thinned to avoid congestion and the oldest removed at the base.

Clematis

For the purpose of pruning, clematis are generally divided into three groups and, while there is an occasional exception, the rules will hold true for practically all the species and cultivars you are likely to grow. A fourth group of herbaceous clematis, such as *Clematis heracleifolia*, *C. integrifolia* and *C. recta*, die down in late autumn when all the dead stems are removed at ground level.

△ Clematis *'General Sikorski' (Group 2): prune in late winter, cutting back to the first pair of healthy buds.*

All newly planted clematis, with the exception of the herbaceous types, should be pruned hard in early spring, unless you have bought the plant in leaf and flower, in which case you should allow it to grow unpruned until the following spring. Take your time examining each stem, working your way down the growths until you come to a pair of healthy, live buds. Prune with sharp secateurs immediately above a pair of buds that will develop into shoots. The tips of these two new shoots should be nipped out in late spring. More growths will be produced and these should also be nipped back a few weeks later, thus building up a framework of stems that will flower at different heights during summer or early autumn. If you leave the plant unpruned, all the flowers will be produced at the top of a couple of straggly stems.

After this initial procedure, it becomes important to know to which group your clematis belongs.

▷▷ Clematis *'Niobe' (Group 3): prune in late winter, cutting all growths back to healthy buds close to the base.*

▷ *C. 'Early Sensation' (Group 1) should be pruned after flowering.*

▷ *Old rampant plants of* C. montana *'Fragrant Spring' (Group 1) may be hard-pruned after flowering, cutting the oldest stems back to a height of 30cm.*

GROUP 1

This group includes the well-known *Clematis montana* and its cultivars, *C. alpina* and the evergreen, winter-flowering *C. cirrhosa* and *C. armandii*, along with their cultivars. The ideal time to prune established plants in this group is immediately after flowering. Where there is sufficient space for these vigorous plants to spread, then little pruning is necessary except to encourage new flowering stems and maintain the plant within bounds.

Cut overlong stems back by two thirds to healthy buds. The plant will naturally, over time, become a tangled mass of shoots that spread beyond their allotted space. At that stage you can thin them drastically to remove the old shoots. One method is to cut the stems into pieces, pulling the pieces out carefully so as not to damage the young, brittle growths. Alternatively, prune and leave the cut stems to wither and die. By the following winter they will have lost their grip and fallen off the support.

After a severe pruning the plant may produce basal shoots. Take the opportunity to build up low, flowering growths that will hide the bare legs of the mature plant. Prune these shoots by nipping out the tips as for newly planted clematis (see page 102).

Where necessary, the clematis in this group can be rejuvenated by pruning hard, cutting the stems down to stumps. There is always a risk that the plant may die from shock, so where possible tackle badly overgrown plants over a 2–3 year period, removing one third of the oldest stems each year after flowering has finished. However, using a chainsaw, I once cut down a *C. montana* var. *rubens* 'Tetrarose' with a stem the diameter of a dinner plate. The idea was to remove it completely in the autumn to prevent it pulling down a client's shed. It took umbrage and produced a mass of shoots. The owner decided to give it a second chance and it has flourished, although the shed itself has become a bit difficult to find.

Pruning clematis – group 1

1 *Clematis cirrhosa* var. *purpurascens* 'Freckles' is well worth leaving to form a mass of flowers.

2 It only needs pruning when it becomes a tangled mass or extends beyond its allocated space.

3 Always make the pruning cut above a pair of healthy buds.

4 Once some of the oldest shoots have been removed, the plant has more room to 'breathe'.

GROUP 2

Included in this group are all the early, large-flowering cultivars, such as C. 'Nelly Moser' (pinkish-mauve with darker central bands), that produce their main flowering display before midsummer. The flowers appear on short growths from shoots produced the previous year. A second, smaller flush of flowers will appear, on the new shoots, in late summer or early autumn. Cultivars such as 'Proteus', with double and semi-double flowers, are also included in this group. 'Proteus', with its large, double, mauve-pink flowers, and other fully double-flowering cultivars can cause confusion by producing single flowers at the second, later flush.

Cut out all the dead or weak, spindly shoots in late winter. Examine each remaining stem from the top down until you come to the first healthy buds. Make a clean cut with sharp secateurs immediately above these buds. If you leave some stems unpruned for a further 7–10 days the flowering will be staggered and prolonged.

If you have a lot of pruning to do, this group can be left for a couple of years without the plants deteriorating. On the other hand, when they have become an untidy mess of stems they will tolerate a hard pruning in late winter by shortening back all the main stems. The first flush of flowers will be lost but the new growths will flower as normal in the late summer.

▽ C. florida sieboldii (Group 2): pruning each plant over a two-week period, a few stems at a time, will extend the flowering time.

Pruning clematis - group 2

1 The plant has become a tangled mass of growths.

2 This group flowers on side shoots produced on the previous year's growth. Remove spindly and thin shoots and shorten last year's growths by working down from the top and pruning at the highest pair of healthy buds.

3 The finished job – a clean, tidy framework ready to produce new growth.

GROUP 3

The late, large-flowering hybrids such as C. 'Ville de Lyon' (carmine-red flowers) and C. 'Jackmanii' (dark purple) are in this group, along with the small-flowering C. *orientalis*, C. *texensis* and C. *viticella* species and their cultivars. They flower late in the season on growth made that year. They simply need to be pruned hard in late winter. Working up from the base, prune off all the growth on each stem, cutting back to just above the first pair of healthy buds, which will probably be 15–45cm above ground level.

Pruning clematis – group 3

1 This late-flowering clematis is a mass of tangled growths. This group flowers on the new growths made during the spring and summer.

2 Work up from the base of each stem, cutting at the lowest, healthy pair of buds.

Roses

There is no great secret to pruning roses. They are simple to manage and the rewards are unbelievably fantastic. What tends to frighten first-time owners of a garden is the diversity of the rose. There are bush roses under the headings of cluster-flowered (floribunda) and large-flowered (hybrid tea).

△ *The quality and quantity of rose flowers, like those of this shrub rose R. 'Chartreuse de Parme', will be improved by regular pruning.*

Shrub roses may be old-fashioned or modern. There are climbers, ramblers, patio, miniature, ground-cover and weeping and upright standards. Their methods of pruning are dictated by their different growing habits, which I will explain as I go along.

The main reason for pruning roses is to encourage vigour and a good, healthy plant. Pruning will also help to maintain a suitable shape, and naturally we all want to prune in a way that achieves the maximum display of flowers.

In warm countries roses tend to flower almost all year round. To avoid losing part of the flower display prune lightly and deadhead continually. Every third year you should be prepared to sacrifice some bloom by pruning harder in spring to reduce plant height and encourage fresh growth from the base of the rose.

Some pruning tips are common to all roses.

▷ *Species roses like this gallica 'Président de Sèze' (the paler pink of the two) and Bourbon 'Honorine de Brabant' are noted for their fragrance. Correct pruning will maximise their flowering potential.*

- If you see black spot disease (see pages 132–133) on leaves or stems you should pick the leaves off, cut out badly infected shoots and burn them.

- Avoid making pruning cuts in very frosty weather as the frost may penetrate the wound, splitting the stem and encouraging dieback disease.

- Pull off unwanted suckers as soon as you see them and before they become large.

- Make each pruning cut immediately above a bud and sloping away from it.

- Prune to a healthy bud that is pointing in the direction in which you would like the shoot to grow.

BUSH ROSES

These are the most popular roses, grown in gardens and municipal parks throughout the world. There are two types that were formerly called hybrid tea and floribunda. Today they are listed in catalogues as large-flowered and cluster-flowered respectively. Large-flowered produce large, individual flowers ideal for use as a buttonhole. Cluster-flowered are exactly that, a cluster of smaller flowers on a single stem.

△ *A well-pruned bush rose with the cuts above buds that are pointing in the direction the shoots need to grow.*

During the dormant season, bare-rooted bush roses are available in garden centres and nurseries. Before planting them, trim any damaged or broken roots, making a clean cut. After planting, prune them hard in spring. Completely remove any stems that are less than pencil thickness by pruning with secateurs as close to the base as possible. Cut out crossing and rubbing stems along with those growing towards the centre of the bush. Prune the remaining healthy stems down to within 7–15cm of the ground, cutting immediately above a healthy, outward-pointing bud.

If you buy container-grown roses in the dormant season when they are without leaves, prune them as for bare-rooted roses. If you buy later in the season, simply cut out any damaged or diseased growths straightaway and prune the following spring as for bare-rooted roses.

In subsequent years, trim bush roses in early winter to reduce their height by one third. This will lessen the risk of strong winds rocking the bushes and loosening the roots in the ground.

Prune bush-type roses in early spring when there is less risk of a hard frost damaging the emerging shoots. If you garden in the northern hemisphere you will, I hope, forgive me for recommending St Patrick's Day (17 March) as the ideal day to prune bush roses. You can prune in winter in mild climates and sheltered gardens, resulting in an early flush of flowers, but this won't work where I live.

▷ *Although R. 'Irish Hope' is cluster-flowered, each flower has the space to show itself off.*

Large-flowered roses Pruning established cultivars consists of removing diseased, weak and spindly stems, and those that are filling the centre of the bush. Shorten any damaged stems, cutting back to healthy wood. Cutting back to outward-pointing buds within a few buds of the older wood will help to produce an open framework of branches.

Shorten the remaining strong, healthy shoots to an outward-pointing bud within 20–25cm of the base of the plant. The pruned stems will be 8–10cm above the previous year's cut. Follow the same procedure the following year, but after that it is time to prune back into the older wood immediately above a dormant, outward-pointing bud to prevent the plant becoming too tall. Where no buds are evident, prune as low as possible without cutting into the oldest wood. Throughout the growing season remove dead flowers and cut off and burn any leaves infected with black spot disease.

Cluster-flowered bush roses With established cluster-flowered roses the only difference in pruning technique to the large-flowered plants is in the pruning of the healthy stems. You are trying to build up a lot of flowering stems, each of which will carry a cluster of flowers. You will still need to cut out all diseased, thin and crossing branches. Cut back the main framework of branches to 30–35cm and shorten any side shoots (laterals) to within 2 or 3 buds of the main stem. Again, select a bud pointing in the direction in which the shoots

Pruning a young bush rose

1 A young bush rose before pruning, with thin and crossing stems…

2 …and afterwards, with an open framework of sturdy stems.

should grow and make the cut at an angle immediately above and sloping away from the bud.

When it is difficult finding a bud to cut above, simply cut at a suitable height to keep the plant in shape. That will encourage a dormant bud to produce a shoot. The stem can then be trimmed down to immediately above the emerging new shoot.

When deadheading, you can remove the individual dead flowers and eventually cut off the whole stem that carried that cluster. Shorten back the stems in early winter to prevent storm damage.

Pruning an established bush rose

1 An established bush rose before pruning. This plant has been pruned regularly throughout its life, so the job is simple, with no congested branches.

2 Remove diseased stems without leaving a stump. Any showing signs of dieback (see page 132) should be burned.

4 Clean, sloping cuts help to keep the plant healthy.

3 After pruning – the centre is open; thin stems have been removed or shortened.

5 New growths are prone to frost damage. In cold areas, prune in late spring so that the growths don't appear too soon.

STANDARD ROSES

The pruning needs of standard roses are similar to those of bush roses. The difference between them is that a standard has a straight, bare, rootstock stem with the bud graft at the top of the stem. Bush roses are bud-grafted at soil level. The cultivar for the standard will have been top-grafted onto *Rosa rugosa* or *R. laxa* rootstocks at a height between 100–150cm. Their tall, bare trunks, with all the stems and foliage high up, makes them prone to wind damage. A strong, timber, supporting stake is a permanent feature of the plant, secured at the top of the stem close to the graft union. Being grafted high up on the stem means that there is more likelihood of stem suckers. These should be pulled off as soon as you see them.

Again, prune at the end of winter or in early spring and, once any diseases, crossing and other unwanted growths have been removed, shorten the main framework of branches. Large-flowered varieties are pruned harder than cluster-flowered roses. It is important to keep the centre of the head of branches open and compact to prevent the plant becoming top-heavy.

Deadhead regularly throughout the flowering season. Shorten back the growth in winter by one third to prevent wind damage.

Weeping standard roses When purchasing a weeping standard it is important to know what type of rose has been top-grafted onto the rootstock. It may be a ground-cover cultivar that trails, or a climber or rambler, and that information will dictate when and how it is pruned. Weeping standards are usually grafted at a height of 1.5–2m.

My advice is to choose the tallest standard rose you can find. A high trunk will allow the stems to grow down for a longer length, providing the maximum show of flowers.

With climbers, the choice is limited to those cultivars such as 'Climbing Shot Silk' (pink and scented) with flexible branches that can be trained downwards. Most cultivars have stiff stems that want to reach for the sky. An umbrella-shaped wire frame attached to the support stake is useful for training the branches. In the first year prune to form an all-round framework of stems by removing the thin stems and pruning the remaining stems back to 2 or 3 buds from the graft. Cut immediately above an outward-pointing bud. Thereafter, prune in autumn, thinning out the centre and cutting old branches back to the wire frame to encourage new growths to replace the old. Shortening the tips of the main branches and the side branches will build up productive stems.

Ramblers have flexible stems that will naturally want to trail downwards. Train a complete circle of weeping stems by pruning to buds that will head in the direction you want. Thereafter, pruning is simply a case of cutting out one third of the oldest shoots annually in summer when they have finished flowering. Prune them close to the centre of the rose. This

◁ A rambling rose pruned and trained on a tripod to keep the stems as near horizontal as possible to encourage side shoots that will carry the flowers.

will allow the new shoots to fill their space. Shorten the side shoots by one half to two thirds to build up more flowering shoots, and shorten any long shoots back to healthy buds. Ramblers are prone to mildew, and retaining too many branches will reduce air circulation and encourage the disease.

Weeping standards never have enough height for extremely vigorous ramblers such as 'Rambling Rector' (white, semi-double, scented). 'Dorothy Perkins' is very vigorous so in late summer you should remove every other shoot that flowered. There will be sufficient new growths to make a great display of small, double pink flowers the following year.

◁ This standard rambler Rosa excelsa will be in constant need of a supporting stake to prevent its head breaking off at the point where it has been grafted.

Even the best of the ground-cover roses will not weep, but gravity will cause them to tumble down. Prune them in the same way as ramblers, removing the flowered stems in summer. Creeping rambler types such as 'Nozomi' (pale pink) and 'Swany' (semi-double, white) will quickly droop to ground level, but if they are not pruned to keep them above the ground the shoots will eventually root, becoming a tangled mess.

PATIO AND POLYANTHUS ROSES

These were originally part of the floribunda group but have been renamed dwarf cluster-cup roses. Patio cultivars such as 'Anna Ford' (salmon-orange, scented) are small, cluster-flowered roses, while polyanthus types such as 'White Pet' (pink buds opening to double, white flowers) are compact versions with clusters of small flowers. They are also ideal when grafted as a standard rose and both excel as container-grown plants.

Pruning is the same as for cluster-flowered cultivars but, being smaller plants, the pruning cuts are closer to the soil, often as low as 2–4cm. Firstly remove any diseased or damaged branches, then any thin and crossing stems. Reduce the remaining framework of branches by one half to two thirds.

MINIATURE ROSES

These charming little gems are at their best in containers. They are easy to manage and pruning is identical to their big sisters, the large-flowered and the cluster-flowered roses, but in proportion.

As a general rule, shorten the main framework by one half to two thirds in early spring, removing completely all the usual unwanted spindly, crossing and diseased stems. The cultivar 'What a Peach' (yellowy-peach, scented) is one of the taller miniatures, growing to 60cm. There are true dwarfs such as 'Baby Betsy McCall' (double, pale pink, scented flowers). This only grows to 20cm but is perfect in every way. A snip to remove the dead flowers and removing the tips of the branches to encourage flowering side shoots serves it well.

△ *Patio roses like this R. 'Queen Mother' are hard-pruned in spring. The compact stems form excellent ground cover.*

◁ *Rambling R. 'Dorothy Perkins' is vigorous and will recover quickly from a hard pruning. Remove all the old stems at ground level.*

CLIMBER ROSES

There is often confusion between rambler and climber roses. The definition is not quite as simple as the fact that ramblers ramble and climbers climb but there is some truth in it. Ramblers have long, pliable, thin stems with large clusters of small flowers during summer. Usually there is only one flush of flowers. Climbers have stiff stems that are more difficult to bend, with larger flowers. Many cultivars are repeat-flowering from early summer through to early autumn.

I know that this is a book on pruning but it is well worth noting that with climbing roses the secret of success lies not only in the pruning but in the training. The side shoots (laterals) will flower profusely if the main stems are arched rather than allowed to grow upright, when only the top of the stem produces flowers.

The time to prune is in autumn and through the winter. I prefer late autumn when exceptionally long stems can be shortened before they are whipped about by winter gales. The old wood can be removed from the centre of the plant without damaging the swelling buds.

When you purchase a climbing rose it will have stems much longer than those of bush roses. Do not prune these, other than lightly trimming any damaged or broken branches and cutting the remainder at an angle immediately above a bud. Before planting, prune any damaged portions of root, making a clean cut. Prune the stems to suitable buds pointing in directions that will encourage a spread of branches that will form a fan with the lowest stems almost horizontal. This well-spread framework of branches will determine the shape of the climber for the next few years.

For the rest of the first season the only pruning necessary is to remove damaged, diseased, thin and crossing branches along with regular deadheading of the spent flowers.

In subsequent years, prune in autumn, removing the oldest branches completely as close to the ground as possible and tying in strong, healthy shoots to replace them. In late summer, cut back the side shoots that flowered to within a few leaves of the main stem to encourage new growths that will flower the following year.

My favourites in this group are 'Dublin Bay' (double, bright red), 'Schoolgirl' (double, deep apricot, scented), 'New Dawn' (double, pale pink, scented) and 'Gloire de Dijon', better known as the 'Old Glory' rose (double, creamy-buff, scented).

Pruning a climbing rose

1 An established climbing rose before pruning and badly in need of thinning and training.

2 Remove the older wood at the base and arch young growths to encourage flowering side shoots.

3 Regular feeding will help to produce strong new growths to replace the older wood each year.

RAMBLER ROSES

Unlike climber roses, newly purchased ramblers should be pruned immediately after planting. Remove dead, damaged and spindly shoots without leaving a stump. Cut all the healthy stems to 30cm above the base to encourage strong shoots from low down on the plant. As they appear, spread them out in a fan and tie them to supporting wires or a trellis.

After the second year, remove one third of the main stems at ground level. Select the oldest branches for pruning, tying in the strong, new growths to replace them. Ramblers flower best on growths made the previous year but each stem will continue to flower for several years. After flowering, shorten exceptionally long stems that are spreading beyond their allotted space.

Where the rambler has made excessive numbers of new shoots then thin them out, retaining the strongest. Too dense a mass of stems and leaves will reduce air circulation and encourage mildew. If you can't let the rose ramble to its full extent you can either train it along wires or a trellis, or curtail it by continually cutting back branches at the base. You should always choose a rambler according to its growing conditions. Check the label when you buy the rose and, if necessary, consult the nursery staff.

My favourite ramblers are 'Dorothy Perkins' (small, double pink), 'Veilchenblau' (deep purple becoming mauve with age), 'American Pillar' (single, pink with a white centre) and 'Kiftsgate' (white with scent) – provided that you have a large tree for 'Kiftsgate' to climb.

▽ *One of my favourite ramblers, R. 'Kiftsgate' is very vigorous and is best suited to growing through an old tree.*

Pruning a rambler

1 Pruning will improve shape and remove congested branches.

2 Remove old growths either at the base or above a strong side shoot. Tie in the main stems, arching them where possible. New shoots will help hide the 'bare legs'.

3 Tie younger shoots on to older branches to cover bare stems.

4 The finished job: by summer it will be a mass of flowers.

△ R. 'Pheasant' makes excellent ground cover. Deadheading faded flowers will encourage a second flush of colour.

GROUND COVER

There are two distinct types of ground-cover roses, both of which are low-growing. Many of them retain their foliage well into winter. The modern ground-cover rose is shrub-like and is used extensively for mass landscape planting of municipal open spaces. In the first spring, shorten the main shoots by one half to two thirds. Only a little pruning is necessary thereafter, other than removing dead and diseased stems and thinning out the centre of the bush. It is worth deadheading the spent flowers if they are accessible. Shorten long, straggly shoots that are spreading too far and remove the tips of the remainder.

I love the County series of cultivars, and especially 'Worcestershire' (single, yellow), 'Surrey' (double, pink), 'Wiltshire' (semi-double, orange-pink) and 'Avon' (semi-double, pale pink to white).

The rambler types of ground-cover roses are fast-growing with long stems that spread over the ground, rooting as they go. In the first year the shoots tend to grow upwards but in the second season the weight of the flowers makes them lie down. Lightly prune in summer after flowering is finished, removing a few of the oldest growths and any stems that are escaping from the bed. These are ideal roses for covering a steep bank while helping to prevent soil slippage.

The Game Bird group of rambler-type, ground-cover roses is sure to please, including 'Grouse' (single, pale pink, scented), 'Pheasant' (double, pink, scented) and 'Partridge' (single, white, flushed pink).

SHRUB ROSES

With their habit of growth and their pruning requirements, the majority of shrub roses could be thought of as deciduous shrubs. But there the similarity ends. Few shrubs can match the variety of flower shapes, colours, perfume or even the history of the shrub rose. According to legend the old species roses were planted in King Midas's garden; the Greeks and Romans certainly loved them, Napoleon's wife Josephine had a superb collection (and even has a rose named after her) and rose lovers throughout the world have their own particular favourites.

For pruning purposes I have divided them into three groups.

Species roses These are the true wild roses such as *Rosa glauca* – also labelled *R. rubrifolia* (single, cerise-pink) – *R. virginiana* (single, bright pink) and *R. moyesii* (single, deep scarlet). They require little in the way of pruning. In spring the occasional long, unruly stem can be shortened and weak stems cut back hard to encourage growth. When the plant becomes untidy, with lots of old, woody branches, you should prune out the oldest stems as close to the base as possible.

Where interesting rosehips are a desirable part of the display, such as with *R. moyesii* (flagon-shaped, red), refrain from snipping until late autumn when the berries have been devoured by birds.

▽ *When rosehips are part of the display, as with this species rose* R. moyesii, *resist the temptation to deadhead – the hips will be less prolific.*

Old shrub roses These are my favourites and I hasten to point out that in this context 'old' represents historic rather than 'past their best'. They have wonderfully romantic names such as gallica, damask and Bourbon.

The gallicas are stunning in summer with their fully double, flat flowers in rich shades of deepest pink, red and purple. They were grown by the Romans and were popular in medieval France for their fragrance. They require little pruning. At planting time, remove thin and damaged stems and shorten any long stems. Tidy established plants in spring, removing diseased and thin stems. In midsummer, after flowering has finished, thin the centre of the bush to reduce congested branches. Every 2–3 years remove a few of the oldest stems as close to ground level as possible. Avoid leaving stumps, as these encourage disease.

The other main types in this delightful group include the damasks (of which one of the best is 'Madame Hardy' – double, white, fragrant), Bourbons ('Souvenir de la Malmaison' – double, pale pink to white, fragrant), albas ('Céleste' – double, light pink, fragrant), Provences ('Fantin-Latour' – double, light pink, fragrant), Portlands ('Comte de Chambord' – double, light pink, fragrant), China ('Cécile Brünner' – double, pale pink) and mosses ('William Lobb' – double,

velvety purple, fragrant). These should all be pruned in the same way as the gallicas.

After planting, trim any long shoots to an outward-pointing bud. Shrub roses mainly flower in summer, although a few will continue into autumn with an occasional bloom. Prune as soon as the main flowering is finished, cutting out dead and diseased stems. At the same time, shorten the main stems and long side branches by one third.

Where the roses are growing strongly, by autumn some shoots may have grown so long as to become a nuisance. Shorten them to the same length as the rest of the plant.

Modern shrub roses such as 'Marguerite Hilling' (semi-double, rose-pink, scented) have been raised over the past 120 years or so. Prune lightly in spring to keep the plant neat and tidy.

The rugosas belong to this group, with cultivars such as *R. rugosa* 'Roseraie de l'Hay' (double, red-purple, scented) and hybrid musk *R.* 'Penelope' (semi-double, creamy-pink, scented) requiring little maintenance. Prune in late winter or early spring by shortening any long shoots of the rugosas and thinning out a few of the oldest shoots as close to ground level as possible. Their big, fat hips are orange or red and resemble tomatoes. Reduce hybrid musk side shoots (laterals) by one half and shorten the main framework of branches by one third.

△ *Once shrub roses like this English Rose R. 'Anne Boleyn' are established, open up the centre by removing the oldest branches.*

▷ *Regular pruning to shape these bushes will prevent the entrance disappearing altogether.*

ENGLISH ROSES

These modern developments must surely represent the future of roses and are the work of one farmer turned nurseryman and rose breeder, David Austin, whose nursery has created over 800 varieties – not bad in a single lifetime. English Roses is a brand name and they have wonderful cultivar names such as 'Gertrude Jekyll' (double, bright pink, scented), 'Mistress Quickly' (sprays of double, soft lilac-pink), 'Jude the Obscure' (large, double, yellow, scented) and 'William Morris' (cupped, soft apricot-pink).

They require little by way of pruning. Deadhead immediately the flowers have faded and remove dead or diseased stems in early spring. A snip here and there to shorten long stems back to healthy buds and to tidy the plant won't do any harm and will let you feel that you have carried out some pruning.

ROSE HEDGES

When in full flower a rose hedge is a thing of beauty. Unfortunately, for most of the rest of the year it looks a bit bedraggled but with its thorns it will deter intruders and prevent young escapees. Some species such as *R. rugosa* have buttery-yellow autumn foliage while *R. glauca* has purple-grey leaves. The rosehips of *R. rugosa* are plentiful, big, fat, orange or red and tomato-like.

After planting, prune out any broken, thin or diseased branches. Cut the remaining stems to within 30cm of the ground to encourage strong, healthy basal shoots that will form the framework of the hedge. Each spring shorten the side shoots to healthy buds to build up a thick mass of flowering shoots and to prevent the base of the hedge becoming thin with gaps.

Every 2–3 years, prune out a few of the oldest branches close to the ground. Cut them into pieces to avoid wrecking the hedge as they are pulled out. Dead stumps should be removed with long-armed pruners.

RENOVATING OLD ROSE BUSHES

There are two very good reasons why it is often worth pruning to rejuvenate an old rose. First, more often than not you will be successful. And second, roses are tough plants and most of them will respond to hard pruning. While the rejuvenated plant may not be as good as a new plant, it is worth remembering that you won't be able to replace the old rose with another new cultivar unless you change the soil in which the old one was growing. In fact, when replacing any plant with another it is as well to add more nutrients to the soil because the first plant will have used most of them.

With very old bush and shrub roses, the best method is to risk all and prune hard. Cut the main branches back to within 15–20cm of the ground. Remove any dead stumps. Water, feed and mulch and, trust me, the plant will push out new growths.

There is no sense in hunting for a suitable bud to prune to. They won't be visible on old stems but the hard pruning will kick-start any dormant buds.

If not pruned every year, climbers and rambler roses will quickly become an untidy mess. Ramblers are normally pruned in summer after flowering but for renovating purposes they can be pruned in the dormant season at the same time as the climbers.

When climbers are badly overgrown with bare lower branches and all the flowers above your head, then the best policy is to cut 3 or 4 of the oldest shoots back to 30cm from the base of the plant.

Cut up the long stems and remove in suitably sized pieces. Any laterals on the remaining stems are shortened by two thirds. Cut just above a bud that is pointing sideways. Alternatively, shorten half the stems by two thirds, pruning the remainder to the same height the following spring.

Ramblers may be renovated by pruning out all the old stems at the base, retaining only new shoots. If there are no new growths and the plant is a tangled mass of branches, then cut all the growths to within 20–30cm of the ground in late summer and wait for new shoots to form.

Examine rejuvenated plants for unwanted suckers, removing them by pulling them off the stem or root when they are small. After a severe pruning, water, feed and mulch the plant to give it the best chance of a full recovery.

△ Rosa 'Comte de Chambord', also known as 'Madame Knorr', is a damask Portland species. It requires little pruning, but benefits from an open centre. Remove the old wood at the base and deadhead for continuous flowers throughout summer and autumn.

◁ This mass of old climbers and ramblers includes R. cooperi, 'Alister Stella Gray', 'Madame d'Arblay' and 'Climbing Josephine Bruce'. Arch the young, pliable stems to fill bare spaces and maximise the summer show.

▷ Good feeding and an ample supply of water will help climbers such as this R. 'Collette' produce its flowers throughout the summer.

DISEASES

The damage caused by some of the more serious diseases of roses may be reduced by timely pruning.

Mildew marks the leaves and flowers, and in serious cases may defoliate the plant. In the case of the rambler 'Dorothy Perkins', the white mildew markings seem to be part of the flower bud. Pruning to keep the centre of the bush open and allowing air to circulate is the best form of prevention.

Dieback and coral spot are killer fungal diseases. Pruning with blunt blades creates ragged cuts that are ideal entry points for fungal spores. Stumps of branches at the base of the plant or where laterals have been cut allow disease spores to enter. The disease can then travel through the plant, causing whole branches to die. To prevent this happening, prune out stumps and tidy up large wounds, using a sharp knife to trim the edges of the cut.

△ Be vigilant: removing infected black spot early offers some control.

▷ Rosa 'Wickwar': the presence of so much ivy around this rambler will cause congested growth, encouraging fungal diseases such as black spot and botrytis. Cut it back and allow the air to circulate.

Black spot disease will attack stems and leaves. Foliage with brown or black spots and yellowing leaves should be picked off and burnt. Where stems show the reddish-brown or black markings they need to be removed, cutting at least 5–7cm below the diseased section of branch. Burn all the prunings and rake up leaves that have fallen. Never put diseased wood or leaves in the compost heap as the spores might survive in compost that doesn't heat up properly.

LAZY PRUNING

Over the last few decades there has been considerable discussion about the merits of rose pruning. There is a school of thought that it is unnecessary to prune above a bud or make a clean, sloping cut with a sharp blade. Instead, the plant as a whole is given a haircut with powered hedge trimmers. In its favour, this would speed up the pruning work and leave the plants uniform and tidy. On the other hand, it goes against the grain to leave ragged and broken stems that are open wounds for the spores of fungal diseases such as dieback and coral spot.

Another method that is gaining support is to prune out any diseased branches but not thin, spindly stems. A rough pruning of the remaining healthy stems would not allow for detailed pruning above selected buds or making sloping cuts.

Time will tell and you can make up your own mind but remember, my method is not only the standard for pruning but it works. The best argument of all is that pruning roses (or any other plant, for that matter) is fun, with a lot of job satisfaction.

Tree fruit

There is something special about growing your own fruit. Eating a crisp, sweet, rosy-red apple straight from the garden tree or biting into a juicy, home-grown peach still warm from the sun is magical. Anyone can grow a fruit tree. You don't even need a garden, because a big flower pot will suffice.

△ *With this nectarine blossom, not every flower will become a fruit, but the small fruits need to be thinned to 10 cm apart along each stem.*

▷ *The fat buds on this apple are the fruit buds, while the thin and pointed ones are growth buds. The fruit bud will open to a cluster of flowers; the growth bud will become a shoot growing in the direction in which the bud is pointing.*

And no plant is better value for money. A suitable variety planted properly in the right position will continue to produce crops for two or three generations. How well the tree grows and crops is largely dependent on the way it is maintained, and that means good pruning.

A very important part of pruning fruit trees is recognising the difference between a growth bud and a fruit bud. The growth bud is slim and pointed and will produce a new shoot that could in time become part of the main framework of branches that make up the tree. On the other hand, it could produce a leafy shoot with fruit buds or, on apple and pear trees, develop into a fruiting spur (a small length of branch that produces many fruit buds and is capable of producing fruit for several years).

A fruit bud is fatter and more rounded, and in the case of apples, pears and peaches it has a downy, outer layer of scales. It opens as a flower or cluster of flowers. Once pollinated, the flowers produce the fruit.

In winter small birds can be a real pest for a fruit tree. They love the fruit buds, especially of apples and plums, and have been known to strip a mature tree in the course of a few days. The best control is to net the tree until the buds are in flower.

A tree that produces too many fruit will naturally thin the young ones, allowing some to fall off (known as June drop).

ROOTSTOCKS

Most fruit trees are produced by budding or grafting onto a rootstock. They don't reliably propagate from cuttings and won't breed true from seed, although I have to admit to producing superb crops of peaches on a south-facing wall on a tree grown from the stone of a shop-bought peach many years ago.

The named variety you wish to grow (the scion) is budded or grafted onto a specially selected rootstock to suit the particular fruit and give you the right size of mature tree.

Each type of fruit has a different species of rootstock and each rootstock is given a code or name that determines the ultimate size of the tree. Thus if you have a handkerchief-sized garden, you can find a dwarf form of apple suitable for a small space. A commercial fruit grower will be able to grow the same variety grafted onto a different rootstock that will result in a much larger tree that will carry a bigger crop of fruit.

Trees that are grafted onto rootstocks are liable to produce unwanted suckers of the stock from below the graft or directly from the roots. These should be pulled off as soon as they are seen (see pages 90–91).

The following rootstocks are those most commonly used for the major hardy fruit. If you take the time to select the correct stock for your needs you will undoubtedly save yourself a lot of unnecessary pruning.

Apple M27 is an extremely dwarfing stock. A mature tree may grow to 2m high. It is ideal for stepover apple trees, cordons and for pot culture.

M9 is also a dwarfing rootstock ideal for the small garden or for trained trees such as fans and espaliers growing against a wall.

MM106 is popular as a medium-sized garden tree where it is trained as a bush, half standard or full standard.

MM111 will produce very large trees. They will carry a large crop of fruit but you will need a ladder to harvest it. This rootstock has the advantage of producing a good crop on poor, gravelly, free-draining soil.

Pear Quince A is the most popular rootstock, forming a mature tree 4–6m high.

Quince C is slightly less vigorous, attaining 3–5m in height. It is most successful when planted in a fertile, loamy soil. It is usually used for cordon- and espalier-trained trees.

Plum St Julien is a vigorous rootstock with mature plum trees reaching 7m.

Pixy is a dwarfing rootstock that is ideal for growing plums as fan-trained trees against walls.

Cherry F12/1 is very vigorous and was once widely used in commercial cherry orchards but has now been largely replaced by less vigorous versions.

Colt will provide a cherry tree with reasonable growth but it is not as dwarf as is sometimes claimed.

Gisela 5 is proving to be the best dwarf rootstock for garden use, forming a compact tree growing to 3m.

Tabel is extensively used by commercial growers in Europe. Although dwarfing, it will become a larger tree than Gisela 5.

Peach, nectarine and apricot St Julien A is a very vigorous rootstock, resulting in a fan-trained tree with a spread of 5m.

Brompton is used by commercial growers but is too vigorous for the average garden.

Pixy will make a small tree but the crop yields are modest. It is an excellent rootstock for pot-grown peaches, nectarines and apricots.

Figs Figs are grown from cuttings on their own roots.

Mulberry Mulberries are grown from cuttings on their own roots.

Quince Quince A or Quince C are used, as for pears.

Medlar Quince A or Quince C are used, as for pears. They used to be grafted onto hawthorn (*Crataegus*) stocks and with old trees it is common to see hawthorn suckers at the base of the medlar. Quince rootstocks form a better root system with fewer suckers.

SHAPES

Once again I will mention that pruning promotes growth and this is used to good advantage when training a fruit tree, which can be done in an amazing range of shapes.

Bush This is the traditional tree shape and is suitable for most types of tree fruit. The framework of branches spreads out, like the spokes of a wheel, from the trunk at a height of 1m above soil level. The centre of the bush is kept open and free of branches.

Half standard This is a bush tree on a taller trunk. It is a large tree with the additional problems of maintenance and fruit picking, making it more suitable for commercial fruit growers.

Standard As for a half standard but with a trunk 2m in height before the branches spread. This size of tree has to be grown on a vigorous rootstock. There is certainly no difficulty using a ride-on mower to cut the grass under the branches!

Cordon This shape is best suited to apples and pears planted in a small space. The single stem is grown at an angle and supported with a stake or tied to horizontal wires. The growth is restricted by regular pruning, resulting in quality fruit easily ripened in the sun.

Double cordon Unlike the single cordon, the two-stemmed tree is usually planted and trained upright with the twin stems 60cm apart. French nurserymen used to produce multiple-stemmed cordons with up to four branches. They resemble overgrown digging forks, with the vertical prongs 45cm apart. They are difficult to train and the crop of fruit from a given length of wall is no better than single cordons, so they have gone out of fashion.

Espalier The horizontal branches are trained in pairs, one on either side of the main trunk. The tiers are uniformly spaced. It is an ideal method for apples and pears growing against a wall.

Fan This shape is suitable for most tree fruit but is ideal for peaches, nectarines, figs and cherries planted to grow against a sunny, sheltered wall, to ensure that the skin colours well and the fruit ripens early. The trunk forms two branches, one heading to either side, and close to the ground. From these two arise the side branches that form the 'bones' of the fan.

Stepover This is an oddity formed from a single cordon bent over and horizontally trained on a wire 30cm from the ground. It may make an attractive low edging to a path but picking the fruit is as sore on the back as picking strawberries!

◁ Prunus persica 'Flat China' – a well-pruned, fan-shaped ornamental peach displaying its flowers.

Fruit pruning techniques

When left to its own devices a fruit tree will produce some fruit, but for the gardener it is a full-time job to balance the amount of stem and leaf growth with the production of the fruit buds that will lead to a bumper crop. Often the balance is upset by soil and weather conditions along with the ravages of pests and diseases.

△ *To be sure of fruit, pollinate almonds by hand, using cotton wool to touch each flower and transfer pollen.*

▷ *Mature fruit trees are well-suited to growing in grass.*

Quick action with the secateurs and pruning saw may well avert disaster and secure a crop of fruit.

The results of heavy or light pruning are easy to understand. If a fruit tree is pruned hard and lots of branches are removed, there are fewer buds for the root system to feed. Plenty of food (nutrients) is therefore available to the remaining growth buds, leading to an excess of new shoots. With light pruning there are more buds to be fed by the same number of roots. Each bud therefore receives fewer nutrients and growth is weaker. This means that you can prune strong growth lightly, and weak shoots hard, to end up with a balanced branch system.

Timing the pruning is all-important. Most fruit trees are pruned in winter or early spring when the tree is dormant. The exceptions are the stone fruits such as plum, damson, greengage, peach, nectarine, apricot and cherry, which should be pruned in summer when there is less risk of the active disease spores of silver leaf and bacterial canker entering the pruning wounds.

Trained trees such as fan, espalier and cordon should be pruned in summer as well as winter. In summer, shorten the side shoots to curtail growth and build up fruiting wood. In winter, when the tree is dormant, remove any additional extension growth to the side shoots, thus building up a fruiting branch or spur without the tree growing too far out from the main trunk, which is supported on wires or trellis.

Apples and pears are hardy trees but their flowers can be damaged by spring frosts. Prune every year (trained shapes twice a year) to build up a framework of branches and encourage fruit buds.

Pears enjoy the warmth of a sunny, sheltered wall, but if there is a risk of early spring frosts they are best sited away from the morning sun.

Specific pruning techniques for the other tree fruits, including apricots, peaches, plums, figs and mulberries, are covered in the directory beginning on page 174.

Pruning a mature fruit tree

1 A well-maintained, established apple tree before winter pruning.

2 After pruning, with the centre opened and long new growths shortened.

3 A few months later…

Pruning a young fruit tree

It is in the first two years that the framework of branches is formed. In early spring of both these years, shorten the leader and side shoots to encourage new branches. Prune thin branches back to two buds and remove any shoots that are growing towards the centre of the tree. Nip off flowers to prevent fruit forming until the third year.

1 A well-branched young fruit tree. Shorten the side shoots to an outward-pointing bud.

2 Drastically shorten a weak side shoot to build up its strength.

3 The finished job.

Pruning an existing spur system

Many pear cultivars are vigorous with stiff, upright growths that have to be trained early before they firm up (for that reason they are difficult to train as stepover trees). Spur systems develop quickly and are in continual need of thinning to prevent overcrowding. Remove those that are dead, diseased or very old with few fruit buds.

1 A pear in winter with an unpruned spur system.

2 Thin healthy spurs to leave plenty of fruit buds, bearing in mind that each bud produces a cluster of flowers, resulting in more than a single pear.

3 The finished job, showing the thinned spurs and shortened side shoots.

Pruning to encourage a spur system

While two-year-old shoots will produce flower buds, it is the formation of multiple spurs made up of lots of fruit buds that provides a large crop of good-size fruit.

1 An established apple tree before pruning, with lots of young growths.

2 After some pruning, with crossing branches removed and the centre of the tree opened up to allow light in.

3 The finished job: the extension shoots have been reduced to encourage side shoots and the formation of spurs.

RENOVATING OLD TREES

Old bush fruit trees that have been correctly and regularly pruned seldom need renovation. However, after a period of neglect, which needn't be longer than a few years, the tree may need serious pruning to rejuvenate it.

The worst thing that you can do is to go in with your chainsaw revving and cut out masses of branches. That will result in the tree producing many new, thin, whippy growths that will never make fruiting wood. Remedial pruning should be staggered over at least two, and probably three, years. How much you do in the first winter depends on the size of the tree.

The first operation is to remove all diseased and damaged branches, cutting well below any visible infection. Large cuts should be trimmed smooth with a sharp knife to reduce the risk of infection. One of the most likely diseases is canker, and where an attack is local and not girdling the branch it may be worth cutting out the infected part with a knife and leaving the branch to callus over the wound. Sterilise the blade of the knife with disinfectant after such work.

The next job is to decide which branches to remove so as to keep the centre of the tree open. It is better to completely remove one large branch rather than a lot of smaller ones. Crossing and rubbing branches are next in importance – remove the oldest, with the least new growth.

In the year following the first pruning, lots of water shoots will form close to

△ Cutting out an apple branch infected with canker. Be sure to make the cut below the damaged area.

where the branches were removed and on the main framework of branches. These thin, unbranched growths won't make suitable replacement branches and should be removed as close to the bark as possible without leaving a stump to re-grow or become infected with dieback disease.

New growths are produced on existing branches so select the strongest and remove the surplus. Shorten the stems by one third to encourage side shoots and fruiting wood.

Trained trees that have been neglected are difficult to renovate without spoiling their shape. Congested branches may be removed and old spur systems thinned out. If, after one year, the tree appears to be producing growth where it is needed you can carry on pruning. If there is little movement and there is only the main framework to work on, it is probably best to cut your losses and remove the tree, planting a new tree in fresh soil.

◁ A heavy crop of apples will bend the branches, changing the shape of the tree. If low branches have to be removed, do the job in winter when the tree is dormant.

Renovating old trees

The apple tree shown here had been left to its own devices for a long time and remedial pruning should probably be spread over three years. You want to promote strong growth, not a mass of thin shoots, and at the same time pay attention to the shape of the tree. Before you remove a large branch, stand back and consider what the effect on the overall look is going to be.

1 The centre of the tree should be cleared of branches to allow sunlight to the fruit – there is less risk of disease if air can circulate through the tree. The branch crossing through the centre of the tree (from left centre to top right of the picture) should be removed completely.

2 When removing a branch, cut from below (called undercutting) to prevent the weight pulling down and ripping the bark on the main trunk.

3 After the undercut, top-cut well out from the main trunk to remove most of the weight of the branch.

4 The top cut leaves a stump like this…

5 …which should then be removed by a final cut close to the trunk.

6 Removing a large branch last time the tree was pruned has encouraged these upright water shoots to form. They will never become fruiting branches and must be removed close to the main branch without leaving stumps to re-grow.

▷ A free-standing quince on a single stem makes a marvellous specimen fruiting tree.

▽ Malus 'High Canon': a sure sign of a well-pruned apple tree is a balanced head uniformly covered in flowers.

PRUNING A BUSH TREE

A tree bought as a maiden (that is, when it is only one year old) is cheaper than a more mature tree but it will have no side shoots. The basic pruning of this single stem will dictate the shape of the tree for the rest of its life. The technique that I recommend is referred to as 'nicking and notching'. There are several variations on this theme but my way works as follows.

Reduce the single leader by one third to encourage side shoots, cutting with a sloping cut away from a healthy bud and immediately above it. Working down from that cut, leave the top bud to grow but, using a sharp knife, make a cut through the bark 0.5cm below the bud to restrict the quantity of nutrients reaching the bud and so reduce the vigour of the new shoot. The next bud down the stem is likely to be very vigorous, competing with the top bud and forming a narrow angle; it should be removed, so push it off with your thumb. The next two buds will form shoots with reasonable growth at good angles to the stem; these should be left untouched. The lower two buds will produce weak growth, so you can divert nutrients to them by cutting a shallow notch through the bark layer 0.5cm above the buds. Lower buds will produce little growth so they are cut off to leave a bare stem. At the end of the first year's growth the tree should have a balanced framework of branches of similar length and vigour.

If you buy a one-year-old tree with a main stem and lots of small side shoots (known as a 'feathered' tree), select the strongest shoots, well spaced to form a well-branched head. Prune off the remainder. After the first year, shorten the main branches in winter to encourage side branches and make all the cuts to buds pointing in the direction in which the new shoots need to grow. Keep the centre open and remove damaged, crossing and diseased branches.

PRUNING A STANDARD

In the first year, stake a maiden tree and train the leader up to the desired height of 150–200cm, supporting it in a vertical position attached to the timber stake with a tree tie. Prune off any side shoots that appear below that height. Thereafter, prune as for the bush tree, the only difference being the height of clear stem that you leave.

Pruning a maiden apple

There are two good reasons for shaping your own apple tree, rather than buying a ready-shaped two- or three-year-old specimen. Firstly, there is a lot of money to be saved by buying a maiden tree. Secondly, doing it yourself is good fun and brings a lot of job satisfaction.

1 A maiden apple tree without side shoots.

2 Reduce the height by one third, making a sloping cut above a bud.

3 Make an upward-sloping cut (a nick) under the top bud to reduce the flow of nutrients to that bud.

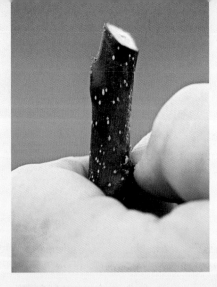

4 Rub out the next bud down the stem as it is likely to form a narrow angle with the main stem.

5 Make a small 'V'-shaped notch above the fifth and sixth buds…

6 …to divert nutrients to them and encourage growth.

Training fruit trees

It is essential that you purchase a tree with a shape that suits your needs. A bush tree is better suited to training as a fan, while a feathered maiden will – with careful pruning – make an excellent cordon or espalier.

△ Whatever the shape you train your fruit tree to be, it is blossom you really want.

▷▷ Summer pruning a cordon involves shortening all the side shoots back to 3 or 4 leaves.

PRUNING A CORDON

Plant a single-stemmed maiden tree at an angle of about 45° to the vertical. Each year prune in both summer and winter, shortening all the side shoots to build up fruiting spurs.

Allow the leader to grow to 2m, then stop it by pruning off the growing tip in early summer. Prune above a weak side shoot to reduce any re-growth at the top. Letting it grow higher makes pruning and harvesting overhead difficult.

The Lorette system of pruning, which was devised in France and in which all the side shoots are pruned to within 5cm of the older wood, is the traditional system for cordons in warm climates. In cooler countries it is modified: cut all the side shoots to 5cm in early summer when the base of the shoots has firmed up. Prune subsequent strong side growths back to one bud. Leave unpruned any side shoots that are shorter than 15cm and shorten them the following spring.

Double cordons are usually planted in an upright position. Select two buds that are close together approximately 30cm above ground level and pointing in opposite directions. Make a notch above the buds (see page 153) and two strong side shoots will be produced. Remove all other side growths.

Train the two shoots in opposite directions at a 45° angle for 20–30cm before changing their direction and tying in the growths vertically to canes. The twin shoots are now 40–60cm apart. The following year, prune the double cordon as for a single cordon. A three-pronged cordon looks great but the central cordon will become much more vigorous than the outer two stems, causing problems throughout the life of the plant.

▷ In the second year the shortened shoots will produce fruit buds.

△ The horizontal
branches of each espalier
are trained to wires. Nip
out the growing tip of
each branch where they
meets on the wire.

PRUNING AN ESPALIER

The secret of a well-shaped espalier is in the supporting horizontal wires, which should be in place before planting. Space them 45–60cm apart. Plant the tree in the centre of the area with a vertical cane for support. Cut the leader back to 5cm above the lowest wire. Make a notch above two buds that are pointing to either side of the main stem, along the wire. Tie the resulting side shoots to bamboo canes at a 30° angle from the wire, then secure these to the wires. Train the leader vertically to another cane. At the end of the season, lower the two side shoots to the horizontal wire. Follow the same process each year, making sure that you cut the leader close to the next available wire above the last two trained stems.

Allow each branch to grow horizontally until it fills the available space, then stop it by nipping out the growing tip of the shoot. When all the tiers have been formed, prune out the leader. Once the framework of the espalier is established, use the modified Lorette system as described for cordons (see page 154), pruning the laterals to three leaves to allow the base of the stem to ripen and develop fruit buds and spurs. Cut the resulting side shoots back to one leaf.

The lower tier of branches will be less vigorous than the upper tiers and in subsequent years may be pruned harder. The spur systems of mature espaliers should be thinned out by removing the oldest wood.

PRUNING A FAN-TRAINED TREE

When there is choice, always buy a fan-trained tree where the branches spread out from two low branches rather than from the main trunk. If you are training the fan yourself, you should prune and train as for an espalier, securing the shoots to bamboo canes fixed at a 45° angle to the main trunk and attached to horizontal wires. Each branch that makes up the fan grows from these two framework branches and should be pruned in summer and winter as for a single cordon.

PRUNING A STEPOVER TREE

With a stepover apple tree the secret of success rather than frustration is to purchase a young maiden with a short stem. Plant it vertically and gradually bend the stem down until it is horizontal and can be tied to a horizontal wire 30–45cm above ground level. Thereafter, prune it in the same way as a cordon tree.

◁ In winter, this fan-shaped pear has a certain stark elegance. In flower it will be beautiful.

▽ Mature stepover trees have so many spurs that they become more like hurdles.

Vines

Grapes may be grown in a greenhouse or outside, preferably in a sunny, sheltered position. Annual pruning in winter is essential, as the vigorous plants quickly grow out of shape.

△ Vitis 'Müller-Thurgau' is attractive in fruit and leaf. It is also hardier than many grape varieties, so can be grown outside against a sheltered wall.

▷ Vitis 'Muscat of Alexandria: each main stem is known as a 'rod' and will carry up to 20 bunches of grapes in a 4m-wide lean-to greenhouse.

▷▷ Vitis 'Lady Hutt': to prevent leaf scorch, keep the vine at least 20–30cm away from the glass.

Under glass, the usual method of growing a grape vine is as a cordon. Tie the main stem of the young plant loosely to a cane and train it vertically up a wall or a side of the greenhouse. Tie the side shoots to horizontal wires that are 30cm apart and 20–25cm away from the glass to avoid scorching. Train the shoots to alternate

wires, the first to the left side and the second to the next wire up on the right. This gives a spacing of 60cm between the horizontal side shoots. During each summer of the first two years after planting, pinch out the tips of the side shoots at the fifth or sixth set of leaves. Remove the flowers to prevent fruit forming and to encourage sturdy growth. In early winter, and again about one month later, shorten the main stem by one half and prune the side shoots again, this time to within 1cm of the main stem. These short shoots are the start of the fruiting spurs.

In subsequent years the pruning system changes. Only one growth bud is allowed to grow away from each pruned spur. Stop the side shoots by pinching out the growing tip at two leaves beyond the small flower cluster on each shoot. Shorten extension side shoots to one leaf. When the main stem is as high and as long as you want it to be, prune the growing tip back to a lateral in winter. At the same time, shorten all the laterals to leave two buds on each spur, one of which will be removed in spring.

Pruning an indoor vine

2 Using a blunt knife so as not to damage the wood, scrape off the loose bark in which pests and diseases can overwinter.

1 Prune the side shoots of an indoor vine back to two buds in winter. When they start to grow, prune back to leave one shoot.

3 Alternatively, pull the old, flaky bark off by hand.

4 Prune side shoots two leaves beyond the clusters of flowers.

5 Indoor vine rods held clear of the glass roof on supports and after winter pruning.

▷ The large dark green leaves of Vitis coignetiae *turn bright red in autumn.*

▽ V. coignetiae is a vigorous plant and needs regular pruning to keep it within bounds.

OUTDOOR VINES

These are usually grown by the double Guyot system, using a post and wire support. The wooden posts are 2–3m apart with the bottom horizontal wire 45cm above ground level and a further four horizontal wires above it spaced 30cm apart.

The idea is to plant the single-stemmed, one-year-old vine below the wires and, leaving two buds, prune it back to about 15cm above ground level. Allow only one shoot to grow and remove the reserve bud, kept in case of an accident damaging either bud. Given a choice, choose the lowest bud. As the shoot grows, shorten any side shoots back to 2cm. The following winter, prune the main shoot back to within 60cm of the ground, leaving three buds. All three shoots will grow vertically during the summer. After leaf-drop in the autumn, prune the top stem back to three buds and train the opposite side shoots to the lowest wires, one to either side. Shorten them back to 1m from the main stem.

The following year allow the side shoots produced from these two horizontal branches (rods) to grow vertically. Thin them out to 20cm apart. Stop them growing by removing the tip 2 or 3 leaves beyond the top wire. These stems carry the flowers and bunches of grapes. In late autumn or early winter prune the two branches that carried the side shoots and fruit, cutting them back to the main stem. Cut the centre shoot back to three buds, and lower the other two shoots and tie to the horizontal wires. Repeat the process each year.

Pruning an outdoor vine

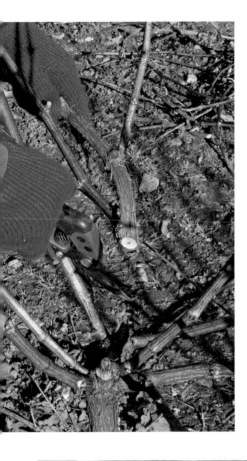

1 The starting point – last year's growth needs to be cut back in winter to encourage the new young growth which will produce fruit.

2 In winter prune the main shoot back, leaving three buds. Train two side shoots in opposite directions and tie them to the wire. They will fruit this year.

3 The three shoots from the main stem will grow vertically during the summer. After leaf drop in autumn, once again prune the top stem back to three buds. Cut out the two stems that have been tied to the wire and have fruited.

4 Lower and tie in two of the side shoots as before. Shorten them to 1m. Cut the other vertical shoot back to leave three buds.

5 Tie in the stems using twist ties or soft string. Cut them out after fruiting in autumn.

Pruning bush and cane fruit

There is a varied selection of berries and currants that are grown as bushes. Gooseberries, blueberries, cranberries and black-, white- and redcurrants are the most popular. Then there are the cane fruit such as raspberries, blackberries and loganberries. Their yields are all improved by regular pruning.

△ *Loganberries are a cross between a raspberry and a blackberry with a sharp taste better suited to culinary use.*

▷ *With regular pruning a blackcurrant bush will crop well for 10–12 years.*

▽ *Summer-fruiting raspberry canes will need support.*

The most important thing with bush fruit is to try to keep the centre of the plant open. This allows air to circulate and the sun to ripen the fruit. The spiny stems of the gooseberry make harvesting difficult in the centre of the bush.

Annual pruning will encourage new growths that may be used to replace older, non-productive stems. In summer, shorten the side shoots of gooseberries, redcurrants and whitecurrants to within 4 or 5 leaves of the base. Remove low branches where the fruit may be mud-splashed when it rains. Any of these fruits may be pruned and trained as cordons against a wall or trellis (see page 154).

Blackcurrants should be pruned after the fruit has been harvested. Cut out the oldest stems as close to soil level as possible. They will have black bark, while younger shoots are brown. Strong new shoots will be produced from low down on the remaining stems: thin these to keep the centre of the bush free of branches. Watch out for coral spot and dieback disease on old stumps (see page 16) and remove any affected parts immediately.

With cane fruit, remove the stems after one crop and train the new shoots in to replace them. Killer diseases such as virus (see page 16) are common and any plants with a majority of distorted, mottled or yellowing leaves should be dug out and burnt.

Prune cranberries and blueberries in winter or early spring, removing any dead, diseased or damaged branches. Old stems that have stopped producing reasonable quantities of fruit should be removed at ground level.

Pruning bush fruit

Of all bush fruit, gooseberries are the most difficult to prune. Most varieties are well endowed with sharp thorns, making it sensible to keep the centre of the bush open for ease of picking the fruit (though even if you leave the bush unpruned for years the tangled mass of branches will continue to produce fruit). It is essential to protect your hands with thorn-proof gloves.

1 A mature gooseberry bush before pruning.

2 With hands well protected and using secateurs, prune out all dead and diseased stems. Remove branches that are growing towards the centre of the bush.

3 In winter shorten the leaders of all main branches by half.

4 Prune side shoots back to two buds.

5 After winter pruning, the branches are well spaced for ease of picking, allowing air to circulate and giving lots of potential for fruit and new growth.

For the second, early summer pruning cut the newly produced side shoots to within 4 or 5 leaves of the main branch. This builds up a well-branched framework and makes access to the fruit easier.

Pruning raspberries

With summer-fruiting raspberries, all the canes that carried fruit should be removed at ground level in early winter. Autumn-fruiting varieties should be pruned in early spring, cutting all the stems close to the soil. A deep mulch of farmyard manure applied in spring will retain moisture, suppress weeds and encourage strong, new shoots.

1 A row of raspberries before pruning. The old canes have already fruited and will be removed; the new canes will fruit next year.

2 When pruning, remove old canes and spindly, weak new canes and thin new ones.

3 Tie the remaining canes in to their supporting wires, 10cm apart, using soft twine.

Pruning loganberries

The canes of loganberries are very vigorous and plants can become a tangled mess after a single season. They are best supported on a strong wire 1.5m above the ground.

2 They fruit on the new growths, so prune the old stems at ground level.

1 Loganberry plants are similar in appearance to raspberries but more vigorous.

3 Remove any weak, spindly stems and those that have fruited.

4 Tie new growths into wire supports to keep the plant tidy. If all the new growths are arched and trained to one side of the wire, then the following winter the new growths can be trained in the same way to the opposite side. After year one it is easy to prune out the old stems.

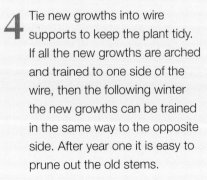

Pruning currants

Currants are easy to prune. After planting blackcurrants, cut all the stems above a bud back to 3–5cm above soil level. The next winter remove any thin or damaged stems as close to soil level as possible. Thereafter in winter remove half the fruited branches at ground level. After 3–4 years remove any remaining old wood.

△ A redcurrant bush grown as a double cordon with all the side shoots pruned back to form fruiting spurs.

Redcurrants and whitecurrants are usually grown as cordons. After planting, prune the main stem back to one half its length and tie it to a vertical cane. Prune the side shoots back to the bud closest to the main stem. In future years shorten the main shoot to leave 15–20cm of new growth and cut the side shoots back to leave one healthy bud. In early summer shorten the side shoots to 4–5 leaves.

▷ Keep side shoots short to prevent leaves from obscuring the fruit.

Pruning blackcurrants

1 Blackcurrants benefit from annual pruning.

2 To remove an old, poorly fruiting branch, cut as close to the base as possible. With blackcurrants, the oldest branches have the darkest bark.

3 The finished job. The young, upright stems will continue to fruit well for several years.

Directory of plants

M any plants will benefit from regular pruning throughout their lives, while others, though old and neglected, may be rejuvenated by a severe pruning. Still others need only be shaped early on and will then reward you by keeping obediently to their allotted space for the rest of their days. Whatever the case, sensible pruning at the right time will help to guarantee a healthy crop of flowers and fruit.

◁ Protea cynaroides (*see page 235*) *seldom requires pruning other than to maintain shape.*

ABELIA
Evergreen or semi-evergreen shrub with arching branches of glossy, green leaves. Terminal panicles of funnel-shaped, pink-tinged, white, fragrant flowers are produced in summer and autumn. Flowers on growths made the previous year. Not totally hardy, succeeding best in a sheltered garden. Height 3m.

In spring tidy the plant, removing dead or damaged stems. After flowering prune 3 or 4 of the oldest branches at ground level. It tolerates hard pruning. To rejuvenate an old plant simply cut all the branches close to the ground in spring, or late spring in frosty areas.

ABELIOPHYLLUM DISTICHUM
(White forsythia)
Deciduous shrub. The matt, green leaves turn purple in autumn. The fragrant, white flowers are occasionally tinged pink, appearing in late winter and early spring on the previous year's growth. Hardy, but in cold areas will do better against a sunny wall. Height 1.5m.

Prune immediately after flowering, removing all flowering stems back to a strong, healthy side shoot. With established shrubs remove one third of the oldest branches as close to soil level as possible.

ABUTILON
Genus of evergreen or deciduous shrubs that need to be pruned in different ways.

One of my favourite evergreens is *Abutilon megapotamicum*, which has arching stems and bright green leaves. Pendant, bell-shaped flowers appear on the new shoots in summer and autumn. Not hardy. Height 2m. This and other evergreen species should be pruned in early spring, shortening the previous year's growths by one third. Young plants tolerate hard pruning, resulting in large leaves on the young growths.

Abutilon vitifolium is a fast-growing, deciduous shrub that resembles a tree with grey, hairy leaves and pendant, saucer-shaped, white or purple-blue flowers in early summer. Cold winds in spring may cause damage. Height 5m.

Prune young plants in summer after flowering. Avoid pruning established plants, other than tidying up dead and broken branches and deadheading.

ACACIA (Mimosa)

Evergreen shrub or small tree with dense branches and pinnate, silver-grey, fern-like leaves and racemes of bright yellow flower heads in winter and spring. Not hardy, preferring to be planted at the base of a sunny, sheltered wall. Height 4–7m.

Prune young plants of vigorous species such as *A. longifolia* by shortening all the stems by 15cm to form bushy plants. For slow-growing species, nip out the growing tips of young plants to encourage side shoots. Prune as soon as the risk of frost is past and as soon after flowering as possible. Trim back frost-damaged stems to a side shoot in late spring. All acacias resent hard pruning.

ACER (Maple)

Genus of deciduous and evergreen trees and shrubs, often with brilliantly coloured autumn foliage and/or attractive bark. Most are fully hardy. *A. platanoides* (Norway maple) can reach 25m; many varieties of *A. palmatum* and *A. japonicum* (Japanese maple) attain no more than 1.5m

Healthy plants need little pruning. If it is necessary to remove broken branches,

▷ Acacia baileyana *is a vigorous species that needs shelter from cold winds, which may damage the young growths.*

do this in winter to avoid sap bleeding from cuts made during the growing season. Variegated cultivars such as *A. platanoides* 'Drummondii' will produce reverted growths with all-green leaves. Prune off these shoots as soon as they are seen. Watch out for narrow-angled branches that will suffer damage in a storm (see pages 26–27).

A. palmatum is prone to dieback (see page 16). Prune in late spring. Break off dead stems or snip with secateurs.

The snake-bark maples, such as *A. grosseri*, are prone to coral spot disease (see page 16).

ACMENA (Lillypilly)
Evergreen tree with glossy leaves and panicles of greenish-white flowers in late spring and early summer. In Australia the white, pink or red autumn berries are eaten. Not hardy but may survive a light frost on a sheltered wall protected from the morning sun. Height 10–12m.

Pruning consists of removing crossing branches. If wall-grown then in late winter prune back the older branches to a strong new shoot or healthy bud.

ACTINIDIA
A. kolomikta is a deciduous climber with dark green leaves, purple-tinged when young, the top half becoming white and pink. Small, fragrant, white flowers are produced in early summer, followed on female plants by yellowish green fruit. Hardy. Height 5m.

Prune in winter to keep the plant within its allotted space. It tolerates hard pruning to rejuvenate an old plant.

A. deliciosa is deciduous and should be pruned in late winter, shortening side shoots back to 2 or 3 buds to form fruiting spurs. During the growing season nip out beyond 5 leaves the growing tips of all side shoots.

AESCULUS (Horse chestnut)
Deciduous trees and suckering shrubs with large, palmate leaves and upright 'candles' of white, pink or rose-red flowers with yellow centres followed by spiny fruit (conkers). Hardy. Height to 25m.

Prune as necessary to maintain shape in late winter when dormant. Retain the central leader. Water shoots that are produced close to large pruning cuts should be removed without leaving a stump. As trees mature the lower branches may be removed to form a standard with 2m-clear trunk.

A. × carnea is prone to competing narrow-angled main branches. Remove the weakest branch as early as possible.

AGAPETES SERPENS
Evergreen climber with small, glossy green leaves and urn-shaped, bright red flowers with V-shaped markings in the leaf axils during late winter and early spring. Not hardy. Height 90cm.

Little pruning is necessary apart from shortening straggly growths. Remove old and bare stems at ground level. It dislikes hard pruning.

AGONIS FLEXUOSA
Evergreen tree with pendant branches and long, thin, willow-like leaves. Clusters of small white flowers are produced in summer. Not fully hardy, preferring a sheltered site and ericaceous compost. Height 6–10m. Pruning is seldom necessary but remove broken or crossing branches in late summer after flowering.

AILANTHUS ALTISSIMA
(Tree of heaven)
Fast-growing, deciduous tree with 60cm-long pinnate leaves and panicles of small green flowers followed by red-brown fruit. Hardy. Height 15m.

Prune in late winter when dormant. Retain a central leader. Suckers from the roots may be a problem and should be pulled off. It responds well to coppicing every second year, forming a multi-branched habit with exceptionally long leaves. Prone to suckers, which will quickly form a thicket if not dug out or pulled off.

AKEBIA QUINATA (Chocolate vine)
Semi-evergreen climber with dark green leaves, blue-green on the underside, turning purple in winter. Pendant racemes of fragrant purplish flowers appear in early spring followed by sausage-shaped, violet fruit. Hardy. Height 12m.

Prune in late spring after flowering by shortening side shoots (laterals) by one half. Cut back vigorous shoots by up to one third to a sturdy side shoot to prevent the climber becoming unruly. Prune out spindly shoots as close to the base as possible.

ALBIZIA JULIBRISSIN
Deciduous tree with fern-like, mid-green leaves and terminal clusters of green-yellow flowers in summer. Not hardy but it will tolerate some frost provided the growths have had a chance to ripen after a hot summer. Height 5–6m.

Prune in spring to remove frost-damaged shoots and crossing branches. It tolerates pruning to reduce size but don't cut into wood more than 2 years old. Prune to a sturdy side shoot pointing in the correct direction.

ALNUS (Alder)
Deciduous trees with conspicuous male catkins. They can be grown with a central leader, although many naturally form multi-stemmed trees. Hardy and happy in damp ground; useful as wind breaks in exposed sites. Height 15–25m.

▷ Akebia quinata *benefits from annual pruning when all risk of frost is over.*

To form a multi-stemmed tree, prune the young, newly planted tree back to 45cm from the base. A mature tree requires only the 3 Ds (see page 20). Prune in winter when the tree is dormant. It tolerates hard pruning.

ALOYSIA TRIPHYLLA (Lemon verbena)

Bushy, deciduous shrub with lemon-scented leaves. The panicles of small, pale lilac or white flowers are produced in late summer. Not hardy. Height 3m.

In cool climates prune in spring to healthy buds 30–45cm from the base. In warm climates shorten all the stems to within 15cm of the main framework. In early summer pinch out the tips of shoots to form a bushy plant.

AMELANCHIER CANADENSIS
(Shadbush)

An erect, suckering, deciduous shrub or small tree with mid-green leaves that turn yellow and orange in autumn. Racemes of small, white flowers appear in early spring followed by edible, blue-black fruit in autumn. Hardy. Height 6m.

Prune in winter to reduce congestion in centre of bush. Remove unwanted stems as close to ground level as possible. Remove suckers as they appear.

AMPELOPSIS BREVIPEDUNCULATA

A vigorous, deciduous climber with dark green leaves and small green flowers in summer followed by blue fruit in late autumn. Hardy. Height 7m.

Prune in winter or early spring, removing unwanted extension growths. Thin out old, bare stems by cutting into lengths and pulling them out of the tangled growths.

ANDROMEDA POLIFOLIA
(Bog rosemary)

Semi-prostrate, evergreen shrub with leathery, dark green leaves and white or pale pink flowers in spring and early summer. Hardy. Height 45cm.

Seldom requires pruning until mature, when old stems bare of leaves may be removed at ground level. The branches root by layering where they are in contact with the ground, and may be potted up.

ANEMOPAEGMA CHAMBERLAYNII
(Yellow trumpet vine)

A vigorous, evergreen climber with tough, claw-like tendrils. Racemes of pale yellow, trumpet-shaped flowers, striped white and purple at the throat, are produced in summer and early autumn. Not hardy but may survive in a sheltered, frost-free corner of the garden. Height 3–4m.

Prune in late winter or early spring, shortening the side shoots to within 2–4 buds of the main framework. It tolerates hard pruning to curtail growth.

ANGOPHORA HISPIDA (Dwarf apple)

A bushy, evergreen shrub or small tree with peeling, orange-brown bark and grey-green leaves with scalloped margins. Clusters of creamy-white flowers appear in late summer. Not hardy but will succeed in sheltered, frost-free gardens. Height 3–6m.

Prune in early spring to keep the centre of the bush open and remove crossing branches.

ANISODONTEA CAPENSIS

Evergreen shrub with upright branches and mid-green, lobed leaves. The racemes of red-purple flowers appear at the leaf axils in summer and early autumn. Not totally hardy but feeding with a high potash fertiliser will firm up the stems before autumn. Height 90cm.

Prune tips in late spring to encourage side shoots and make a bushy plant.

ANNONA CHERIMOLA
(Custard apple)

In cool conditions it is only semi-

△ Aralia elata 'Variegata': prune in early spring to remove all green shoots and diseased, dead or damaged branches.

evergreen with dark green, aromatic leaves and fragrant, pale yellow flowers with a purple-spotted base, followed by 15–20cm pale green, edible fruit. Not hardy. Height 6m.

Cut back the young plant and allow 3 or 4 laterals to grow. Prune the tips of these in summer to encourage more side shoots. Prune back by one third any vigorous shoots that are spoiling the shape or are refusing to produce flowers. Keep the centre of the bush open, with no crossing branches.

ARALIA

Deciduous shrubs and small trees with spiny stems and enormous, dark green leaves. There are variegated cultivars. Large umbels of small, white flowers are produced in summer and autumn. Hardy. Height 8–10m.

Take great care when pruning as the spines are dangerous. Prune in early spring, removing crossing or damaged branches. Variegated cultivars may revert and the all-green shoots should be pruned out as soon as they are seen.

ARAUCARIA ARAUCANA
(Monkey puzzle)
An evergreen, coniferous tree with whorled branches and leathery, glossy, bright green leaves that become duller as they age. The large male and female cones are conspicuous. Hardy. Height 20–25m.

Occasionally a young tree will produce a side shoot from the base. Remove it as soon as possible to prevent it spoiling the tree shape. Mature trees will lose their lower branches, leaving dead stumps. Cutting these off close to the trunk will improve the look of the tree.

ARBUTUS (Strawberry tree)
Bushy, evergreen shrubs or small trees with peeling red-brown bark and leathery, dark green leaves. The panicles of small, urn-shaped, white or pink flowers are produced in autumn with the strawberry-like fruit appearing at the same time one year later. Hardy but protect from cold, biting winds. Height 2–15m.

Prune in spring when all risk of frost is over. Little pruning is necessary but dead branches should be removed and the centre of the plant kept open.

ARCTOSTAPHYLOS (Bearberry)
Prostrate or upright evergreen shrubs and small trees with panicles of small, urn-shaped, white or pink flowers in winter, spring or early summer. Hardy but prefer to be sheltered from cold winds. Height 10cm–10m.

Prune in early spring to remove crossing branches. Low-growing shrubs may be trimmed after flowering with the loss of the fruit.

▷ Arbutus × androsterilis *will seldom need pruning once mature, provided you have allocated it enough space.*

◁ Ardisia crenata: *in the first growing season nip out the tips of the shoots to encourage a bushy plant and avoid 'bare legs'.*

ARDISIA
Erect, evergreen shrubs with mid- to dark green, leathery leaves and terminal clusters of small, star-like, pink flowers in summer followed in winter by bright red berries. Not hardy, requiring a very sheltered site to survive a mild winter. Height 90–150cm. Prune established shrubs in late winter. Shorten summer growth that spoils the plant's shape.

ARGYRANTHEMUM
(Chrysanthemum)
Evergreen sub-shrubs with green, lobed leaves and single or double, white, pink or yellow flowers in spring, summer or autumn. Not hardy. Height 50–100cm.

Pinch out the growing tips to encourage side growths and disbud to increase the flower size.

ARGYREIA NERVOSA
(Woolly morning glory)
A twining, evergreen climber with silver-backed, dark green leaves. The lavender-blue flowers are flushed red-purple on the inside and appear in summer and autumn. Not hardy. Height 8m.

Prune in late winter to curtail the growth. In a large container, summer pruning may be necessary to keep the plant within bounds.

ARISTOLOCHIA (Dutchman's pipe)
Evergreen and deciduous twining climbers with heart-shaped, dark green leaves and petalless summer flowers, with curved calyces and inflated bases. They may be white, brown or purple with darker blotches. *A. macrophylla* is reasonably hardy but most species are not hardy. Height 5–10m.

Prune after flowering, shortening long shoots. Where growth has to be curtailed all the laterals may be cut back in late summer to within 3 or 4 buds of the main framework of branches.

ARISTOTELIA CHILENSIS (Macqui)
Evergreen shrub with glossy, dark green leaves and greenish-white flowers in summer. Hardy but requires shelter from cold winds and hard frosts. Height 5m.

Prune in spring to shape the plant and remove crossing branches. Male plants may be deadheaded after flowering. Female plants produce black fruit.

ARONIA (Chokeberry)
Deciduous, suckering, bushy shrubs with mid- to dark green leaves that colour to red and purple in autumn. White flowers on the previous year's growth in spring. Hardy. Height 2–3m.

Prune in spring, removing dead branches and those filling the centre of the bush. After flowering, shoots may be cut back to within 3 or 4 buds of the framework to allow new growths to be produced. On mature plants, cut out one third of the oldest branches at the base.

ARTEMISIA (Wormwood)
Evergreen and deciduous shrubs with aromatic, grey-green, fern-like leaves and panicles of unattractive yellowish flowers in late summer. *A. dracunculus* is the herb tarragon. Hardy. Height 60–120cm.

Regular pruning is essential to prevent the plant becoming woody and bare at the base. Pinch out unwanted flowering buds. Hard pruning will encourage new growths from the base.

ARTOCARPUS (Breadfruit, jackfruit)
Evergreen trees with dark green leaves and edible fruit. Not hardy. Height 15–25m. With young plants train four healthy laterals to canes to lower them and form an open, branched head. *A. altilis* (breadfruit) tends to produce vigorous, upright shoots. After fruiting prune to encourage new shoots that will fruit the following year. Mature branches are brittle and easily damaged.

ASTERANTHERA OVATA

An evergreen climber or crawling shrub with deep green, hairy leaves on white stems and bright, deep pink, long-tubed flowers in summer. Hardy, but avoid drying, cold winds. Height 3–4m.

Prune out dead or damaged stems at ground level in late spring after all risk of frost is past. Prune back old, bare stems. Severe pruning may kill the plant.

ATRIPLEX

Evergreen and semi-evergreen shrubs, perennials and annuals, usually with grey-green leaves and insignificant green or greenish-white flowers in summer.

Shrubs are hardy but benefit from shelter from cold winds. Height 1.2–2m.

Prune in late spring, reducing the previous year's growths by one third to one half. A light clipping in summer will keep the plant compact and tidy.

AUCUBA (Spotted laurel)

Evergreen shrubs with large, glossy green leaves, often spotted and blotched with yellow. The inconspicuous, red-purple flowers are produced in spring and are followed on female plants by bright red fruit. Hardy. Height 3m.

Prune the non-fruiting varieties in winter and those with fruit in mid-spring.

New plants should have the stems shortened by one half to encourage a bushy shrub. Strong-growing, vertical shoots should be removed. Dieback is common and blackened stems should be cut back to healthy wood. Rejuvenate old plants over 2 years by cutting out the oldest shoots at the base.

AVERRHOA CARAMBOLA (Star fruit)

A slow-growing, semi-evergreen tree or shrub with pendant branches and dark green leaves glaucous on the underside, and dark red flowers. Not hardy but will tolerate light frost. Height 10m.

Prune in the early years to form an open framework of branches. Shorten the main stems to encourage laterals and a multi-branched head. Thereafter the 3 Ds (see page 20) are the only pruning needed.

AZARA

Evergreen shrubs and trees with mid- to dark green or variegated leaves and small clusters of fragrant, yellow flowers in winter and early spring. Not reliably hardy, requiring the shelter of a sunny wall. Height 4–10m.

Little pruning is required. It does not tolerate hard pruning. Remove crossing or dead branches in late spring.

BACCHARIS HALIMIFOLIA
(Sea myrtle)

Vigorous, upright, deciduous shrub with grey-green, deeply notched leaves and small, white flower heads in autumn. Hardy. Height 4m. Prune in spring by trimming over the whole plant, removing one third of each stem.

◁ Artemisia frigida: *annual pruning in late spring will result in a bushy plant without leafless stems.*

BANKSIA

Evergreen trees and shrubs with leathery leaves that are often lobed. The cylindrical or globe-like yellow, orange or red flowers are produced in spring, summer or autumn. Not hardy. Height 2–10m.

Prune after flowering by reducing the length of the previous year's stems. *B. coccinea* dislikes hard pruning.

BARLERIA CRISTATA

(Philippine violet)

Evergreen shrub with bristly-hairy stems and dark green leaves. The small pink, white or violet flowers appear in summer. Not hardy. Height 90cm.

Prune after flowering, cutting the stems that flowered back by one third. Mature plants may be thinned by removing the old stems close to the ground.

BAUERA RUBIOIDES

Low-growing, bushy, evergreen shrub with dark green leaves and individual white or pink flowers on long stalks during spring and summer. Not hardy. Height 15cm–2m.

Prune after flowering by removing crossing branches and shortening shoots that are spoiling the shape of the plant.

BEAUFORTIA SPARSA

(Swamp bottlebrush)

Evergreen shrub with mid- to deep green leaves. The bright cerise-red flowers are produced in summer and autumn. Not hardy. Height 2m.

Prune in late spring, shortening any long stems and removing crossing branches. Deadhead after flowering.

BEAUMONTIA GRANDIFLORA

Evergreen climber with reddish-brown young leaves maturing to glossy, deep green. The fragrant, white, trumpet-shaped flowers appear in late spring and summer. Not hardy. Height 5–8m.

Prune in late winter to keep the plant within bounds. Side shoots may be shortened in early spring to within 3 or 4 buds of the permanent framework to build up flowering stems.

BERBERIDOPSIS CORALLINA

(Coral plant)

Evergreen climber with dark green, spiny leaves glaucous on the underside. Clusters and racemes of dark red flowers on long stalks are produced in summer and early autumn. Hardy but avoid cold winds. Height 3–4m.

Prune in spring to keep the plant within bounds, but it is not a strong grower so there is seldom the need.

BERBERIS (Barberry)

Deciduous and evergreen shrubs with glossy, green, spine-toothed or red-purple leaves and spiny stems. The pale to dark orange-yellow flowers are produced in clusters or racemes during spring. Hardy. Height 30cm–4m.

Prune in early summer if the blue-black fruit are not wanted. Otherwise prune in winter to open the centre of the plant and remove the oldest branches. To rejuvenate, cut the branches to within 30cm of ground level. Varieties grown for their foliage, such as the deciduous *B. thunbergii* 'Rose Glow', may be pruned hard each winter to encourage new growths to develop.

BERCHEMIA

Deciduous climbers with mid- to dark green leaves with prominent, parallel veins, and long panicles of small green flowers during summer. Hardy. Height 4m.

Prune in late winter or early spring, shortening long growths and thinning out congested, old stems.

BETULA (Birch)

Deciduous trees and shrubs with mid- to dark green leaves and male and female catkins on the same plant. Peeling bark may be silver, white, cream or orange-brown. Hardy. Height 60cm–25m.

Prune in winter when the plant is dormant. Avoid spring when the sap is rising, as any pruning at that time will make the plant bleed. Remove crossing and dead branches. If 'witches' brooms' are considered unsightly they may be pruned out (see page 17).

BILLARDIERA

Evergreen climbers with thin stems and dark green leaves. In spring or summer they produce greenish-yellow, green or purple bell-shaped flowers followed by white, pink, red, dark green or purple berries. Not fully hardy but will survive in a sheltered position. Height 2–4m.

Prune after flowering to reduce height.

BOENNINGHAUSENIA ALBIFLORA

Deciduous sub-shrub with pinnate, dark green leaves and panicles of cup-shaped, white or pale yellow flowers in late summer. Hardy. Height 90cm.

Prune in early spring, removing the flowering stems close to the base.

BOMAREA

Tuberous, deciduous climbers with mid- to dark green leaves with tubular or bell-shaped, yellow, orange or red flowers during summer and autumn. Not hardy, although *B. edulis* may survive in a sheltered garden on a warm wall. Height 2–3m.

Prune at ground level all the stems that flowered. Cut out any dead growths.

▷ Berberis thunbergii *is deciduous, quickly becoming large and bushy. It will make a formidable hedge with good colour.*

△ Bomarea caldisii *loves to scramble over other plants (here a cotoneaster), which can make it difficult to prune off shoots once they have finished flowering.*

BOMBAX CEIBA (Red silk cotton tree)
Deciduous tree with a spiny stem and palmate, mid-green leaves. The bright cerise-red flowers have fleshy petals appearing in early spring, before the leaves. Not hardy. Height 20m.

Prune in winter when dormant to restrict growth and remove crossing branches. Cut the stems back to the main framework.

BORONIA
Evergreen shrubs with deep green leaves that are often aromatic. The bell- or cup-shaped flowers range in colour from reddish-brown to deep pink and are produced from late winter to summer. Not hardy, although *B. megastigma* may survive in a sheltered, frost-free area.

After planting, prune the tips to form a bushy plant. Prune after flowering, shortening the flowered shoots by one third. They dislike hard pruning so avoid cutting into old wood or leaving the plant with few leaves.

BOUGAINVILLEA

Evergreen and deciduous, spiny-stemmed climbers, grown for their brightly coloured bracts, which are usually white, apricot, magenta, red or purple. Not hardy, although *B. glabra* and *B. spectabilis* may survive outside in a sheltered, frost-free garden. Height 5–7m and vigorous.

Prune in early spring before growth commences. *B. spectabilis* is pruned after flowering in late summer. After planting, prune young climbers back hard to encourage strong growths from the base of the plant. Thin out weak and spindly shoots. Prune established plants by shortening the long growths by three quarters of their length. Prune badly placed shoots to within 3 or 4 buds of the main framework. Cut back all the laterals to produce flowering spurs.

BOUVARDIA

Bushy, compact, evergreen shrubs with mid-green leaves and long-tubed scarlet or fragrant white flowers produced on the current year's growth from late summer to early winter. Not hardy. Height 60–100cm.

Immediately after flowering or in late winter prune out at ground level old growths, crossing stems and weak branches. Reduce flowering stems by half. Prune the tips of the new growths to encourage side shoots.

◁ *Boronia 'Lipstick' should be pruned lightly immediately after flowering. Shorten the stems that flowered by one third. Feed a high-potash liquid fertiliser to firm up late growth.*

△ Bouvardia ternifolia *flowers at the tips of new shoots, so prune early to encourage side shoots.*

BRACHYCHITON (Bottletree)
Evergreen and deciduous trees, some with bottle-shaped trunks, and mid- to dark green leaves, some of which are palmate. The panicles of petalless flowers have white, pink or red bracts during summer. Not hardy. Height 6–20m.

Prune when dormant in late winter or early spring, removing old stems and those cluttering up the centre of the tree.

BRACHYGLOTTIS
Evergreen trees and shrubs plus herbaceous perennials with silvery-grey-green leaves and terminal clusters of white or yellow, daisy-like flowers in summer or autumn. Hardy but some species require a sheltered position. Height 1–4m.

Prune in spring when risk of frost is past. Clip into shape after flowering. Rejuvenate plants by pruning in early summer, cutting back to the old wood. Woody stemmed, straggly plants may not produce new growths.

BROUSSONETIA PAPYRIFERA
(Paper mulberry)
Deciduous, suckering tree with hairy, grey-green, deeply lobed leaves. The male (green-white, pendant anthers) and female (spherical with purple stamens followed by edible fruit) flowers are produced on separate plants. Hardy. Height 7m.

Prune in late winter to remove dead, damaged or crossing branches, cutting back to within 3 or 4 buds of the older wood. Remove suckers before they form a thicket.

BROWNEA
Evergreen trees and shrubs with young bronze pinnate foliage turning deep green. The clusters of orange-red flowers and bracts are produced in summer. Not hardy. Height 7m.

Prune in late winter or early spring to remove dead and crossing branches. Prune back strong growths to half their length in late summer to keep the plant in shape.

BRUGMANSIA (Angel's trumpets)
Evergreen and semi-evergreen shrubs and small trees with lobed, mid-green leaves. The large, pendant, trumpet- or tubular-shaped, white, yellow, pink or orange flowers are usually fragrant, appearing in summer and autumn. Not hardy but container-grown plants enjoy being outside in summer. Height 2–10m.

Wear gloves when pruning. Both the leaves and flowers are toxic. Prune in winter before new growth commences. Cut back the previous year's growths to within 20cm of the framework of branches. Rejuvenate by hard pruning, leaving stumps. New growths will quickly appear from the old wood.

BRUNFELSIA
Evergreen shrubs and small trees with glossy, dark green leaves and white or creamy-yellow flowers in summer. *B. pauciflora* produces wavy-margined, purple flowers that fade through pale blue to white and are produced from spring to late summer. Not hardy. May survive outside in a sheltered, frost-free site. Height 1–3m.

Prune after flowering, shortening the stems that have flowered. Prune the tips of young plants to build up a framework of branches.

BUDDLEJA (Butterfly bush)
Fast-growing, deciduous and evergreen shrubs with mid- to dark green and variegated leaves. The long panicles of usually fragrant flowers appear in spring, summer or autumn. Hardy. Height 3–4m. Prune in spring, cutting all the previous year's growths back to within 5cm of the main framework.

B. alternifolia flowers in early summer and is pruned after flowering, shortening all the shoots back to healthy side shoots. Old branches are cut back to the base. *B. colvilei* and *B. globosa* flower in early summer but require little pruning apart from keeping the centre of the bush open and removing broken branches.

BUPLEURUM FRUTICOSUM
(Shrubby hare's ear)
Bushy, evergreen shrub with blue-green leaves and terminal umbels of small, star-shaped, yellow flowers in summer and early autumn. Hardy. Height 2m.

Prune in late spring, clipping the tips of the shoots to keep the plant in shape. It will tolerate hard pruning to encourage new growths.

BUXUS (Box)
Evergreen shrubs and small trees with small, glossy, dark green, rounded leaves.

Small, insignificant flowers appear in spring. Hardy. Height 1–4m.

Prune by clipping in mid- to late summer. Old plants tolerate hard pruning to within 15cm of ground level.

CAESALPINIA

Evergreen shrubs and climbers with fern-like leaves. Racemes of yellow or orange-yellow flowers appear in spring, summer or autumn. Not hardy but will survive in a sheltered, frost-free garden. Height 3–4m.

Prune after flowering, shortening shoots that are spoiling the shape of the plant. Prune wall-grown plants in spring, shortening the previous year's growth to within 15cm of the main branches. Prune the tips of young shrubs to encourage a bushy plant.

CALLIANDRA (Powder-puff tree)

Evergreen shrubs and small trees with dark green leaves. Spherical heads of funnel-shaped, red, pink, white or greenish-yellow flowers with brightly coloured stamens are produced in summer or throughout winter. Not hardy. Height 2–5m.

Prune to tidy after flowering. Cut out old shoots close to the main framework.

CALLICARPA

Evergreen and deciduous shrubs with pink flowers in summer followed by pink, lilac, purple or violet fruit in autumn and winter. Hardy. Height 1–3m.

Prune in early spring to within 5cm of the main branches. Plants tolerate hard pruning with the older stems cut close to the ground.

CALLISTEMON (Bottlebrush)

Evergreen shrubs with narrow, leathery, mid-green leaves and terminal spikes of small, white, green, yellow, pink, red or purple flowers with long stamens. Hardy but avoid cold, windy sites and frosty areas. Height 2–15m.

Prune in summer immediately after flowering. Straggly branches may be shortened to a strong side shoot. Cut to shoots that are upward-pointing to help lift the pendulous branches. They tolerate hard pruning with the plants being rejuvenated over a 2–3 year period. Prune the tips of young plants to encourage bushiness.

◁ Calliandra haematocephala *should be pruned by shortening the side shoots to form a well-branched head on a single stem.*

CALLUNA VULGARIS (Heather)

Evergreen shrub with small, dark green leaves that turn purple-tinged in winter. The racemes of small, bell-shaped, white, pink, red and purple flowers appear from midsummer to late autumn. Hardy. Height 10–50cm.

Prune in spring or after flowering, removing all the flowered stems as close to the older wood as possible.

CALOTHAMNUS (Netbush)

Evergreen shrubs with leathery, needle-like leaves and nodding, pendulous, bright red flowers with bundles of red stamens. Not hardy. In cooler climates pot-grown plants enjoy the summer outdoors. Height 2–3m.

Prune after flowering to shape the plant. No other pruning is necessary. It dislikes hard pruning.

CALYCANTHUS (Allspice)

Deciduous shrubs with dark green leaves, aromatic when crushed, and dark red, fragrant flowers, brown-tipped during summer. Hardy. Height 2–3m.

Prune in early spring, removing all the stems back to the main framework of branches. In cold, exposed gardens prune when all risk of frost is past.

CAMELLIA

Evergreen shrubs and trees with glossy, green leaves and white, yellow, pink or red flowers in autumn, winter or spring. Hardy, although early spring flowers are often spoilt by morning frost followed by sun. Height 1–15m.

▷ Callicarpa bodinieri *var.* giraldii *'Profusion': after a hard pruning feed and mulch in spring.*

Prune immediately after flowering to maintain shape. They tolerate hard pruning; old plants may be rejuvenated by cutting to stumps. *C. sasanqua* flowers in late autumn and should be pruned in spring before the new growth buds open.

CAMPSIS (Trumpet vine)

Deciduous climbers with mid- to dark green leaves. Panicles of trumpet- or funnel-shaped, dark orange, orange-red or red flowers are produced during late summer and autumn. Hardy but provide shelter from cold winds. Height 10m.

Prune in late winter or early spring. After planting cut all stems to 15cm from the base to encourage vigorous growth. Remove weak or damaged shoots. The framework of stems will take 2–4 years to grow. Thereafter reduce the side shoots to 3 or 4 buds from the main framework to build up a flowering spur system.

CANTUA BUXIFOLIA

(Sacred flower of the Incas)
This is the species most likely to be grown. Semi-scandent shrub with mid-green, softly hairy leaves. The long-tubed, pendant, pink to purple flowers with bright red petal lobes appear in spring. Not hardy but will survive outside in a sheltered, sunny site. Height 2–4m.

When necessary, prune after flowering when all risk of frost is past. Prune the tips and remove old stems. It dislikes hard pruning.

CARICA PAPAYA (Papaya, Pawpaw)

Evergreen tree with long-stalked leaves that are shed as the plant grows upwards. The white, yellow or green flowers form in the leaf axils and both male and female plants are required for pollination. The enormous green fruits hang from the main trunk. Not hardy but makes an attractive pot plant that may be grown outside in summer. Height 2–6m.

Prune after harvesting the fruit, which can be produced at any time of the year. The height of plants may be reduced by shortening the main trunk by half. Allow the top side shoot to grow vertically and remove the remainder. Rejuvenate an old plant by cutting it close to ground level and training in a new main stem.

CARISSA MACROCARPA (Natal plum)

Bushy, evergreen, spiny shrub. White, waxy, jasmine-like, fragrant flowers appear in late spring followed by plum-like, red-black, edible fruit. Not hardy but may be grown outside in a sheltered, sunny position. Height 2–3m.

Prune after flowering to keep the plant in shape and remove dead or spindly branches. Its spiny stems and attractive foliage make it an ideal boundary hedge. Clip after flowering.

CARMICHAELIA

Deciduous shrubs. The seedling plants have pinnate leaves but mature plants are leafless or with few leaves. The creamy-yellow, pink or purple flowers are pea-like, usually fragrant and are produced in early spring or summer. Hardy in well sheltered, sunny gardens. Height 2–3m.

Prune in late winter or early spring, removing dead and diseased branches. Remove shoots to prevent the centre of the plant becoming congested.

CARPENTERIA CALIFORNICA

Evergreen shrub with peeling bark and leathery leaves. Cup-shaped, fragrant, white flowers with bright yellow stamens are borne in summer. Hardy, but needs shelter in cold, exposed gardens. Height 2m.

Prune after flowering. Remove a few of the oldest branches annually, cutting at ground level. Remove frost-damaged tips of shoots in late spring back to a healthy bud. It seldom fully recovers from a severe pruning.

CARPINUS (Hornbeam)

Deciduous trees with mid-green, toothed leaves that turn to butter-yellow in autumn. The yellow male catkins and greenish-yellow female catkins are produced in spring. Hardy. Height 25m.

Prune while dormant in late winter to remove dead and diseased branches. They tolerate hard pruning. When new growths appear, shorten the stumps back to above the top shoot. Prune *C. betulus* in late summer when grown as a hedge.

CARYA (Hickory)

Deciduous trees, some with ornamental bark and mid-green foliage that turns yellow in autumn. The male (pendant, yellow-green catkins) and female (small, green spikes) flowers are produced in spring and early summer on the same plant, followed in autumn by nuts. Hardy, but *C. illinoinensis* (the pecan nut tree) requires shelter from prolonged frost. Height 25m.

Prune in late winter or early spring to remove the 3 Ds (see page 20). Avoid narrow-angled branches and double leaders. Stumps are prone to dieback.

CARYOPTERIS

Deciduous shrubs with aromatic, grey-green or yellow leaves and blue flowers produced on the current growths during late summer and autumn. Hardy. Height 1–1.2m.

Prune in late spring after the last of the frosts and immediately before the buds break into growth. At planting time, shorten all the growths by two thirds to build up a framework of branches. Thereafter, shorten the growths back to within 2–5cm of the old wood. Never cut below where buds are visible as the shrub will not recover.

CASSIA (Golden shower tree)

Deciduous and evergreen shrubs with bright green leaves, the oldest of which are shed in winter. Panicles or racemes of bowl-shaped, fragrant, yellow, pink or crimson flowers are produced in spring and summer. Not hardy. Height 8–15m.

Prune in late winter or early spring to retain shape. When grown under cover, curtail growth by pruning after flowering to shorten vigorous shoots.

CASSINIA

Evergreen, heather-like shrubs with needle-like, dark green leaves. The clusters of tiny, often fragrant, funnel-shaped, white flowers are produced in summer. Hardy. Height 2–3m.

Prune in mid-spring by reducing flowered shoots to within 3cm of older wood. Won't survive hard pruning where the stems are cut close to the ground.

CASSIOPE

Dwarf, evergreen shrubs with tiny, scale-like, dark green leaves pressed to the stems. The solitary, urn- or bell-shaped flowers are white or creamy white and are produced in late spring and early summer. Hardy. Height 8–25cm.

Prune after flowering just before the new growths appear by clipping off the flowered stems with hedge clippers or secateurs. Remove the prunings rather than letting them lie on the plant. Don't prune into the older wood.

CASTANEA (Chestnut)

Deciduous trees and shrubs with matt or glossy, mid- to dark green leaves. The catkins of small, creamy-white, fragrant flowers appear in summer on the young growths and are followed by nuts that in the case of *C. sativa*, *C. dentata* and *C. mollissima* are edible. Hardy. *C. sativa* (Spanish chestnut) is the most successful for cool climates. Height 20–30m.

Prune in late winter or early spring to remove dead or damaged branches. They tolerate hard pruning and are traditionally coppiced for chestnut fencing poles. In the US, where chestnut blight is a killer, regular pruning will protect the tree from the spores, which only attack older wood.

CASTANOPSIS

Evergreen trees and bushy shrubs with glossy, dark green leaves, bronze on the underside. The erect catkins appear in summer and are made up of small white flowers followed by acorn-like nuts. *C. cuspidata* is the most commonly grown species. It is hardy but needs to be protected from cold winds. Height 8m.

Prune in late winter to maintain the shape. Thin out congested growths, shortening them to a low, healthy bud.

CATALPA

(Indian bean tree, Western catalpa)
Deciduous trees with large, pale or mid- to dark green or yellow leaves and panicles of white or yellowish-white, bell-shaped flowers marked with yellow and purple or orange and purple. The flowers are followed by long, thin, bean-like, pendant pods of seeds. Hardy. Height 10–15m.

Prune in late winter before buds open. To coppice, prune all the stems to within 2 or 3 buds of the base of the plant and remove completely the oldest stems to prevent congestion.

CEANOTHUS (California lilac)

Deciduous shrubs and small trees with panicles of small, white or blue flowers in spring, summer or autumn. Hardy, although tips of shoots may be damaged by spring frost. Height 1–6m.

▷ Catalpa bignonioides *'Aurea': when coppiced in spring, the young shoots produce large leaves without flowering.*

◁ Ceanothus 'Cynthia Postan' is evergreen and benefits from a light pruning after flowering in summer.

They dislike hard pruning and it is difficult to successfully renew old, straggly, bare branches. Prune evergreen species such as C. arboreus 'Trewithen Blue' after flowering, reducing the flowered shoots by half their length. Prune deciduous plants such as C. × delileanus 'Gloire de Versailles' in early spring, cutting the previous year's growths back to within 5cm of the main framework of branches.

CEDRUS (Cedar)
Evergreen, coniferous trees with sharply pointed, pale or mid- to dark green leaves and male and female cones. Hardy. Height 5–40m.

Prune as necessary in autumn to remove misshapen branches. Watch out for double leaders and remove the weaker one.

CEIBA (Kapok)
Deciduous trees with spiny branches and mid-green leaves. Cup-shaped white, yellow or pink flowers are produced in winter and early spring before the leaves. Not hardy. Height 25–30m.

C. pentandra is the species that is most usually grown. It normally forms a single-stemmed tree. Prune in winter to keep the tree in shape. Where necessary it will recover from a severe pruning.

CELASTRUS (Bittersweet)
Deciduous shrubs and climbers with mid-green leaves that turn yellow in autumn. Panicles of green, male and female flowers are often on separate plants. Female flowers are followed by clusters of small, orange-yellow fruit with red or pink seeds. Hardy. Height 8–12m.

Prune in winter or early spring to keep within bounds. Cut out the oldest stems as close to the ground as possible and then cut them into short lengths to make removal from the other growths possible.

CELTIS (Nettle tree)
Deciduous and evergreen trees and shrubs, most with glossy leaves. The small, green flowers are produced in spring with the male clusters at the base of the stems. The females appear at the leaf axils, followed by sweet, orange-red edible fruits. Hardy. Height 8–20m.

Prune in winter before the plant starts to grow. Has a habit of occasionally sending up a vertical shoot from a side branch. If left to grow it will take over and spoil the shape of the tree. Remove it before it becomes large, as pruning wounds are slow to callus.

CEPHALANTHUS (Button bush)
Deciduous and evergreen trees and shrubs with glossy, mid-green leaves and clusters of small, funnel-shaped, white or cream flowers that are produced in late summer and early autumn. C. occidentalis has glossy leaves with red veins. Hardy. Height 2–5m.

Prune shrubs in early spring, removing the previous year's growths back to the main framework.

CEPHALOTAXUS (Plum yew)
Evergreen conifers with mid- to dark green, yew-like leaves with silver bands on the underside. The clusters of male flowers are produced at the leaf axils. Female plants produce small, olive-green fruit. C. harringtonia fruit ripen to purple-brown. Hardy. Height 4–10m.

Prune in early summer. They tolerate hard pruning and will rejuvenate from stumps. Clip to shape in summer if grown as a hedge.

CERATOSTIGMA (Plumbago)
Deciduous and evergreen shrubs with bristly stems and mid- to bright green leaves that turn red in autumn. The bright blue or purple-blue flowers are produced on the current season's growths in late summer or autumn. Hardy but prefer a sheltered site. Height 45–100cm.

Prune in late spring, removing all the dead stems (in cold climates they will die back to ground level in winter). Shorten the remaining stems to 5cm from ground level.

CERCIDIPHYLLUM JAPONICUM
(Katsura tree)

A vigorous, deciduous tree with mid-green leaves that are bronze when young and turn to yellow, orange and red in late autumn. The fallen leaves smell of home-made fudge. Tiny, red flowers are produced in spring before the foliage. Hardy, but opening leaves may be damaged by a late frost. Height 18m.

Prune in late winter or early spring (late spring in cold, exposed areas) before growth commences. Thin young branches to keep the centre of the tree open. Don't leave stumps as these are subject to coral spot disease (see page 16).

CERCIS (Redbud, Judas tree)

Deciduous trees and shrubs with glossy, green or bluish-green leaves that turn yellow in autumn. The pink, magenta, red, purple or occasionally white clusters of flowers are produced on the previous year's stems before the leaves emerge. The flowers will also appear directly from the bark of older branches. Hardy but young, unripened shoots may suffer from frost damage. Height 3–10m.

Prune in late winter or early spring, removing frost-damaged shoots in early summer. Remove congested branches in the centre of the tree. They tolerate rejuvenation and will re-grow from stumps. Multi-stemmed plants are prone to produce weak, narrow-angled branches. The weakest should be removed before a split occurs.

▷ Cercidiphyllum japonicum: *prune in late spring in cold, exposed gardens.*

CESTRUM

Evergreen and deciduous shrubs whose leaves have an unpleasant odour when crushed. The funnel- or tubular-shaped, fragrant flowers appear in spring and early summer or summer through to late autumn in orange, pink, red or crimson followed by white, red, purple-red or black berries. Not hardy. *C. parqui* (willow-leafed jessamine) may be grown outside in a sheltered position. Height 1–3m.

Prune early-flowering evergreens such as *C. aurantiacum* immediately after flowering to keep the plant within bounds. Late-flowering evergreens such as *C. psittacinum* are pruned in late spring, removing straggly stems and opening the centre of the shrub. *C. parqui* is deciduous and is pruned in early spring, cutting last year's stems back to the main framework of branches.

CHAENOMELES

(Japonica, Flowering quince)
Deciduous, spiny shrubs with glossy leaves. Single or double, cup-shaped, white, pink, magenta or red flowers are borne in early spring, before or at the same time as the leaves, followed by apple-like, edible, hard, green fruits that ripen to yellow. Hardy. Height 1–3m.

Prune after flowering, removing the flowered shoots back to strong-growing lower laterals. With mature shrubs, remove one in four of the older stems at ground level. Wtih wall-trained plants, cut all the flowered shoots back to 2 or 3 buds of the main framework of branches.

CHAMAECYPARIS (Cypress)

Evergreen conifers with tiny, overlapping, pale to dark green and variegated leaves and small male and female cones. Hardy. Height 1–30m. Prune from early summer to early autumn. When grown as a hedge, clip in summer to allow nesting birds to breed. Pruning into old wood will not produce new growth.

CHAMELAUCIUM (Geraldton wax)

Evergreen shrubs. *C. uncinatum* has thin, dark green leaves hooked at the tip and clusters of white, pink, red or purple flowers during spring and summer. Not hardy but will survive in a sheltered, frost-free garden. Height 2–4m.

Prune after flowering to retain a good shape. It dislikes hard pruning.

CHIMONANTHUS (Wintersweet)

Deciduous and evergreen shrubs with glossy, mid-green leaves and pendant, bowl-shaped, fragrant, waxy, yellow flowers in winter. Hardy. Height 4m.

Prune immediately after flowering to remove dead or damaged branches. With wall-trained plants, cut all the flowered shoots back to within 2–5cm of the main framework of branches.

CHIONANTHUS (Fringe tree)

Deciduous and evergreen trees and shrubs with glossy, dark green leaves and terminal panicles of fragrant, white flowers in summer followed by blue-black fruit. Hardy. Height 3m.

Prune in late winter or early spring before growth starts. Removing low-growing laterals will encourage a tree-like appearance rather than a bushy shrub.

◁ Cestrum fasciculatum *is evergreen and vigorous. Prune in midsummer, shortening the arching stems by one third.*

CHOISYA (Mexican orange blossom)
Evergreen shrubs with aromatic, glossy
green or yellow leaves and star-shaped,
fragrant, white or pink-tinged white
flowers in spring and again in late
summer and autumn. Hardy, although
C. arizonica prefers a sheltered, sunny
site. Height 1–3m.

Prune in late spring after main
flowering period to retain the shape of
the plant. They tolerate hard pruning.

CHORISIA SPECIOSA (Floss silk tree)
Semi-evergreen tree with a spiny trunk
and long-stalked, mid-green leaves. The
funnel-shaped, single, white or creamy-
white flowers are purple-red on the upper
part and are produced at the leaf axils in
autumn. Not hardy. Height 13m.

Prune in late winter or early spring,
removing dead or damaged branches. It
dislikes hard pruning.

CHRYSOLEPIS CHRYSOPHYLLA
(Golden chinkapin)
Evergreen tree with dark green leaves,
golden hairy on the underside. Creamy-
white, fragrant catkins are produced in
summer followed 12 months later by
spiny fruit. Hardy but dislikes strong
winds. Height 10m.

Prune in winter or late spring to
remove crossing and dead branches.
Cut out competing leaders.

CINNAMOMUM
Evergreen trees and shrubs, of which *C.
camphora* (camphor tree) is the best
known, with glossy, dark green, aromatic
leaves and small greenish-yellow flowers
in spring and summer followed by black
berries. Not hardy. Height 15–20m.

Prune in late winter or spring to
remove damaged and crossing branches.

▷ Citrus limon: *prune immediately above a
leaf or side shoot to avoid leaving stumps that
will die back.*

CISSUS
Evergreen climbers with pale to mid- or
dark green, glossy leaves and small, green
or yellow flowers in summer. Not hardy.
C. striata will grow outside in a sheltered,
sunny position. Height 3–12m.

Prune in spring to keep the plant
within bounds. The tips of young plants
should be pruned to make them bushy.
They tolerate severe pruning.

CISTUS (Rock rose, Sun rose)
Evergreen shrubs with grey-green to dark,
sometimes glossy, green leaves and
saucer-shaped white to dark pink flowers,
the petals often marked with chocolate
brown. Hardy but prefers shelter from
frosty sites. Height 30cm–3m.

Prune after flowering, cutting misplaced
branches back to healthy buds. This is a
short-lived plant liable to become leggy. It
won't tolerate pruning into the old wood.

**× CITROFORTUNELLA
MICROCARPA** (Panama orange)
Evergreen shrub or small tree with bright
green, leathery leaves and occasionally
spines on the stems. The pure white
flowers are produced in spring and
summer and are followed by yellow fruit
colouring to orange. Not hardy but will
survive outside against a sheltered, sunny
wall. Height 3–5m.

Prune in late winter or early spring,
removing dead or damaged branches. Keep
the centre of the shrub clear of branches.

CITRUS
Evergreen shrubs often with spiny stems
and light, mid- or dark green leaves. The
fragrant, white or purple-tinted flowers
are produced during spring, summer or
early autumn, followed by edible fruit

such as oranges and lemons. *C. limon*
(lemon tree) frequently produces flowers
and fruit at the same time. Not hardy
but pot-grown plants may be grown
outside during the summer. Height
2–10m.

To allow new wood to firm up before
winter in cool climates, young trees
should be pruned in spring. Otherwise,
prune at any time of year.

Grafted trees are prone to suckers,
which should be removed as soon as
possible. Prune established trees when,
or immediately after, picking the fruit.
Mature plants need to be pruned only to
retain the shape and remove crossing
branches. Lemon trees occasionally
produce strong, upright stems that need
to be taken out. Water shoots are
common and should be removed without
leaving a stump.

Old, neglected citrus trees may be
rejuvenated, but this must be a gradual
process with only a single branch being
cut out annually.

CLADRASTIS (Yellow wood)
Deciduous trees of which *C. lutea* is the most commonly grown. The light green leaves turn a brilliant yellow in autumn. Panicles of pea-like, pendant, fragrant, white flowers with yellow markings are produced in spring and early summer. Hardy. Height 10m. Prune in early winter or after flowering to retain the shape of the tree and keep the centre open.

CLEMATIS (Old man's beard)
See pages 102–109.

CLERODENDRUM
Deciduous and evergreen trees, shrubs and climbers with panicles or clusters of white, pink, red, scarlet or blue and white flowers in summer and autumn. The flowers are often fragrant. *C. bungei* (glory flower) and *C. trichotomum* are hardy but prefer a sunny, sheltered site. Height 1–5m.
   Prune climbers such as *C. splendens* immediately after flowering to thin out

congested areas and old, non-flowering shoots. Deciduous shrubs are pruned in late winter before growth commences. *C. bungei*, although deciduous, is pruned in early spring, cutting the stems back to within 5cm of the main framework. Evergreens are pruned in late spring to maintain the plants' shape. Deadheading will encourage new growths.

CLETHRA
Deciduous and evergreen trees and shrubs with mid- to dark green or blue-green leaves. The terminal racemes of cup- or bell-shaped, white or cream, fragrant flowers are produced in summer and autumn. Hardy. Height 2–8m.
   Prune deciduous species in late winter or early spring before growth buds open. *C. arborea* (lily-of-the-valley tree) is not hardy and is pruned in late spring to maintain shape and keep it within the allotted area. *C. alnifolia* (sweet pepper-bush) produces lots of suckers. The strongest of these are used to replace old stems that are cut out at the base of the plant.

CLEYERA
Deciduous and evergreen trees and shrubs with mostly dark green leaves. The bowl-shaped, white or yellowish-white, fragrant flowers appear in the leaf axils in summer. Not hardy but *C. japonica* may survive outside if planted against a warm, sunny, sheltered wall. Height 3m.
   Prune after flowering to retain shape. Deadheading will help to produce strong shoots but occasionally small, red fruits appear in autumn. This is unlikely outside in a cool climate.

◁ Clerodendrum bungei *is deciduous and if you are lucky it will produce suckers that are worth potting up.*

CLIANTHUS PUNICEUS
(Lobster claw)
Evergreen shrub with dark green leaves and narrow leaflets. The pendant racemes of brilliant red, white or pink, lobster-claw-like flowers are produced during spring and early summer. Not hardy but will succeed when it is planted against a sheltered, sunny wall. Height 4–5m.
   Prune immediately after flowering, reducing the flowered shoots by one third. It will frequently produce strong growths from the base and these may replace old branches, which need to be cut as close to soil level as possible.

COBAEA
Evergreen and herbaceous climbers of which *C. scandens* (cup-and-saucer plant) is the most commonly grown. The bright green, evergreen leaves are equipped with hooked tendrils for support. The creamy-green, fragrant flowers age to a deep purple and appear in summer and autumn. Not hardy but will survive in a sheltered, frost-free site. Height 10–15m.
   Prune in late winter or early spring, or after flowering to tidy the plant.

CODIAEUM (Croton)
Evergreen trees and shrubs with leathery, often brightly variegated leaves. The tiny, creamy-yellow, star-like flowers appear throughout the summer. Not hardy. Height 1–2m.
   Prune in mid- to late spring. Removing the growing tip of a single-stemmed plant will encourage it to branch. Hard pruning to remove 'leggy', bare stems will allow shoots to grow from the base.

COLLETIA
Deciduous shrubs with grey-green, sharply pointed spines and few if any leaves. The small, tubular and fragrant

△ Clianthus puniceus: *thin out congested stems, cutting back to a strong side shoot.*

flowers are produced in summer and autumn on or below the spines. Hardy but needs protection from cold, drying winds. Height 3m.

Prune in late winter or early spring before growth starts. Old plants may be rejuvenated by pruning hard over a 2–3 year period. To encourage bushiness, reduce shoots on newly planted shrubs by one third.

COLQUHOUNIA

Evergreen and semi-evergreen shrubs of which C. *coccinea* is the species most commonly grown. The sage-green leaves are aromatic and woolly on the underside. The terminal spikes of tubular, orange, yellow or scarlet flowers appear in late summer. Hardy but

succeeds best in a sheltered, frost-free site. Height 2m.

Prune in early spring, reducing the stems to within 2–5cm of the main framework of branches. Plants damaged by frost will re-sprout from the base.

COLUTEA

Deciduous shrubs with pale green or blue-green, pinnate leaves and pea-like red-brown or yellow flowers in summer followed by translucent seed pods. Hardy. Height 2–3m.

Prune in late winter before growth commences to tidy the plant. Plants tolerate hard pruning.

COLVILLEA RACEMOSA

An evergreen tree with long, fern-like, pinnate leaves and long racemes of scarlet flowers in late autumn and winter. Not hardy. Height 8–12m.

Prune in winter or early spring before growth commences. Retain a single trunk. Under glass, prune after flowering in winter to curtail growth.

CONVOLVULUS

Climbing annuals and perennials and evergreen shrubs. C. *cneorum* is an evergreen shrub with silky, silver-green leaves. The clusters of funnel-shaped, white flowers with yellow centres open from pink buds during spring and early summer. Hardy but dislikes cold, wet soil in winter. Height 60cm.

Prune after flowering by trimming long shoots and trimming the tips of the stems to ensure a bushy plant. It dislikes hard pruning and is unlikely to produce new growths from old wood.

COPROSMA

Evergreen trees and shrubs with light to dark green, variegated, purple or brown, sometimes leathery leaves. Where male and female plants are grown together the tiny, inconspicuous flowers are followed in late summer and autumn by white, orange, red or blue translucent berries. Hardy but provide shelter from late frost. Height 45cm–2m.

Prune after flowering to keep the shape of the plant.

CORDYLINE

Evergreen perennials and shrubs with long, leathery, mid-green, variegated or purple leaves. The terminal panicles are made up of hundreds of tiny, fragrant, creamy-white or purple flowers. Not fully hardy but will grow outdoors in gardens sheltered from biting, cold winds and frost. Height 2–10m.

Prune by pulling off the leaves that die as the plant grows upwards. They usually start turning brown when the main trunk is 6m high. Start with the lowest leaves and pull each one downwards. Don't cut

them off. Remove the dead flower stalks low down in the centre of the rosette of leaves. Removing the growing tip will encourage the plant to become multi-branched. *C. australis* (cabbage palm) tolerates coppicing, producing lots of shoots from the stump. These should be thinned to leave 2–4 stems to form a branched specimen.

CORIARIA

Deciduous trees and shrubs with arching stems and mid- to dark green leaves that often turn red in autumn. The terminal racemes of small, green flowers are produced in late spring followed by fleshy, black, purple, dark red or yellow fruit. Hardy but prefers a sheltered, frost-free site. Height 1–2m.

Prune in late winter or early spring to remove dead and crossing branches. Old branches that are not flowering should be removed at the base in spring.

CORNUS

Deciduous trees and shrubs, often with coloured bark and mid- to dark green or variegated leaves, some of which turn orange and red in autumn. The clusters of small, white flowers of *C. alba* (dogwood) appear in late spring and early summer and are followed in autumn by white or white-tinged blue fruit. Hardy. Height 3m.

C. kousa forms a deciduous tree with flaking bark and dark green leaves. The small, green flowers are produced in summer and are surrounded by 4 large, pure white bracts followed in autumn by fleshy, red, strawberry-like fruit. Hardy. Height 6m.

Prune the dogwoods and those with young coloured bark in spring, cutting

◁ Cordyline australis: *to remove dead leaves, pull downwards, working up from the bottom of the plant.*

all the stems to within 2–5cm of the base of the main framework. This will encourage more strong shoots with good bark colour.

C. *kousa* should be pruned in late winter to remove the 3 Ds (see page 20) and branches crossing the centre of the plant. It dislikes hard pruning.

COROKIA
Evergreen shrubs with glossy, dark green or grey-green leaves, sometimes silvery-grey on the underside. Clusters, panicles or racemes of small, yellow flowers, sometimes fragrant, are produced in late spring and early summer followed by yellow, orange, red or black fruit in autumn. Hardy but need to be sheltered from both cold winds and late frosts. Height 2–3m.

Prune after flowering to retain the shape. They tolerate hard pruning, and old stems lacking in flowers may be cut out at ground level.

CORONILLA
Evergreen and deciduous shrubs with bright green or variegated leaves. Umbels of pale or bright yellow flowers, often fragrant, are borne in either late winter and early spring (C. *valentina*) or from late spring to autumn (C. *emerus*, also known as *Hippocrepis emerus*). The flowers are followed by thin seed pods. Hardy. Height 1–2m.

Prune in late winter to remove damaged branches.

CORREA (Australian fuchsia)
Evergreen shrubs and small trees with matt or glossy, mid- to deep green leaves that are aromatic when crushed. The tubular or bell-shaped, white, cream, green, pink or red flowers are produced in clusters or singly from late autumn to spring or from early summer to autumn. Not hardy. Height 1–3m.

Prune after flowering to keep the plant tidy and remove straggly shoots. Prune the tips of young plants to make them bushy.

CORYLOPSIS
Deciduous shrubs and small trees with pale to dark green leaves, occasionally blue-green on the underside. The pendant racemes of bell-shaped, yellow flowers are fragrant and are produced in early to mid-spring. Hardy but prone to frost damage on the early flowers. Height 1–5m.

Prune immediately after flowering to tidy up the plant. Prune to reduce congestion in the centre of the shrub.

CORYLUS (Hazel)
Deciduous shrubs and trees with mid- to dark green, yellow or purple leaves. The long, bright yellow male catkins are produced in winter with tiny, insignificant red female flowers followed in autumn by edible nuts. Hardy. Height 5–20m.

Prune in winter or early spring to remove dead or diseased branches. Take out crossing branches. C. *avellana* and C. *maxima* respond to hard pruning and may be cut back to within 2 or 3 buds of the base. C. *avellana* 'Contorta' (corkscrew hazel) has manic, twisted stems. It is grafted on to a rootstock of the common hazel and will produce straight suckers, which should be removed.

COTINUS (Smoke bush)
Deciduous trees and shrubs with green, purple or red leaves that colour well in autumn. The panicles of tiny flowers are followed by plume-like clusters of small, grey fruit. The leaves of C. *obovatus* (American smoke tree) colour beautifully in autumn. Hardy but the brittle branches are prone to wind damage. Height 5–10m.

▽ Corylopsis glabrescens *should be pruned after flowering, keeping the centre of the plant open.*

Prune in late winter or early spring to retain a neat shape. If all the branches are coppiced in early spring the new growths will produce very large leaves.

COTONEASTER
Deciduous, semi-evergreen and evergreen trees and shrubs with dull to bright green, and occasionally variegated, leaves. The small, white or pink flowers are produced in late spring and summer followed in autumn by yellow, orange-red or red fruit. Hardy. Height 30cm–10m.

Prune evergreens after flowering to retain shape. Deciduous plants are pruned in winter or early spring when dormant to shape the plant. Cotoneasters tolerate hard pruning. Hedges should be clipped back in summer to leave the flowers or berries.

CRATAEGUS (Hawthorn)
Semi-evergreen and deciduous trees and shrubs with spiny stems and mid- to dark green, glossy leaves, some of which provide good autumn colour. The clusters of small, white, pink or red flowers appear in spring followed by red 'haws'. Hardy. Height 6–10m.

Prune in winter or early spring when dormant to remove the 3 Ds (see page 20). Trim hedges in autumn. It responds well to rejuvenating, growing away happily from stumps.

CRINODENDRON
Evergreen shrubs and small trees with dull, dark green leaves. The urn- or bell-shaped, deep red, red-pink or white-fringed flowers are produced in spring and summer or late summer. Hardy but

◁ Crataegus laevigata punicea: *please don't risk the wrath of the little people by pruning a 'fairy thorn' in the middle of a garden.*

flower buds and early growths may be damaged by frost. Height 6–8m.

Prune C. *hookerianum* after flowering, shortening shoots that spoil the tree shape. C. *patagua* is pruned in late spring to remove crossing branches.

CRYPTOMERIA JAPONICA
(Japanese cedar)
Evergreen conifer with small, deep green leaves. Some varieties have yellow foliage, others turn a deep plum-bronze in autumn. The small, female cones are mid-brown. Tiny, male cones are clustered at the tips of the shoots. Hardy. Height 6–20m.

Other than removing damaged branches, pruning is not normally necessary. It tolerates coppicing.

CUNNINGHAMIA LANCEOLATA
(China fir)
Evergreen conifer with fibrous, red-brown bark and glossy, bright green leaves with 2 white bands on the underside. The small, female cones are green-brown with the tiny, yellow-brown male cones in clusters. Hardy. Height 15–20m.

Prune to retain shape. Young plants tend to be bushy. When necessary, prune back young plants in spring to produce growths and then train in a leader by tying the top shoot to a cane.

CUPHEA
Evergreen shrubs, perennials and annuals. Shrubs produce racemes or panicles of tubular white, orange, pink, red or deep violet flowers in late spring and summer or summer and autumn. Not hardy but may be grown in a sheltered, frost-free site. Height 30–70cm.

Prune after flowering or in spring, shortening the shoots that have flowered to within 2–5cm of the old growths.

×CUPRESSOCYPARIS LEYLANDII
(Leyland cypress)
Fast-growing, evergreen conifers with flattened growths of small, scale-like, dark grey-green or golden-yellow leaves. The tiny, female cones are dark brown. Hardy. Height 25–35m.

Prune to retain shape and remove double leader shoots. Trim hedges without cutting into the old wood. Don't prune after early autumn.

CUPRESSUS (Cypress)
Evergreen conifers with pale to dark green, blue-green or yellow, scale-like leaves. Hardy but some require shelter from cold winds. Height 10–30m.

Prune in early summer. Don't cut into the old wood as it is unlikely to produce new shoots.

CYDONIA OBLONGA (Quince)
Deciduous tree or large shrub with dark green leaves. The white or pale pink flowers appear in the leaf axils in late spring followed by edible, aromatic, yellow fruit in autumn. Hardy. Height 5m.

Prune mature plants in winter when dormant to prevent congestion of branches. Wall-trained plants are pruned in summer, shortening the new growth to form fruiting spurs.

CYTISUS (Broom)
Deciduous and evergreen shrubs with mid-green or silvery-grey leaves. Some shrubs are leafless when mature. The clusters or racemes of pea-like, white, cream, yellow, pink or red flowers are followed by pea-like seed pods. Hardy but the new growths of some species may be damaged by frost. Height 60cm–7m.

Prune in winter before growth starts or after flowering, cutting all the flowering shoots to healthy buds or 3–5cm from the older wood. Don't prune into the older wood.

DABOECIA (Heath)

Evergreen shrubs with wiry stems and thin, dark green leaves, silvery-grey on the underside. Racemes of urn-shaped, pink, purple or magenta flowers are produced in early or late summer and autumn. Hardy but new growths may be damaged by late spring frosts. Height 20–40cm.

Prune in early spring by shortening the flowered shoots back to within 2–4cm of the older wood. Old, straggly, neglected plants may be clipped hard but not into the very old wood.

DAIS COTINIFOLIA

Evergreen shrub but deciduous in cool climates with glossy, blue-green leaves. The rounded umbels of lilac-pink, fragrant flowers are produced in summer. Not hardy but may survive in a sheltered, sunny, frost-free site. Height 2–3m.

Prune in late winter or early spring before growth commences. Remove dead, damaged and crossing branches. It doesn't tolerate heavy pruning.

DANAE RACEMOSA
(Alexandrian laurel)

Shrub-like, evergreen perennial with glossy, leaf-like stems and terminal racemes of greenish-yellow flowers in summer followed by orange-red berries. Not fully hardy. Protect from cold winds and late spring frosts. Height 1m.

Prune by cutting the old shoots at ground level in spring.

DAPHNE

Deciduous, semi-evergreen and evergreen shrubs with mid- to dark green, often glossy, leaves. The tubular, white, pink, yellow, lilac or deep purple-red flowers are usually fragrant, appearing in

▷ Daphne cneorum, *like all daphnes, resents pruning and hard pruning will kill it.*

late winter, spring or summer and sometimes followed by white, pink, orange, deep red or purple-black fruit. Hardy but prefer to be sheltered from cold winds. Height 10cm–4m.

Prune in late winter or early spring or after flowering to remove crossing or damaged branches. They dislike pruning of any sort and will suffer if main branches are cut.

DAPHNIPHYLLUM HIMALAENSE SUBSP. MACROPODUM

Evergreen shrub or small tree with large, leathery, dark green leaves, glaucous on the underside. The racemes of deep purple flowers have no petals and are produced in late spring and early summer. Hardy but needs shelter from cold winds. Height 6m.

Prune in late summer after flowering to maintain the shape of the plant. It tolerates hard pruning.

DARWINIA

Evergreen, heather-like, bushy shrubs of which *D. citriodora* (lemon-scented myrtle) is the best known. Its small, grey-green leaves are lemon-scented. The bell-shaped, pinkish-orange flowers have bright green outer bracts and are produced in late spring. Not hardy. Height 1–2m.

Prune in summer after flowering, cutting the flowered stems to within 2–5cm of the older wood.

DAVIDIA INVOLUCRATA

(Handkerchief tree)
Deciduous tree with red-stalked, mid-green leaves, softly hairy on the underside. The small flowers appear in spring with a pair of large, pure white bracts of unequal size followed by pendant, greenish-brown, ridged fruit. Hardy but succeeds best in a sheltered site. Height 15m.

Prune in late winter to keep the plant in shape before growth commences. Make sure that the young plant grows with a single leader to prevent it becoming an untidy, bushy, shrub-like tree.

DECAISNEA FARGESII

Deciduous shrub with 1m-long, pinnate, dark green leaves, paler green on the underside. The pendant panicles of bell-shaped, yellowish-green flowers are petalless, appearing in early summer and followed by bean-like, deep blue fruit. Hardy but protect from late spring frosts. Height 6m.

Prune in late winter or early spring before growth commences to retain the shape of the plant.

DECUMARIA

Deciduous and evergreen climbers with glossy, dark green leaves. Yellow or creamy-white flowers are produced in late spring or in summer. Hardy but protect from cold winds. Prefers to be grown against a warm, sunny wall. Height 2–8m.

Prune in late winter to retain the shape of the plant. If wall-trained, prune after flowering, shortening the stems to within 2–5cm of the main framework of branches.

DELONIX REGIA (Flame tree)

Semi-evergreen tree with 2-pinnate, bright green leaves. The scarlet and pale yellow flowers appear from spring to summer. Not hardy. Height 10m.

Prune in late winter to remove damaged or crossing branches. It tolerates hard pruning in summer.

DESFONTAINIA SPINOSA

Dense, bushy, evergreen shrub with glossy, dark green, spiny leaves and pendant, tubular, red flowers with yellow tips during summer and autumn. Hardy. Height 2m.

△ Decaisnea fargesii: *in spring nip out the growing tips of young plants to encourage a bushy plant.*

Prune in late spring to keep the shape. Thin congested plants by cutting a few of the oldest branches at the base.

DESMODIUM

Deciduous shrubs with pale or dark green, 2-pinnate or palmate leaves and panicles or racemes of small, pea-like, white, pink or purple flowers in late summer and autumn. Hardy. Height 1–4m.

Prune in early spring, removing the oldest shoots as close to the base as possible. Prune off the dead flowers.

DEUTZIA

Deciduous shrubs with bright, mid- or dark green leaves. Clusters of cup- or star-shaped, white, pink or purple-pink flowers appear in summer and are occasionally fragrant. Hardy. Height 1–3m.

Prune after flowering, cutting the flowered shoots back to young, healthy shoots or strong buds. Old plants may be rejuvenated each year by removing one third of the oldest branches as close to the base as possible.

DIERVILLA (Bush honeysuckle)
Deciduous, suckering shrubs, the most commonly grown being *D. sessilifolia* with bronze-tinted young leaves. The tubular, sulphur-yellow flowers are produced in summer. Hardy. Height 1.5m.

Prune in early spring, cutting the stems back to within 2–5cm of the permanent framework of branches.

DIOSPYROS KAKI
(Chinese persimmon)
Deciduous tree with glossy, dark green leaves that turn yellow, orange and red in autumn. Pale yellow flowers are followed by large, tomato-like, edible fruit. Hardy but grow it against a warm, sunny wall for crops in a cool climate. Height 6m.

Pruning is important when the plant is young. The branches are very brittle, so it is essential that a sturdy framework is built up. Prune out any narrow-angled branches where they join the main framework. Suckers should be pulled rather than cut. The tree fruits on new growths, so prune in winter to encourage new shoots. A mature tree requires little pruning, apart from thinning out weak branches and opening the centre of the tree to allow air to circulate.

DIPELTA
Deciduous shrubs with peeling bark and glossy leaves. Bell-shaped or tubular flowers appear in late spring and early summer. Hardy. Height 3m.

Prune after flowering, cutting the shoots that have flowered back to healthy buds or strong shoots. Remove a few of the oldest branches as close to ground level as possible.

◁ Diospyros kaki *should be pruned in winter. Removing large branches will result in lots of weak shoots, so remove crossing branches and any growing into the centre of the tree while they are small.*

DIPTERONIA SINENSIS

Deciduous tree with dark green, pinnate leaves and panicles of greenish-white flowers in summer followed in late autumn by clusters of flat, red-brown fruit. Hardy. Height 10m.

Prune in winter or early spring before growth commences to retain the shape of the plant.

DISANTHUS CERCIDIFOLIUS

Deciduous shrub with glaucous, blue-green leaves turning yellow, red and purple in autumn. The spidery, bright red, fragrant flowers appear in pairs in autumn as the leaves colour. Hardy although late spring frosts may damage young shoots. Height 3m.

Prune in spring before growth starts. Thin out any congested branches in early summer.

DISCARIA

Deciduous, spiny shrubs of which *D. toumatou* (wild Irishman) is the most commonly grown. The slender, green stems are covered with pairs of green spines and glossy, green leaves. Clusters of star-shaped, greenish-white flowers are produced in spring. Hardy but prefers a sheltered, sunny site. Height 2–3m.

Prune after flowering in late spring to retain the shape of the plant. Wear thorn-proof gloves.

DISTYLIUM

Evergreen shrubs and trees with glossy, dark green leaves and racemes of small, petalless flowers made up of bright red calyces and deep purple stamens. Hardy but requires shelter from cold winds and late spring frosts. Height 3m.

Pruning is not normally necessary but remove any damaged branches in late winter.

DOMBEYA

Evergreen and deciduous shrubs with mid- to dark green, long-stalked leaves and clusters of white, yellow, pink or red flowers on long, pendant stalks during late summer or winter and spring. Not hardy. Height 2–6m.

Prune deciduous species in early spring, cutting back the growths to within 2cm of the main framework. Evergreens are pruned after flowering simply to retain the plant shape.

DREGEA

Evergreen climbers with mid-green leaves, grey-green on the underside. The umbels of fragrant, yellow or creamy-white, red-speckled flowers are produced in summer followed by pairs of seed pods. Not hardy but will survive in a sheltered, frost-free site. Height 3–4m.

Prune after flowering to keep the plant within its allotted space. Remove dead and damaged stems in late winter.

DRIMYS

Evergreen shrubs and trees with glossy, dark green, aromatic leaves and clusters or umbels of white flowers in spring and summer. Hardy but need to be sheltered from cold winds. Height 4–12m.

Prune out dead, damaged and diseased wood in early spring. Prune to shape the plant after flowering.

DURANTA

Evergreen trees and shrubs with arching branches and sometimes spiny stems and mid-green to dark, glossy, green leaves. The racemes or panicles of white, blue or purple flowers are produced in summer and early autumn followed by small, poisonous, yellow fruit. Not hardy although *D. erecta* will survive a light frost. Height 2–6m.

Prune in late winter to retain the plant's shape. It dislikes hard pruning.

DURIO ZIBETHINUS (Durian)

Evergreen tree with mid-green leaves, silvery on the underside. Greenish-white or pink flowers are followed by long-stalked, pungent, edible, green fruit that ripen to yellow. Not hardy. Height 25–30m.

Prune to remove vertical shoots that are unlikely to produce fruit. Remove epicormic growths that will appear on the branches as well as the trunk (see page 92). Thin out the large clusters of fruit when they are 4–5 weeks old.

ECCREMOCARPUS SCABER
(Chilean glory flower)

Vigorous, evergreen climber with pale green or grey-green leaves. The racemes of tubular, orange-red flowers are produced from late spring to autumn. Not fully hardy but will grow in a sheltered, sunny site. Height 3–4m.

Prune after planting by pinching out the growing tips. Prune in early spring, cutting back all the previous year's growth to within 30–45cm of the base.

EDGEWORTHIA

Deciduous and evergreen shrubs of which *E. chrysantha* (paper bush) is the most recognised. It is a deciduous shrub with dark green leaves. Rounded heads of small, fragrant, bright yellow flowers are produced in late winter and early spring. Hardy but late spring frosts may damage the flowers. Height 1.2–1.5m.

Prune in late winter before growth starts, removing any dead or damaged stems.

ELAEAGNUS

Deciduous and evergreen shrubs and small trees with mid-green to dark glossy, green leaves, often silver-scaly on the underside. The small, bell- or tubular-shaped, white, cream, silvery-white or yellow flowers are often fragrant and are produced in late spring or summer followed by yellow, red or brown edible fruit. Hardy. Height 3–5m.

△ Enkianthus campanulatus *seldom needs to be pruned as a mature shrub.*

Prune deciduous shrubs after flowering, shortening the shoots back to a healthy side shoot. In late winter remove dead or damaged branches and a few of the oldest stems as close to the ground as possible.

Prune evergreen shrubs in late spring to retain the shape of the plant. On variegated cultivars, remove all green-leafed, reverted shoots as they appear.

ELSHOLTZIA
Semi-evergreen and deciduous shrubs and sub-shrubs, plus annuals and perennials, of which *E. stauntonii* is most usually grown. It is a deciduous sub-shrub with mid-green, mint-scented leaves that turn red in autumn. The panicles of tiny, purple-pink flowers are produced in summer and autumn. Not fully hardy but will succeed in a sheltered, sunny site. Height 1–1.5m.

Prune in early spring, cutting back to the main framework of branches. Tolerant of severe pruning.

EMBOTHRIUM
Evergreen trees and shrubs of which *E. coccineum* (Chilean fire bush) is the best known. It is an evergreen, suckering shrub with deep green leaves and racemes of scarlet flowers (occasionally yellow) in late spring and early summer. Hardy but provide shelter from cold winds. Height 10m.

Prune in winter or early spring to remove crossing branches. The suckers are replicas of the parent plant so dig them out with a piece of root attached and pot them up in ericaceous, soil-based compost.

ENKIANTHUS
Deciduous shrubs of which *E. campanulatus* is the most frequently grown. It is open-centred with clusters of pale green leaves at the tips of the shoots turning to deep yellow and red in autumn. The pendant racemes of bell-shaped, creamy-yellow flowers are streaked with deep pink, appearing in late spring and early summer. Hardy. Height 4–5m.

Prune in late winter to remove crossing branches and retain the shape of the plant.

EPACRIS
Evergreen, heath-like shrubs of which *E. impressa* (common Australian heath) is the most widely grown. It is usually a slender shrub with upright branches and small, deep green leaves with sharp tips. The cylindrical, pendant racemes of white, pink or red flowers are produced in spring and summer. Hardy but requires a sheltered, sunny site. Height 60–100cm.

Prune after flowering, cutting the flowered shoots to within 3cm of the older wood.

ERCILLA VOLUBILIS
Evergreen, climbing perennials with deep green leaves patterned with pale veins. The green or purple flower spikes appear in spring followed by purple berries. Not hardy but if the shoots have had time to harden they will tolerate some frost. Height 6–7m.

Prune in early summer after flowering to contain the growth. Old wood may be cut out at ground level in early summer. Feed with high potash in late summer to harden the new stems.

EREMOPHILA (Emu bush)

Evergreen shrubs and trees as well as perennials. The mid- or grey-green leaves are often hairy. The tubular, 2-lipped, green, yellow, orange, pink, red or purple flowers are produced in the axils of the top leaves during late winter and spring or from spring to early autumn. Not hardy although *E. maculata* will survive outside in a sheltered, frost-free site. Height 0.5–3m.

Prune after flowering by deadheading and removing older wood to avoid congestion in the centre of the plant.

ERICA (Heath)

Evergreen shrubs from prostrate to tree-like with tiny, linear, mid- to dark green or yellow, gold, red or bronze leaves. The panicles or racemes of urn- or bell-shaped, white, pink, red or purple flowers may be produced at any time of year, depending on the species. Hardy. Height 10cm–2m.

Prune after flowering, cutting the flowered stems to within 2cm of the old wood. Deadhead tree heathers such as *E. arborea* after flowering and trim to keep the shape. It is worth trying to rejuvenate old plants by pruning into the old wood but some won't recover.

E. spiculifolia (spike heath) is a low-growing, hardy, evergreen shrub with small, thin, glossy, dark green leaves and bell-shaped, white or pink flowers in summer. Prune after flowering by cutting all the growths back to within 4cm of the previous year's wood.

ERINACEA ANTHYLLIS
(Hedgehog broom)

Evergreen sub-shrub with spiny stems and small, palmate, dark green leaves. The clusters of violet-blue-white flowers appear in late spring and early summer. Hardy. Height 30cm. No pruning necessary – this is a well-behaved plant that is unlikely to become untidy or to spread beyond its allotted space.

ERIOBOTRYA JAPONICA (Loquat)

Evergreen shrub or tree with strongly veined, glossy dark green leaves and large panicles of fragrant, white flowers in autumn and winter, followed by edible, deep orange-yellow fruit. Not fully hardy but will survive outside in a sheltered, sunny site. Height 7m.

Prune just before the plant starts into growth. Shorten main stems by one third to encourage side shoots on young plants. Fruit is produced on this year's growth, so where there are too many side shoots, thin them out rather than reducing their length. When picking the fruit remove the entire group, cutting the stem back to a healthy bud or strong shoot.

ERIOGONUM (St Catherine's lace)

Evergreen shrubs and sub-shrubs with grey-green or deep green leaves, often white-woolly on the underside. The dense clusters of long-lasting, white, yellowish-green or pink flowers are produced in late spring or summer. Not hardy, although *E. crocatum* tolerates moderate frost but dislikes wet winters. Height 30cm–2m.

▽ Eriogonum umbellatum *is a well-behaved sub-shrub that seldom needs to be pruned.*

Prune in late winter before growth commences. Remove crossing or damaged branches.

ERIOSTEMON (Waxflower)
Evergreen shrubs with leathery, thin or sometimes warty, pale or deep green, often aromatic, leaves. The star-shaped, white, pink, red or mauve flowers are produced in winter and spring, or from spring to autumn. Not hardy. *E. australasius* tolerates some frost when grown in a sheltered site with well-ripened shoots. Height 1–6m.

Prune in winter to retain shape.

ERYTHRINA (Coral tree)
Evergreen, semi-evergreen and deciduous trees, shrubs and perennials often with spiny stems and mid- to dark green, variegated leaves. The pea-like, orange-red, dark red or scarlet flowers are

▽ *Erythrina crista-galli is deciduous and hardier than many others of this genus. Prune only to maintain shape and remove crossing or damaged branches.*

produced in spring or summer and autumn. Not hardy, but *E. crista-galli* will tolerate light frosts if it is sheltered from cold winds. Height 2–18m.

Prune in late winter to remove crossing and damaged branches. It does not respond well to hard pruning.

ESCALLONIA
Mostly evergreen shrubs (*E. virgata* is deciduous) and small trees with mid-green to dark, glossy, green, and occasionally aromatic, leaves. The terminal racemes or panicles of white, pink, red or scarlet flowers are produced during summer and autumn. Hardy although most cultivars prefer a sheltered, sunny site. Height 60cm–7m.

Prune in late spring. Hedges are pruned in late summer. They tolerate rejuvenation in spring by cutting them back to stumps.

EUCALYPTUS (Gum tree)
Evergreen trees and shrubs with attractive bark and aromatic, grey-green or bright green, juvenile and mature leaves. The umbels of petalless flowers

have white, cream or red stamens. A few species such as *E. gunnii* and *E. coccifera* are hardy while others will succeed in a sheltered, sunny site. Height 2–20m.

Prune in late winter to tidy the tree and remove damaged branches. For juvenile foliage, trees may be coppiced, cutting the previous year's growths to within 5–10cm of the base.

EUCOMMIA ULMOIDES (Gutta-percha tree)
Deciduous tree with glossy, dark green, prominently veined leaves and tiny, green, petalless flowers in early spring followed by winged, green nuts on female plants. Hardy. Height 10m.

Prune in late winter before growth commences, removing dead or damaged wood. It dislikes heavy pruning.

EUCRYPHIA
Evergreen trees and shrubs with leathery, bright to dark green leaves. The cup- or saucer-shaped, fragrant, white or creamy-white flowers are produced in early to midsummer or late summer and autumn. Hardy but succeeds best when sheltered from cold winds. Height 6–15m.

Prune in late winter or early spring to retain the plant's shape and remove dead or damaged branches. Where frost has killed young growths, prune in late spring to reshape the plant. Prune *E. lucida* after flowering, shortening the flowered shoots and shaping the plant. It dislikes hard pruning.

EUONYMUS (Spindle tree)
Evergreen, semi-evergreen and deciduous trees and shrubs, many with good autumn leaf colour. The small, insignificant, greenish-white or deep red flowers appear in late spring or summer followed by ribbed or winged fruit that contain seeds often with brightly coloured arils. Hardy. Height 30cm–10m.

△ Euphorbia characias *has sap that may irritate the skin, so wear gloves when pruning.*

Prune deciduous plants in late winter before growth commences to thin out congested plants and remove dead or damaged branches. Evergreens are pruned after flowering by shortening long shoots that are spoiling the plant's shape. Variegated, evergreen cultivars may revert to all-green leaves, which should be removed as soon as they are seen.

EUPATORIUM

Evergreen shrubs with light to deep green leaves and fragrant, creamy-white, pink or violet flowers in autumn or winter. Not hardy. Height 2–5m.

Prune after flowering to remove the flowering stems back to a healthy bud or strong side shoot.

EUPHORBIA (Spurge)

Evergreen and deciduous trees, shrubs and succulents with light to dark green leaves and a milky-white, irritant sap. The flower-like growths (called cyathia) form an umbel or cluster, usually greenish-yellow, red, brown or purple. Many are hardy. Height 20cm–15m.

Prune tree-like shrubs in late winter before growth commences. Prune shrubs in early spring, cutting back to the main framework.

EUPTELEA

Deciduous trees and shrubs of which *E. polyandra* is the most usually grown. It is a suckering shrub with glossy, bright green leaves that turn yellow, orange and red in early autumn. The clusters of reddish-green flowers are produced in early spring before the leaves. Hardy. Height 7m.

Prune in late winter before growth commences. Late spring frosts may damage new growths.

EURYOPS

Evergreen shrubs with hairy grey or silvery-grey, leathery leaves and daisy-like bright or deep yellow flowers. Hardy. Height 20cm–1m.

Prune after flowering to retain the shape of the plant.

EXOCHORDA (Pearl bush)

Deciduous shrubs often with arching branches and pale or mid-green leaves. The cup- or saucer-shaped, white flowers are produced in late spring and early summer. Hardy. Height 2–3m.

Prune after flowering, cutting flowered shoots back to healthy buds or a strong side shoot. Each year, remove a few of the oldest branches at the base.

FABIANA

Evergreen, heath-like shrubs of which *F. imbricata* is the most commonly grown. The tiny, needle-like, dark green leaves crowd the upright stems. The tubular, pale mauve or white flowers are produced in early summer. Hardy but benefits from shelter from cold winds. Height 2–3m.

Prune in early spring to remove old, woody stems and branches that are bare at the base. Make a sloping cut, leaving 15–20cm of stump that will produce strong shoots from dormant buds. Shorten straggly branches after flowering, pruning to above a side shoot, thus retaining the plant's shape.

FAGUS (Beech)

Deciduous trees with grey bark and mid-green to dark, glossy, green, purple or yellow leaves turning yellow and then pale brown in autumn. The tiny, male and female flowers appear with the leaves. Hardy. Height 5–25m.

Prune in winter before growth commences. Little pruning is needed apart from removing dead, damaged or crossing branches. Where branches are rubbing together, remove the weakest and check that the remaining branch is not damaged.

FALLOPIA (Russian vine)

Vigorous, twining, deciduous climbers with mid- to dark green leaves and panicles of tiny, funnel-shaped, white-tinged-pink or greenish-white flowers produced in late summer and autumn. Hardy. Height 12–15m.

Prune in early spring to keep the plant within bounds and remove old, woody, non-flowering stems. For mature plants, cut out 2 or 3 of the thickest, oldest stems as close to the base as possible each spring. If you can't disentangle the stems after pruning, allow them to wither and then cut into manageable portions and remove each piece.

△ Fatsia japonica *should always be pruned to above a side shoot.*

× FATSHEDERA LIZEI (Tree ivy)

Evergreen shrub with leathery, dark green leaves and greenish-cream flowers in autumn. Not fully hardy. Height 2m.

Prune in late winter or early spring to thin out the centre of the plant. Prune the upright stems back to just above a strong, healthy side shoot. Each year remove 1 or 2 of the oldest stems as close to ground level as possible.

FATSIA JAPONICA (Japanese aralia)

Suckering, evergreen shrub with leathery, glossy, dark green, palmate leaves and umbels of tiny, creamy-white flowers in autumn followed by clusters of small black fruit. Not fully hardy. Height 2–4m.

Prune in late spring to encourage a balanced plant. Older bare stems are pruned down to above a healthy side shoot. Select a shoot that is growing up and outwards rather than a horizontal stem. Remove suckers that are congesting the centre of the plant.

FELICIA AMELLOIDES (Blue daisy)

Bushy, evergreen sub-shrub often treated as an annual, with grey-green leaves and blue flowers in summer and autumn. Not hardy. Height 30–50cm.

When grown as an annual, little pruning is required other than pinching out the tips of the shoots in early summer to encourage flowering side shoots. If overwintered, prune half the stems back to side shoots in late spring to make the plant bushy.

FICUS

Evergreen trees, shrubs and climbers with large or small, usually leathery, dark green or variegated leaves and insignificant flowers followed by ornamental or edible fruits. Many are not hardy. Height 2–60m.

F. carica is the edible fig. It is deciduous with an open-branched habit of growth and large, lobed, mid-green leaves. The inconspicuous flowers are followed by fruit with green or purple skin. I choose to class it as a tree fruit but others may call it a soft fruit. Hardy but prefers a sheltered, sunny wall. Height 3–5m.

For growing on a wall it is advisable to purchase a 2–3-year-old fig already trained as a fan. Prune in early spring to remove damaged branches or those killed by frost. Cut them back to healthy wood or a suitably placed side shoot. Rub off any buds pointing away from the wall.

In early summer shorten the shoots, cutting beyond the fifth leaf and tying the shoots to horizontal wires. After the ripe fruit has been harvested in early autumn remove any small- to medium-sized fruit. If they are allowed to overwinter they will not swell and will prevent further fruit forming. Tiny fruit that have formed in the leaf axils close to the ends of the shoots and only twice the size of the head of a pin are allowed to overwinter.

Old branches and those that are bare are cut back to about 5cm to leave one bud that will produce a healthy, strong shoot. The roots of the fig must be contained or pruned regularly or it will make too much growth at the expense of fruit. A word of warning: the sap of the fig can irritate the eyes.

FIRMIANA SIMPLEX

(Chinese parasol tree)

Deciduous tree with large, dark green leaves turning yellow in autumn. Large terminal panicles of small, greenish-yellow flowers appear in summer followed by papery fruit that split to reveal the seed. Not hardy but will survive some frost in a sheltered, sunny position. Height 13m.

Prune in late winter or early spring to remove damaged or diseased branches. In a conservatory, shorten the side shoots by half in summer to maintain size.

FORSYTHIA (Golden bell)

Deciduous shrubs with grey-green to dark green leaves and 4-petalled, pale or bright yellow flowers in early spring before the leaves. Hardy. Height 2–4m.

Prune immediately after flowering. Shorten the flowered stems back to just above healthy buds or to strong side shoots. To encourage strong new shoots on mature plants, remove one third of the oldest branches as close to ground level as possible.

FORTUNELLA JAPONICA (Kumquat)

Evergreen shrub or small tree with spines in the leaf axils and glossy, mid-green leaves. Clusters of fragrant, white, waxy flowers appear in spring and summer followed by edible, golden-yellow citrus fruit. Not hardy. Height 2–4m.

Prune at any time in frost-free climates, otherwise prune in late spring to allow the new growths to ripen before the cold winter weather. The head of the tree can be kept compact by shortening the main branches to strong side shoots during winter. These branches are again shortened by one third, allowing the tree to build up a neat, uniformly branched head.

Kumquats are usually grafted onto *Poncirus trifoliata* (an ornamental orange with long, sharp spines), which provides a dwarfing effect. Any suckers which emerge from the rootstock should be pulled off when young.

FOTHERGILLA

Deciduous shrubs with dark green and toothed margins to the leaves, which turn yellow, orange and red in autumn. The bottlebrush-like spikes of fragrant, white flowers are produced in late spring. Hardy. Height 1–3m.

Prune in late winter before the leaves open to remove any damaged or crossing branches, but otherwise keep pruning to a minimum.

FRANKLINIA ALATAMAHA

Deciduous tree with glossy, dark green leaves that turn red in autumn. The large, cup-shaped, fragrant, white flowers have yellow stamens appearing in late summer and autumn. Hardy. Height 4–5m.

Prune in early spring before the tree comes into leaf. Keep pruning to a minimum, but encourage flowering by completely removing congested branches in the centre of the tree to allow more sunlight to penetrate.

FRAXINUS (Ash)

Deciduous trees with pinnate, light to dark green leaves and panicles or racemes of usually insignificant, sometimes fragrant, flowers followed by winged seed capsules. Hardy. Height 15–25m.

Prune in late winter to remove dead, diseased or crossing branches. Where large branches are removed smooth the surface of the wound (see page 25). The following year, thin out the new growths from around the cut branch.

FREMONTODENDRON (Flannel bush)

Evergreen and semi-evergreen trees and shrubs with hairy, young shoots and dark green, lobed leaves. The saucer-shaped, deep yellow or orange-yellow flowers are produced from late spring until autumn. Not fully hardy but will succeed on a warm, sheltered, sunny wall. Height 2–7m.

Prune in midsummer to shape the plant and remove damaged branches. Shorten shoots that have flowered back to healthy side shoots. This plant tends to be short-lived and dislikes hard pruning, so leave old, bare branches untouched. The leaves and stems are covered in irritant hairs so wear goggles when pruning.

▷ Fuchsia 'Mrs Popple': *If growing a fuchsia as a standard, remove any side shoots that appear on the bare stem.*

FUCHSIA

Deciduous, upright shrubs with ballerina-like flowers followed by purple or black fruit. Not hardy but will grow outdoors in a sheltered position. Height 1–5m.

Prune the species, such as *F. magellanica*, in early spring to remove growths that have been killed by frost. Shorten main branches by one third and remove a quarter to a fifth of the oldest branches as close to the base as possible. Hybrid fuchsias that are grown indoors are made bushy by nipping out the tips of the young shoots in spring.

To produce a standard, train a shoot up a bamboo cane. Remove all the side shoots below the desired height. Nip out the growing tip and the tips of side shoots above that height to form a bushy head.

△ Genista aetnensis (*Mount Etna broom*) *flowers in summer on new growths. Prune lightly in early spring.*

GARDENIA

Evergreen shrubs and small trees with fragrant, white or cream flowers. Not hardy. Height 2–10m.

With early-flowering species such as *G. thunbergia*, remove dead flowers and shorten by one third any shoots that have outgrown the rest of the plant. Prune summer-flowering species such as *G. augusta* in late spring to remove congested branches. Cut dead flower stems back to strong buds.

GARRYA ELLIPTICA (Silk-tassel bush)

Evergreen shrub with leathery, grey-green leaves and pendant, grey-green catkins in winter and early spring. Hardy. Height 4m.

Prune in early spring as the catkins fade. Remove shoots growing outwards on wall-grown plants. Old plants may be rejuvenated by hard pruning all the old growths over a 3-year period. Strong new shoots will be produced from dormant buds on the branch stumps.

GAULTHERIA

Evergreen shrubs with glossy or leathery, dark green, occasionally aromatic, leaves and small white flowers followed by white, pink, red or purple fruit in autumn. Hardy. Height 15–150cm.

Prune excess young growths after flowering. In late winter clip over mature plants to keep them compact. Remove suckers by pulling or digging them out to prevent them forming a thicket.

GAYLUSSACIA BACCATA
(Black huckleberry)

Deciduous shrub with dark green leaves that turn red in autumn. Pendant racemes, of tiny, urn-shaped, red flowers appear in late spring followed by edible, glossy, black fruit. Hardy. Height 1m.

Prune in late winter to keep the centre of the plant open. Old, woody, bare branches may be cut out as close to the ground as possible. Prune low-growing stems to an upward-pointing bud.

GENISTA (Broom)

Deciduous and often spiny shrubs with small, palmate leaves, or leafless. The small, pea-like, yellow flowers appear in spring and early summer. Hardy. Height 15cm–3m.

Prune in early spring to remove damaged branches. After flowering lightly clip over the plants to make them bushy. Don't cut into the old wood of any species as the plant will not produce new growths. Do not prune *G. lydia.*

GEVUINA AVELLANA (Chilean hazel)

Evergreen tree with large, leathery, glossy, dark green leaves and spider-like white flowers in summer. Hardy but needs shelter from cold winds. Height 8m.

Shorten the side shoots in early spring if the shrub needs to be kept within bounds. No other pruning is required.

GINKGO BILOBA (Maidenhair tree)

Deciduous conifer with bright green, fan-shaped leaves that turn yellow in autumn and clusters of male, yellow, catkin-like flowers. The single, female flowers produce yellow-green fruit with a rotten smell. Hardy. Height 30m.

Established trees dislike being pruned and often suffer from dieback as a result of being cut. Prune young plants to ensure that there is only one leading branch. There are two types of shoot on a mature tree: short stems with leaves at the tip; and longer, fast-growing branches with lots of side shoots. It is the latter that will try to take over as leader.

GLEDITSIA

Deciduous trees, usually with spiny stems and glossy, green or yellow, pinnate leaves. The small, inconspicuous, greenish-white flowers are followed by long, pendant seed pods. Hardy but young trees may suffer frost damage. Height 5–30m.

Pruning is seldom necessary but remove broken branches in late summer or autumn. Young growths that have been damaged by late frosts are pruned back to healthy buds in late spring.

GORDONIA

Evergreen trees and shrubs with leathery, dark green leaves and camellia-like white, flowers during winter and spring or in

▷ Ginkgo biloba *should be trained to a single leader when young. Mature trees seldom need pruning.*

summer. Not fully hardy but if *G. lasianthus* is sheltered from cold winds it will survive a few degrees of frost. Height 6–18m.

Pruning is not normally necessary but remove broken branches and shorten long shoots that unbalance the head of the tree during early spring.

GREVILLEA

Evergreen trees and shrubs with broad or needle-like, often pinnate, leaves. The summer flowers are petalless with red or yellow calyx tubes. Not hardy but some species such as G. 'Canberra Gem' will survive light frosts. Height 90cm–4m.

Prune the tips of young plants in late spring to encourage side shoots and make a bushy plant. Remove frost-damaged shoots back to the main stem. Don't leave stumps as they are prone to dieback.

GREYIA SUTHERLANDII

(Natal bottlebrush)
Evergreen large shrub or small tree with stiff, upright branches and leathery, light green leaves. Racemes of brick-red, bell-shaped flowers are produced in spring. Not fully hardy. Height 2–4m.

Prune after flowering, removing the old flower stems. Prune one fifth of the upright branches in early summer; removing one quarter to one third of their length back to outward-pointing buds will open up the bush to make it spread.

GRISELINIA

Evergreen shrubs with leathery, glossy leaves and inconspicuous yellow flowers in spring followed in summer by purple fruit. Not fully hardy but *G. littoralis* will withstand some frost. Height 5–9m.

Prune in late spring to remove frost-damaged shoots. Clip hedges in summer using secateurs to avoid cutting large leaves that will turn brown. Plants may be pruned hard, leaving stumps that will re-grow from dormant buds.

GYMNOCLADUS DIOICA

(Kentucky coffee tree)
Deciduous tree with large panicles of creamy-white flowers in early summer, followed, on female flowers, by long, pendant pods. Hardy. Height 20m.

Pruning is not normally necessary except to remove damaged or dead branches in spring. When there are two leading branches, remove one, leaving no stump.

HALESIA (Snowdrop tree)
Deciduous trees and shrubs with mid-green leaves that turn yellow in autumn. The pendant, bell-shaped, white flowers are produced in late spring or early summer followed by winged fruit. Hardy. Height 6–10m.

Prune in late autumn or during winter to tidy up the appearance of the plant. Cut out crossing branches. Older branches may be thinned out in late winter. To rejuvenate a neglected tree, prune the oldest branches out at soil level immediately after flowering.

× HALIMIOCISTUS
Evergreen shrubs with dark or grey-green leaves and white or creamy-yellow flowers with maroon bands during late spring and early summer. Hardy. Height 45–60cm. Pruning is seldom needed for this compact plant.

HALIMIUM
Evergreen shrubs with grey-green leaves and saucer-shaped yellow or white flowers in late spring and early summer. Hardy but prefer to be sheltered from cold winds. Height 45cm–1.5m.

Pruning is seldom necessary but a light clipping in late spring will encourage bushy growth.

HALIMODENDRON
HALODENDRON (Salt tree)
Deciduous, spiny shrub with pinnate, grey-green leaves and small racemes of pea-like, purple-pink flowers in midsummer. Hardy. Height 2m.

Prune in late winter to remove dead or damaged branches. Remove one quarter of the oldest branches each year in winter, cutting as close to the ground as possible.

▷ Hamamelis × intermedia: *mature plants need pruning only to maintain shape. You can do this while they are in flower and bring some of the wonderful fragrance indoors.*

HAMAMELIS (Witch hazel)
Deciduous shrubs and small trees with mid- to bright green leaves turning yellow in autumn. The spider-like, fragrant, yellow or red flowers appear in winter before the leaves. Hardy. Height 2–4m.

Prune in early spring after the flowers fade and before the leaves appear. Cut broken or crossing branches back to strong side shoots or buds. Pull off suckers from grafted plants. Where rejuvenation is necessary remove one quarter of the oldest branches close to soil level each spring.

HARDENBERGIA (Coral pea)

Evergreen climbers with bright green, palmate leaves and pendant racemes of white, pink, violet or purple flowers with green or yellow spots in winter and spring or spring through to summer. Not hardy although *H. violacea* will tolerate light frosts if grown in a sheltered site. Height 2m.

Prune after flowering to remove old, bare stems that are not flowering. Cut back to a strong side shoot or remove the shoot at soil level.

HEBE

Evergreen shrubs with leaves that may be scale-like or large and pale to deep, glossy green or variegated. The racemes or spokes of small, tubular flowers are white, pink, red, violet, blue or purple during summer. Mostly hardy but some are prone to frost damage. Height 30cm–3m.

Prune in late spring, removing older branches close to the ground. Species that are naturally mounded are clipped over after flowering. Removal of large, faded flower spikes will encourage new growths. Variegated cultivars are prone to reverting to all-green. Remove these branches as soon as possible, cutting them back to the main branch.

HEDERA (Ivy)

Evergreen, trailing and self-clinging climbers with glossy, mid- to dark green or variegated leaves. The umbels of greenish-yellow flowers appear in autumn followed by yellow or black fruit. Hardy. Height 2–12m.

Prune in early spring before growth commences. After planting pinch out the tips of the shoots to encourage the plant to produce strong growth. During the growing season, shorten shoots that are heading in the wrong direction. To keep the plant within bounds, prune back in spring to a strong side shoot or bud. To

rejuvenate an old, leggy plant, cut the stems back to 45cm from the base in winter before the sap rises. Train in the new growths as they appear.

Where ivy has taken over a tree, the mass of evergreen leaves acts as a sail and during a storm can cause the tree to fall. Where it is not wanted, cut the ivy 30cm above ground level. Eventually the ivy will lose its grip on the tree bark and fall.

HELIANTHEMUM (Rock rose)

Evergreen and semi-evergreen shrubs with small, mid- to dark green, grey-green or silver leaves and saucer-shaped, brightly coloured flowers during spring and summer. Hardy. Height 15–50cm.

Prune after flowering, cutting all the flowering stems back to within 2–3cm of the older wood. Old, woody plants are unlikely to produce new growths and are best replaced with young plants.

HELICHRYSUM

Evergreen shrubs and sub-shrubs as well as perennials and annuals. The stems are woolly or hairy with silver or grey-green, hairy and often aromatic leaves. The 'everlasting' flowers are often daisy-like in shades of yellow during summer and early autumn. Hardy but some are prone to frost damage. Height 15–120cm.

Prune in early spring (late spring in cold areas), cutting the flowered shoots back to within 2–5cm of the older wood. They dislike hard pruning into the very old wood.

HIBBERTIA

Evergreen trees, shrubs and climbers with bright or deep, glossy green, sometimes leathery, leaves and bright yellow flowers in winter and spring or in summer. Not hardy. Height 1–4m.

Prune climbers after flowering, removing older stems to prevent congestion. Prune shoots to keep them

△ Hardenbergia violacea: *cut old, non-flowering stems at ground level.*

within their allotted space, cutting above a side shoot or healthy bud. Prune shrubs after flowering, cutting the flowered stems back to strong side shoots.

HIBISCUS

Deciduous and evergreen shrubs with trumpet- or saucer-shaped, white, pink, yellow, orange, red or blue flowers in summer and autumn. The deciduous *H. syriacus* is hardy; others such as the evergreen *H. rosa-sinensis* are not. Height 1–4m.

Pruning is seldom necessary. If a deciduous plant spreads beyond its allocated space or becomes cluttered, prune in late winter or early spring when dormant. Prune evergreens in late spring, cutting the main shoots back by one quarter. Always prune immediately above a strong bud as a stump will attract coral spot disease (see page 16). Both deciduous and evergreen shrubs are tolerant of hard pruning, producing strong shoots from the base.

HIPPOPHAE RHAMNOIDES
(Sea buckthorn)
Deciduous shrub or small tree with spiny shoots and grey-green or pale green leaves. The racemes of tiny, greenish-yellow flowers appear in spring followed on female plants by bright orange fruit. Hardy. Height 6m.

Prune in late summer, removing dead wood back to a healthy side shoot. Suckers should be removed before they form a thicket. The plant will recover from hard pruning with the oldest shoots cut as close to the base as possible but will produce additional suckers.

HOHERIA
Evergreen and deciduous shrubs and trees with hairy, dark green or grey-green leaves. The juvenile leaves of seedlings have a silvery appearance. The cup-shaped, fragrant, white flowers are produced in mid- to late summer. Hardy but shoots of evergreens are subject to frost damage. Height 6–12m.

Pruning is seldom necessary but remove frost-damaged shoots and broken branches in late spring or after flowering.

▽ Hippophae rhamnoides *should be pruned to keep the centre of the plant open.*

HOLBOELLIA
Evergreen, twining climbers with dark green leaves and racemes of small, mauve or greenish-white male flowers and purple female flowers in spring. Occasionally female flowers are followed by sausage-shaped, red or purple fruit. Hardy but succeed best when protected from cold winds. Height 4–7m.

Prune in late spring, removing old, bare stems close to ground level. Thin out congested stems, reducing their length by one third to a strong bud.

HOLODISCUS
Deciduous shrubs with softly hairy, grey-green leaves and large, plume-like panicles of tiny, cup-shaped, creamy-white flowers in summer. Hardy. Height 2–4m.

Prune after flowering, shortening the flowered shoots back to healthy buds or strong side shoots. Rejuvenate old plants by pruning one third of the oldest wood back to the base.

HOVEA
Evergreen shrubs, often with spiny, rust-red stems with glossy or matt, dark green leaves. The clusters of purple or violet, pea-like flowers appear at the leaf axils in spring. Not hardy but *H. montana* will survive in a sheltered, sunny position. Height 40–150cm.

Prune after flowering, removing the flowered stem back by one quarter to a side shoot. Thin out congested branches of *H. chorizemifolia*, cutting as close to the base as possible without leaving stumps.

HOVENIA DULCIS (Raisin tree)
Deciduous tree with glossy, dark green leaves, downy on the underside. The tiny, greenish-yellow flowers appear in summer. After flowering the flower stalk swells, becoming red and edible with a sweet taste. Black fruit form in autumn. Hardy. Height 10m.

Prune in late winter or after the last of the frosts in cold, exposed areas. Remove broken or crossing branches. It tolerates hard pruning to thin out the head of the tree.

HOYA (Wax flower)

Evergreen climbers with leathery or succulent, mid- to dark green leaves. The umbels of waxy, fragrant, white, cream, pink, red or purple flowers appear in spring or summer from the leaf axils. Not hardy. Height 1–10m.

Wear gloves when pruning as the cut stems exude a white latex that is a skin irritant. Pruning is not usually necessary but old, non-flowering stems are removed at the base after flowering. They dislike hard pruning. Leave the old flower stumps as they often produce new flowers.

HUMULUS (Hop)

Perennial climbers with light or dark green leaves. The spikes of female flowers are green and produced in summer. Hardy. Height 3–6m.

Being perennial, they die down in late autumn so prune the dead growths off at ground level in early spring.

HYDRANGEA

Evergreen and deciduous shrubs and climbers with mid- to dark green, bronze or variegated leaves. The terminal flower heads are produced in summer and autumn. They are flat, domed or conical with both tiny, fertile flowers and showy, sterile flowers with white, pink, red or mauve, petal-like sepals. Hardy although some species require protection from late spring frosts. Height 1.5–15m.

Prune climbers such as *H. anomala* subsp. *petiolaris* after flowering. Where wall-trained, shorten back to 5cm any side shoots that are growing away from the wall. *H. paniculata* is pruned in spring, shortening the previous year's

growths to within 5cm of the main framework of branches. This will result in fewer but larger flowers.

Prune the well-known mop heads such as *H. macrophylla* in spring, cutting the old flower stems back to the first pair of healthy buds. They respond to hard pruning and one third of the oldest wood should be cut out at the base each spring.

Other species require little or no pruning, except in late winter to remove broken or crossing branches.

HYMENOSPORUM FLAVUM (Australian frangipani)

Evergreen shrub or small tree with glossy, dark green leaves, pale green on the underside. The large panicles of tubular, fragrant flowers are produced from spring to late summer, creamy-white becoming orange-yellow with age. Not hardy but will survive in a sheltered, frost-free area. Height 4–10m.

Prune after flowering to remove misshapen and broken branches back to a strong side shoot. It tolerates hard pruning, cutting old stems back to stumps that will produce shoots from dormant buds.

HYPERICUM

Deciduous, semi-evergreen and evergreen shrubs with light to dark green and bronze leaves, some of which colour in autumn. The yellow flowers, usually with prominent stamens, appear in late spring, summer and autumn followed by red or black fruit. Hardy. Height 15cm–2m.

Prune evergreen species in spring, shortening old, non-flowering shoots back to healthy buds. Prune deciduous species in early spring, cutting the previous year's flowering stems to within 5cm of the main framework.

Most hypericums tolerate hard pruning to rejuvenate old plants. *H. calycinum* is pruned to ground level in late spring.

HYSSOPUS OFFICINALIS (Hyssop)

Semi-evergreen, aromatic shrub with thin, mid-green leaves and slender spikes of funnel-shaped, deep blue flowers during summer and early autumn. Hardy. Height 50–70cm.

Prune in mid-spring, cutting all the growths back to within 2cm of the main framework of branches. Remove old, non-flowering wood at the base.

IDESIA POLYCARPA

Deciduous tree with glossy, dark green leaves and long, pendulous panicles of small, fragrant, greenish-yellow flowers in summer. These are followed on female plants by red berries. Hardy. Height 10m.

Pruning is seldom necessary but remove dead, diseased or crossing branches in late winter before the sap flows.

ILEX (Holly)

Evergreen trees and shrubs with glossy, dark green or variegated, often spiny, leaves. The small clusters of white, cream, pink or blue, male or female flowers appear in the leaf axils in early summer followed by white, yellow, orange, red or black berries in autumn. Hardy. Height 30cm–20m.

Trim hedges in early spring. Young plants are pruned to remove double leaders. Mature trees seldom require pruning but deal with the 3 Ds (see page 20) in late winter or early spring.

ILLICIUM (Anise)

Evergreen trees and shrubs with thick, glossy, dark green, aromatic leaves and star-shaped, fragrant, cream, yellow, pink or red-purple flowers in spring or summer. Hardy but require shelter from cold winds. Height 2–15m.

Pruning is seldom necessary but remove congested branches in summer after flowering. Leave stumps that will produce new shoots from dormant buds.

INDIGOFERA

Evergreen and deciduous trees and shrubs with pinnate, glossy leaves and racemes of white or pink, pea-like flowers in summer and early autumn. Hardy but most species require protection from cold winds. Height 70cm–2m.

Prune in late spring before new growth appears. In frosty areas prune back last year's flowered shoots to the main framework of branches. They tolerate rejuvenation with all the branches cut to within 10cm of ground level.

ITEA

Evergreen trees and shrubs with holly-like, glossy, dark green leaves often with autumn colour. The racemes of fragrant, white, greenish-white or cream flowers are produced in summer and early autumn.

▽ *Indigofera's early growth is prone to frost damage, so prune in late spring before this appears.*

Hardy but most species succeed best in a sheltered, sunny site. Height 1–5m.

Prune evergreens in late spring to remove crossing branches, cutting back to a strong side shoot. Deciduous species are pruned after flowering by removing one quarter to one fifth of branches at the base. Wall-trained plants are pruned after flowering or in late winter, shortening flowered shoots back to the main framework of branches.

IXORA

Evergreen shrubs and trees with mid- to dark green leaves and white, pink, orange or red, 4-petalled, fragrant flowers in summer. Not hardy. Height 1.5–2m.

Prune young plants by nipping out the growing tips of shoots to make the plant bushy. Immediately after flowering, remove up to half the flowered shoot to above a healthy bud. Rejuvenate an old plant by pruning all the stems back to 20cm from the base in late winter.

JACARANDA MIMOSIFOLIA

Deciduous tree with pinnate, fern-like, bright green leaves. The upright panicles of blue-purple, white-throated, foxglove-like flowers are produced during spring and early summer, often before the leaves appear. The flowers are followed by hard, disc-shaped seed pods. Not hardy. Height 15m.

Pruning is seldom necessary but damaged or low branches can be removed in late winter before the sap starts to flow.

JAMESIA AMERICANA (Wax flower)

Deciduous shrub with peeling bark and rough-textured, dark green leaves. The small panicles of fragrant, star-shaped, white flowers appear in late spring and early summer. Hardy. Height 1–2m.

Prune after flowering, shortening the flowered stems back to strong side shoots or healthy buds. Remove one quarter of the stems at ground level.

△ Jasminum nudiflorum: *to avoid mine becoming a tangled mass of shoots, I cut it to the ground every three years, leaving the one-year-old green stems.*

JASMINUM (Jasmine)
Evergreen and deciduous shrubs and climbers with white, yellow or pink flowers, often fragrant, in winter or summer. Some need protection from spring frost. Height 1.5–5m.

Prune mature climbers immediately after flowering, removing the old dead wood as close to the base as possible. Reduce the shoots on newly planted climbers by half to encourage strong growths from the base. They tolerate hard pruning in spring, producing new shoots from stumps 45cm long. Where the stems twine, cut and allow the shoots to wither. Those that are dead are then visible and can be cut out in sections.

JUGLANS (Walnut)
Deciduous trees with pinnate, mid- to dark green leaves. The male and female flowers are greenish-yellow and are produced in spring and early summer followed by edible nuts within a brown, furrowed shell. Hardy but late frosts can cause damage. Height 10–25m.

Prune in midsummer to prevent the tree bleeding sap. Young wood has hollow stems with segmented pith and this is a cause of dieback on badly pruned stems. Prune to immediately above a strong side shoot. Where stumps are left they must be removed as soon as possible.

Walnuts dislike hard pruning so early pruning and shaping to keep the centre open for sunlight is essential. Cut large branches back, making sure the collar is left intact (see page 25).

JUNIPERUS (Juniper)
Evergreen conifers with scale- or needle-like, pale to dark green, blue-green, grey or golden leaves. The tiny male and female cones are followed on the females by fleshy fruit. Hardy. Height 15cm–20m.

Pruning is not normally necessary but where branches have to be removed it is possible to cut into the older wood where new shoots will be produced. Nipping out the growing tips of young plants will encourage a bushy habit of growth. Where reverted growths appear on junipers, remove them before these more vigorous shoots smother the plant and turn the leaves brown.

KADSURA
Evergreen climbers with glossy, dark green leaves. *K. japonica* is the commonly grown species with cup-shaped, yellowish-green flowers appearing in summer and autumn at the leaf axils. Female flowers are on separate plants and are followed by deep red, blackberry-like fruit. Hardy but prone to frost damage on the new growths. Height 4m.

Prune in late winter, removing older stems to avoid congestion. Prune back to strong buds close to the base, or where grown on a wall shorten the side shoots to the main framework of stems.

KALMIA
Evergreen shrubs with leathery, glossy, deep green leaves and racemes of cup- or saucer-shaped, white, pink or red flowers often with other coloured markings. Hardy. Height 15cm–3m.

Pruning is seldom necessary. To retain the shape of the plant, remove damaged or crossing branches after flowering. With the exception of *K. angustifolia*, most species dislike hard pruning. To rejuvenate, remove just a few branches each summer as close to ground level as possible.

KALOPANAX SEPTEMLOBUS
(also named *Kalopanax pictus*)
Deciduous tree with spines on the main branches and lobed, dark green leaves. The large panicles of small, white flowers appear in late summer followed by blue-black fruit. Hardy but succeeds best in a sheltered site. Height 10m.

Pruning is seldom necessary but broken or crossing branches are removed in late winter or early spring. Stumps are prone to coral spot disease (see page 16).

KERRIA JAPONICA (Jew's mallow)
Deciduous shrub with bright green leaves and golden-yellow flowers in late spring. Hardy. Height 2m.

Prune after flowering, cutting the flowered stems down to healthy side shoots close to the base of the plant. Stumps are liable to dieback. Prone to suckers, which may be dug out with their roots and transplanted.

△ Kolkwitzia amabilis: *rooted suckers can be potted up for friends.*

KOELREUTERIA

Deciduous trees and shrubs with pinnate, mid-green leaves that, in the case of *K. paniculata*, open pink-red and turn yellow in autumn. Panicles of yellow flowers are produced in summer and autumn followed by red-brown bladder-like fruit pods. Hardy but young shoots may suffer frost damage. Height 10m.

Pruning is seldom necessary but remove broken or diseased branches during winter when the tree is dormant. Stumps are subject to dieback so prune immediately above a side shoot. They dislike hard pruning.

KOLKWITZIA AMABILIS (Beauty bush)

Deciduous shrub with bell-shaped, light to dark pink flowers with yellow throats produced in late spring and early summer. Hardy, but new growths may be damaged by late frosts. Height 3m.

Prune after flowering, cutting the flowered stems back to strong side shoots low down on the branch. It tolerates hard pruning. Rejuvenate by removing one quarter of the old stems at the base in summer. Remove suckers to prevent the plant becoming a thicket.

KUNZEA

Evergreen shrubs, some species with white margins to the leaves. The short spikes or small, rounded heads of scarlet or pink-mauve flowers are produced in spring and early summer. Not hardy but *K. baxteri* will survive in a sheltered, frost-free site. Height 1–2m.

Pruning is not normally necessary but broken, diseased or congested branches are removed in late winter or early spring. Cut back to strong side shoots without leaving a stump.

+LABURNOCYTISUS 'ADAMII'

Deciduous tree with 3-palmate, dark green leaves and racemes of pea-like flowers in late spring and early summer in 3 separate colours on the same plant: yellow, purple and mauve-pink with a yellow flush. Hardy. Height 7m.

Pruning is seldom required. Broken, diseased or crossing branches are removed in winter when the plant is dormant. Avoid leaving stumps. Remove suckers from below the graft.

LABURNUM (Golden rain)

Deciduous trees with 3-palmate, dark green leaves. The pendant racemes of pea-like, bright yellow flowers are produced in late spring and early summer. Hardy. Height 7–9m.

Pruning is not normally necessary apart from removing damaged and crossing branches in late winter.

LAGERSTROEMIA

Evergreen and deciduous trees and shrubs with peeling bark and grey-green or dark green leaves. The panicles of white, pink, red, mauve or purple flowers with crinkled petals are produced from late spring through to autumn. Not hardy. Height 3–12m.

Prune in late autumn or winter to remove damaged branches. To thin out congested branches and allow light to the centre of the plant, prune in early spring by removing one fifth of the laterals back to the main framework of branches. The new growths may flower in late summer.

△ Lapageria rosea: *too lovely to prune!*

◁ Laburnum × watereri *'Vossii': remove crossing branches in winter. Do not leave stumps, as these will be prone to dieback.*

LANTANA

Evergreen shrubs with deep green, often wrinkled leaves and terminal heads of white, cream, yellow, orange, pink, red or purple flowers from late spring to autumn. Not hardy. Height 20cm–2m.

Prune in late winter to remove broken or congested stems. Cut back to a strong bud or side shoot. Deadhead on a regular basis. Nip out the growing tips of young plants to make the plant bushy.

LAPAGERIA ROSEA

(Chilean bell flower)

Evergreen climber with bell-shaped, fleshy, red or pink flowers in the leaf axils during late summer and autumn. Not fully hardy but may be grown on a sheltered, warm, shaded wall. Height 4m.

Do not prune unless stems have to be thinned – do this after flowering. *Lapageria* spreads by suckers that may be lifted and transplanted.

LARDIZABALA BITERNATA

Evergreen climber with dark green leaves. The white and brown-mauve flowers appear in late autumn and early winter, the males are in pendant racemes while each female is produced in the leaf axils, followed by purple, sausage-shaped, edible berries. Hardy but protect from biting, cold winds. Height 3m.

Prune after flowering to remove damaged or congested branches. Cut back to a strong side shoot. Don't leave stumps. It tolerates hard pruning with the oldest stems cut out at the base.

LARIX (Larch)

Deciduous conifers with spirals of needle-like leaves that turn butter-yellow in autumn. Yellow or pink male cones appear in spring. Female cones are purple, turning woody and brown. Hardy. Height 30m.

Pruning is not usually necessary. Occasionally a young plant will produce two leading shoots. The weaker should be removed in early spring.

LAURELIA SEMPERVIRENS

Evergreen shrub or small tree with aromatic, bright green, leathery leaves and panicles of inconspicuous, cup-shaped, pale green flowers in early summer. Hardy. Height 15m.

Pruning is seldom necessary but congested or damaged branches are removed in late winter or early spring. Prune to a strong side shoot. It tolerates hard pruning but leave stumps to produce shoots from dormant buds.

LAURUS NOBILIS (Bay laurel)

Evergreen shrub or small tree with aromatic leaves. Clusters of greenish-yellow flowers appear in spring followed by black berries. Hardy but does best when sheltered from cold winds. Height 13m.

Prune in late winter or in spring in cold areas. Nip out the growing tips of young plants to make them bushy. Where grown as topiary, clip over 2 or 3 times in summer to maintain shape.

LAVANDULA (Lavender)

Evergreen shrubs with aromatic grey, grey-green or green leaves and long-stalked spikes of fragrant, white, pink, blue, purple or mauve flowers in spring and summer or in late summer. Hardy but some species are prone to spring frost damage. Height 30–100cm.

With new plants nip out the growing tips of all the shoots to make the plant bushy. In cool climates remove the old flower stalks in autumn and prune in spring, cutting the previous year's growths back to within 2–5cm of the older wood. In warm climates where there is little or no risk of frost, prune in autumn, cutting back to within 2–5cm of the main framework of branches. Lavender will not recover from hard pruning into the old wood.

LAVATERA (Mallow)

Deciduous and evergreen shrubs, perennials and annuals often with grey-green leaves. The saucer- or funnel-shaped, white, pink or cerise flowers are produced in summer. Hardy. Height 60cm–2.5m.

Prune in early spring, cutting all the previous year's flowered shoots back to the main framework of branches. Lavatera are not suitable for hard pruning. They are short-lived plants prone to wind damage.

LEDUM (Labrador tea)

Evergreen shrubs with aromatic leaves and terminal clusters of small, white flowers in spring and early summer. Hardy. Height 60–120cm.

Pruning is seldom necessary. If straggly, the flowered shoots may be pruned to healthy buds in summer.

△ Leonotis leonurus: *in cold, exposed gardens prune in late spring.*

▷ Leptospermum *'Red Falls': prune flowered stems back to a side shoot.*

LEONOTIS LEONURUS (Lion's ear)

Semi-evergreen or evergreen shrub with square stems and deep green leaves. The whorls of tubular, red or orange-red flowers appear in late autumn and winter. Not hardy but will survive in a sheltered, sunny site. Height 2–3m.

Prune in early spring, cutting the flowered shoots back to within 3–5cm of the old wood. Avoid leaving stumps as they are prone to dieback.

LEPTOSPERMUM (Tea tree)

Evergreen trees and shrubs with dark green leaves that are often silky, hairy and aromatic. The single or clusters of star- or cup-shaped, white, pink or red flowers appear from the leaf axils in late spring and summer or late summer. *L. rupestre* is fully hardy while others suffer frost damage on young growths. Height 20cm–7m.

Prune after flowering to maintain shape, reducing all flowering shoots by one third to strong side shoots. Leptospermums dislike hard pruning. Where there is old wood, remove a single branch at the base each autumn.

LESPEDEZA (Bush clover)

Deciduous shrubs with 3-palmate, dark or blue-green leaves. The racemes of small, pea-like, pink-purple flowers are produced in late summer or autumn. Hardy. Height 2m.

Prune in late spring, reducing all the shoots to within 2–4cm of the permanent framework of branches. It tolerates hard pruning. Remove bare stumps when the new shoots appear.

LEUCOPOGON FRASERI

Evergreen sub-shrub with tiny, glossy, dark green leaves turning red in autumn. The fragrant, white flowers are produced at the tips of the shoots in summer followed by edible, sweet, orange fruit in autumn. Hardy. Height 15cm.

Prune in mid-spring, nipping out the tips of strongly growing shoots.

LEUCOTHOE

Deciduous, semi-evergreen and evergreen shrubs with glossy, dark green or variegated leaves and panicles or racemes of white, urn-shaped flowers in spring or early summer. Hardy. Height 1–3m.

Pruning is seldom necessary but damaged branches are removed in late winter. They tolerate hard pruning to renovate, producing shoots from 30cm-high stumps. Suckering species (such as *L. racemosa*) quickly form a thicket if the suckers are allowed to remain.

LEYCESTERIA

Deciduous shrubs with hollow, cane-like stems and dark green leaves. The terminal racemes or pendant spikes of yellow or white flowers surrounded by dark, purple-red bracts are produced in late spring and summer or from early summer until autumn. They are followed by green or deep purple berries. Hardy but require a sheltered site in frosty areas. Height 2m.

Prune in spring to prevent the plant becoming congested. Cut the flowered stems back to immediately above a strong side shoot. Remove thin, spindly shoots. Where stumps die and turn pale brown they need to be pruned back to the base. To rejuvenate, prune all the shoots to the base.

LIGUSTRUM (Privet)

Deciduous, semi-evergreen and evergreen shrubs and trees with glossy, green or variegated leaves. The terminal panicles of small, white flowers have an unpleasant, sickly sweet smell and are followed by black fruit. Hardy. Height 2–10m.

Prune in late winter or in early spring in frosty areas. Newly planted hedges should be reduced to half their height after planting. To reduce congestion in the centre of the plant, thin out one quarter of the stems at ground level. Where stumps are left they will produce shoots from dormant buds. These should be thinned out when small. Hedges are lightly clipped 2 or 3 times in summer.

LINDERA (Spice bush)

Deciduous and evergreen trees and shrubs with aromatic, bright or dark green leaves, some of which turn yellow in autumn. The umbels of tiny, star-like, yellow or greenish-yellow flowers appear in early or late spring, followed on female plants by red berries. Hardy. Height 3–5m.

Prune in late autumn or winter to thin out surplus flowering side shoots. It tolerates hard pruning but water shoots will form close to the cut branches. Remove these without leaving stumps. For coppicing, cut back to 20–30cm every second or third year, in winter.

LIQUIDAMBAR (Sweet gum)

Deciduous trees with palmate, mid-green to dark, glossy green, purple or variegated leaves turning orange, red and purple in late autumn. The inconspicuous, greenish-yellow, female flowers are followed by spiky fruit clusters. Hardy. Height 6–25m.

Pruning is not normally necessary. Remove broken or low-growing branches in winter when the tree is dormant. Prune out dead wood in summer. When young, check for double, competing leaders and remove the weakest without leaving a stump. It dislikes hard pruning.

LIRIODENDRON (Tulip tree)

Deciduous trees with saddle-shaped, almost square, deep green leaves turning yellow in autumn. The cup-shaped, green flowers are marked orange or yellow and are produced in summer. Hardy. Height 25–30m.

Prune in winter when dormant to remove wind-damaged branches. Remove dead branches in summer. Wounds are susceptible to dieback and coral spot disease (see page 16) so prune as little as possible and always leave a smooth wound.

LITHOCARPUS

Evergreen trees and shrubs with leathery, dark green leaves. The upright panicles of tiny, white flowers appear in summer or late autumn and winter followed by clusters of acorns. Hardy but succeed best when sheltered from cold winds. Height 10m.

Prune in winter or in late spring in cold areas. Young plants may produce competing leaders; allow one to remain. Remove congested and crossing branches back to the main framework of branches.

▷ Liriodendron tulipifera: *prune to remove crossing branches. Avoid leaving stumps.*

LOMATIA

Evergreen trees and shrubs, some with felted young shoots and dark green leaves. The racemes of white, cream or yellow-red, often fragrant, flowers are produced during summer. Not fully hardy but will succeed in a sheltered site. Height 1–10m.

Prune in winter or early spring to remove damaged branches. Where frost has killed the tips of branches, prune back to a strong side shoot. If *L. silaifolia* becomes congested in the centre, remove some branches at the base. *L. tinctoria* is prone to suckering, becoming a bushy clump. Remove the suckers by pulling them away from the roots.

LONICERA (Honeysuckle)
Deciduous and evergreen shrubs and climbers with light to dark green, yellow or variegated leaves. The funnel- or bell-shaped, white, cream, yellow, orange or red flowers are often fragrant and are followed by red or black berries. Hardy. Height 2–14m.

Prune climbers in early spring. Cut young plants back by two thirds to build up a framework of strong stems. Nip out the growing tips when the stems have reached the required height. Mature plants tolerate hard pruning. To rejuvenate, prune all the shoots back to 45cm in early spring and thin out the new growths, leaving the strongest.

Shrubs require little or no pruning. Shape and thin out congested plants in summer. Rejuvenate by cutting the old branches close to the base. Hedges are clipped 3 or 4 times from late spring to early autumn.

LOPHOMYRTUS
Evergreen shrubs with leathery, dark green leaves, puckered between the veins. In summer, single, cup-shaped, white flowers are produced in the leaf axils followed by red-black berries. Not hardy but will survive in partial shade in a sheltered site. Height 2–7m.

Pruning is not normally necessary. Broken or crossing branches are removed in spring. If there are any frost-damaged shoots, prune them back to strong side shoots in late spring.

LOROPETALUM CHINENSE
Evergreen shrub with mid-green leaves, rough on the upper surface, paler green on the underside. Small, fragrant, white, spider-like flowers are produced in late winter or early spring. Not hardy but will succeed in a sheltered site. Height 2m.

Prune after flowering, cutting the flowered stems back to healthy side shoots. Thin out congested shoots, cutting back to within 15cm of the base. Dormant buds will produce strong shoots.

LOTUS
Deciduous, semi-evergreen and evergreen sub-shrubs with palmate or pinnate leaves. The pea-like, white, cream, yellow, red or purple flowers are produced in spring and early summer or from summer through to autumn. Hardy with some species prone to frost damage. Height 20–90cm.

Pruning is not normally required. Deadhead after flowering and shorten straggly shoots back to a healthy bud or side shoot.

LUMA (Myrtle)
Evergreen shrubs and small trees, some with peeling bark. The leathery, dark green or variegated leaves are aromatic. The small, white flowers are produced in summer and autumn. Hardy, but young growths may be damaged by frost. Height 3–10m.

Pruning is not normally necessary. Thin out congested and crossing branches in late winter and prune back any frost-damaged tips to healthy side shoots. They tolerate hard pruning. The stumps will produce vigorous, upright shoots from dormant buds.

LUPINUS ARBOREUS (Tree lupin)
The most commonly grown evergreen, shrubby lupin with silky, young shoots and palmate, grey-green leaves. The upright racemes of bright yellow, fragrant, pea-like flowers are produced in late spring and summer. Hardy. Height 2m.

After flowering, prune straggly shoots by half to three quarters of their length back to strong buds. Deadhead after flowering unless you want to save the seed.

Perennial cultivars such as Russell lupins may be deadheaded after flowering, cutting down to a side shoot that will in turn produce flowers later in the summer.

LYCIUM BARBARUM
(Duke of Argyll's tea-tree)
The most commonly grown species with spiny stems and mid- to grey-green leaves. Clusters of small, funnel-shaped, pink, lilac or purple flowers are produced in late spring and summer followed by yellow or orange-yellow berries. Hardy. Height 3m.

Prune after flowering, especially those plants with a scandent habit, cutting back by one third to a strong side shoot. It tolerates hard pruning, so cut one third of the branches to within 15cm of the base. Clip hedges in early summer.

LYONIA
Deciduous and evergreen shrubs with glossy, leathery, dark green leaves and clusters or racemes of white or pale pink flowers in late spring and summer or winter and early spring. Hardy but prefers a sheltered, shady site. Height 2–5m.

Prune after flowering, shortening the flowered shoots back to the first strong shoot. Thin out congested stems, cutting them close to the base.

LYONOTHAMNUS FLORIBUNDUS
(Catalina ironwood)
Evergreen tree with peeling, red-brown bark and glossy, deep green leaves. The terminal panicles of small, star-shaped flowers are produced in spring and summer. Hardy but succeeds best in a sheltered site. Height 12m.

Pruning is not normally necessary but damaged branches are removed in late winter or in cold areas in late spring. Shorten side branches in late summer to retain the conical shape of the tree.

MAACKIA

Deciduous shrubs and trees with pinnate, dark green leaves. The panicles or racemes of small, pea-like, white flowers are produced in late summer followed by flat seed pods. Hardy. Height 10–15m.

Prune in late winter or early spring, removing diseased, damaged or crossing branches. Prune to a sturdy side shoot. They dislike hard pruning.

MACADAMIA (Macadamia nut)

Evergreen trees with racemes of white or pink flowers in the leaf axils in late winter or spring followed by clusters of edible nuts. Not hardy, needing a hot growing season and lots of rain but will survive in a sheltered site. Height 6–20m.

Prune young trees to maintain a central leader. They are prone to forming narrow angles that weaken the tree. The leaves are in whorls, each with 3 buds. The centre bud will form an upright leader but is too weak for a main side branch. Allow the leader branch to grow, shortening the 2 side shoots back to 1cm. These produce strong, well-angled side branches. Space the branches 30–45cm apart. Once established, trees require minimal pruning.

MACKAYA BELLA

Evergreen shrub with wavy-margined leaves and racemes of funnel-shaped, pale lilac flowers with dark purple veins from spring to late summer. Needs a sheltered site. Height 1–2m.

Prune young plants by shortening shoots by one third to encourage bushiness. Deadhead after flowering, cutting the flowered stems back to a strong side shoot.

MACLURA

Evergreen and deciduous trees, shrubs and climbers, often with thorny branches and dark green leaves. The cup-shaped, greenish-yellow flowers are produced in

early summer, often followed on female plants by orange or green-yellow fruit. Hardy but young growths may suffer frost damage. Height 6–15m.

Prune in late winter or spring in frosty areas. Cut frost-damaged stems back to healthy side shoots in late spring.

MAGNOLIA

Deciduous and evergreen trees and shrubs with mid-green to dark or glossy green leaves. The solitary, star-, goblet- or saucer-shaped, often fragrant, flowers are white, cream, yellow, green, pink, wine-red or purple. They are produced in late winter and spring or early to late summer, followed by cone-like fruits often with red-skinned seeds. Most are hardy but some suffer from frost damage. Height 3–15m.

Trees and deciduous shrubs are pruned in late winter, removing dead and damaged branches back to a strong side shoot. Where shrubs are congested remove thin, spindly branches back to the main framework. Wounds are prone to dieback so don't leave stumps. Prune evergreens in early spring or late spring in frosty areas by shortening long shoots back to strong side shoots.

MAHONIA

Evergreen shrubs with glossy, spiny leaves, often purple-red or orange-purple when young. Racemes or panicles of small, bright yellow, fragrant flowers in winter or spring are followed by black or purple berries. Hardy but *M. lomariifolia* is prone to frost damage. Height 30cm–4m.

Prune after flowering. Tall, extended shoots are cut back to a strong side shoot at the same level as the remainder of the stems. They tolerate hard pruning in early summer. Over 2 years, cut back all the branches to within 45cm of the ground. New shoots will be produced from the stumps. Tidy the plant by trimming the stump back to the new shoots.

MALUS (Apple)
See pages 134–157.

MANDEVILLA

Twining climbers with bright green leaves, occasionally purple-green on the underside. Racemes of funnel-shaped, white or rose-pink and yellow, sometimes fragrant, flowers are produced in summer and early autumn. Not hardy. *M. laxa* will tolerate temperatures close to freezing for short periods. Height 3–6m.

Prune in late winter or early spring before growth starts, shortening all the side shoots to within 3–4 buds of the main framework of branches.

MANGIFERA INDICA (Mango)

Evergreen trees with bright green leaves and yellow-red or pinkish-red flowers, followed by large, green, yellow or red, edible fruit. Not hardy. Height 20–30m.

With young trees, prune between periods of growth, forming a well-branched head similar to that for an apple. Remove weak, spindly branches as they need to be strong to support the fruit. Avoid narrow-angled branches, removing the weaker branch. Reduce long branches by one third to keep the fruit within reach. Mature trees require little pruning but keep the centre of the tree open and remove damaged branches after harvesting fruit.

MAYTENUS BOARIA (Maiten)

Evergreen tree or occasionally shrub with glossy, dark green leaves. The clusters of tiny, tubular, pale green flowers appear in late spring with the females producing orange-red capsules with red seeds. Hardy but succeeds best in a sheltered site. Height 5–20m.

▷ Mahonia lomariifolia: *wear gloves when pruning as the spiny leaves are hard on hands and arms.*

Prune in late winter to remove damaged branches; otherwise no pruning is usually needed.

MEDICAGO ARBOREA
(Moon medick)
Evergreen shrub with dark green leaves and racemes of yellow flowers from late spring until autumn followed by spiralled and flattened brown seed pods. Not fully hardy. Height 2m.

Prune in late winter to thin congested branches, cutting them back to healthy side shoots. Remove dead shoots in late spring. Don't leave stumps.

MELALEUCA (Paperbark)
Evergreen shrubs and trees with peeling bark and small, leathery, mid-green leaves. Dense spikes of small flowers with conspicuous, pink, red, crimson or purple stamens resembling a bottle brush are produced in spring and early summer. Not hardy. Height 1–6m.

Prune in late winter to remove crossing branches and thin out congested stems. Cut back to a strong side shoot or at the base of the plant without leaving a stump.

MELIA AZEDARACH (Pride of India)
The most commonly grown species. Deciduous tree with deeply furrowed grey bark and pinnate, mid- to dark green leaves. The pendant panicles of small, star-shaped, fragrant, pink-white flowers appear in spring and early summer followed by small yellow fruit. Not hardy. Height 10m.

Prune in late winter to keep the tree within bounds. Keep the tree to a single main stem with the side shoots well spaced. Remove the lower branches, but where a number of branches need to be removed only prune out 2 or 3 each year.

▷ Melianthus major: *avoid damaging the new growths when cutting back in spring.*

MELIANTHUS MAJOR (Honey bush)
Evergreen shrub with hollow stems and sharply toothed, grey-green or blue-green leaves. Racemes of brick-red flowers are produced from late spring to summer. Not fully hardy, but well-ripened stems will survive in a sheltered site. Height 2–3m.

Prune back the old growths to the base in spring. In hot climates prune the flowered stems in early autumn, shortening them to above a healthy leaf.

MELICYTUS
Evergreen and semi-evergreen shrubs with leathery, dark green, fragrant leaves. Tiny, yellow or greenish-yellow flowers are produced in spring or summer followed by small, purple berries. Hardy but succeed best when protected from cold winds. Height 1–1.5m.

Pruning is seldom required. A light trim of straggly, non-flowering shoots in summer will keep the plant's shape.

MELIOSMA
Deciduous and evergreen shrubs and trees with mid- to dark green, occasionally pinnate leaves. Large panicles of cup- and saucer-shaped, fragrant white or creamy-white flowers are produced in late spring or summer followed by tiny, dark red or violet fruit. Hardy but new growths may be damaged by late frosts. Height 2–10m.

Pruning is seldom necessary. Remove crossing or damaged branches in late winter. Prune frost-damaged shoots back to a strong side shoot or healthy bud in late spring.

MENISPERMUM CANADENSE
(Canadian moonseed)
Deciduous climber with rounded, dark green leaves. The racemes of tiny, bowl-shaped, greenish-yellow flowers are produced in summer followed by glossy, black fruit. Hardy but succeeds best in a sheltered site. Height 5m.

Prune in early spring to keep the plant within bounds. Nip out the tips of young plants to encourage bushiness. To rejuvenate, cut out the old, straggly, bare stems at ground level. Prone to suckers, which will cause congestion if not removed by pulling off or digging out.

MENZIESIA

Deciduous shrubs with mid- to dark green, clustered leaves. Some turn red in autumn. Umbels of bell- or urn-shaped, pink-purple or red-flushed yellow flowers appear in late spring and early summer. Hardy but new growth may be damaged by late frosts. Height 1–2m.

Prune after flowering, cutting long, straggly shoots back by one third to side shoots. Thin out congested branches in midsummer. They dislike hard pruning. Don't leave stumps.

MESPILUS GERMANICA (Medlar)

Deciduous tree with dark green leaves that turn deep yellow in autumn. The large, single, white or pink-tinged flowers appear in late spring and early summer at the tips of the branches, followed by fleshy, brown edible fruit. Hardy. Height 5m.

Prune young trees by shortening the side shoots to form a well-branched head of stems. Prune to an outward-pointing bud. Remove crossing branches and branches cluttering the centre. With mature trees, remove old, congested branches. They dislike hard pruning and produce strong, vertical, non-flowering shoots from the stumps.

METASEQUOIA GLYPTOSTROBOIDES (Dawn redwood)

Deciduous conifer with fibrous, orange-brown bark and soft, bright green leaves, turning golden, red-brown in autumn. Small, brown, male and female cones are produced in the crown of the tree. Hardy. Height 30m.

Pruning is not normally necessary. Watch for double leaders on young plants and remove the weaker one. Remove broken branches in late spring.

MICHELIA

Deciduous and evergreen trees and shrubs with glossy, dark green leaves, paler on the underside. Bowl-shaped, fragrant (banana-scented), white, yellow or greenish-white flowers, sometimes with maroon petal edges, are produced in spring and summer. Not hardy but *M. figo* will survive in a sheltered, frost-free site. Height 3–14m.

Pruning is seldom necessary but damaged branches are pruned in late winter, or spring in cold areas.

MITRARIA COCCINEA

Evergreen shrubs with leathery, glossy, dark green leaves. Single, tubular, scarlet flowers are produced from spring to autumn. Hardy but succeeds best in a sheltered, shady site. Height 2m.

Prune in spring (late spring in cold areas), shortening back straggly shoots to healthy side shoots or strong buds. Deadhead immediately after flowering.

MONSTERA DELICIOSA

(Swiss cheese plant)

Evergreen climber with long-stalked, leathery, glossy, mid- to dark green leaves with holes between the main lateral veins. The creamy-white spathes appear in summer followed by cone-shaped, edible, cream-coloured fruit. Not hardy. Height 10m.

Prune in spring to keep the plant within its allotted space, cutting above a side shoot or leaf stalk. To rejuvenate older plants, cut back half the main stems to within 45cm of the base in late spring, repeating the operation with the remainder the following year. Leave the aerial roots intact.

MORUS (Mulberry)

Deciduous trees and shrubs that become gnarled with age, with light or dark green leaves and tiny, pale green, male and female catkins on the same plant in late spring and early summer. The female flowers are followed by solitary, raspberry-like, edible fruit in autumn. Fruit colour may be white turning to deep pink, or red turning to dark purple. Hardy but unripened shoots are killed by frost. Height 8–12m.

Prune in late autumn or early winter to avoid bleeding. They seldom require pruning and dislike hard pruning, producing unwanted water shoots in the area of the cut. Old branches can be removed over a period of several years to avoid overcrowding.

MUEHLENBECKIA

Deciduous and evergreen shrubs and climbers with mid-green or glossy dark green leaves. The tiny, cup-shaped, fragrant, yellowish-green or green flowers are produced in spring, summer or summer and autumn, occasionally followed by white, fleshy fruit. Not fully hardy but will survive in a sheltered, frost-free garden. Height 20cm–3m.

Prune after flowering, removing straggly shoots. They tolerate hard pruning: shorten the stems by one third to one half, cutting immediately above a side shoot or strong bud.

MUTISIA

Evergreen shrubs and climbers with mid-green or glossy, dark green, occasionally pinnate, leaves. Daisy-like, orange or pink, single flowers appear in summer and autumn. Hardy but will suffer in frosty areas. Shelter from cold winds. Height 1.5–3m.

Prune in spring, reducing flowered shoots by one quarter to one third and cutting above a side shoot or strong bud.

They tolerate hard pruning. *M. decurrens* is prone to suckering. Thin out suckers by pulling them off the plant to prevent congestion.

MYRICA (Bog myrtle)

Evergreen and deciduous trees and shrubs with dark green, often aromatic, leaves. Yellow-green or yellow-brown male catkins appear in late spring followed by waxy, off-white or yellow-brown fruit. Hardy. Height 1–5m.

Prune in late winter to thin out congested branches. Prune back by one third to a suitable side shoot. Thin out suckers by digging them out to prevent a thicket forming.

MYRTUS (Myrtle)

Evergreen trees and shrubs with aromatic, glossy, green leaves and fragrant, creamy-white flowers in late spring or summer and early autumn followed by purple-black or aromatic red berries ripening to black. Hardy. Height 1.5–6m.

Pruning is not normally necessary but broken or diseased branches are pruned in late spring. Cut back straggly branches by one quarter to healthy side shoots. Old, bare branches tolerate hard pruning.

NANDINA DOMESTICA (Heavenly bamboo)

Evergreen or semi-evergreen shrub with long, pinnate leaves reddish-purple when young and again in late autumn. Panicles of small, star-shaped, white flowers are produced in summer followed by bright red fruit in autumn. Hardy. Height 2m.

Pruning is seldom necessary but remove broken branches in late spring. Thin out the upright stems in spring, cutting one third back to a side shoot.

NERIUM OLEANDER (Rose bay)

Evergreen shrub or small tree with leathery leaves. Clusters of up to 60 white, pink or red flowers are produced in summer. Not fully hardy but will survive in a sheltered site. Height 2–5m.

Prune in late spring, shortening the flowered shoots back by one third to a pair of leaves or a strong side shoot. Deadhead after flowering.

NOTHOFAGUS (Southern beech)

Deciduous and evergreen trees and shrubs with glossy or leathery, dark green leaves turning yellow, orange or red in autumn. Hardy. Height 15–20m.

Pruning is seldom necessary but remove damaged branches in late winter.

◁ Nandina domestica *needs to be pruned only when the plant has become congested.*

NOTOSPARTIUM

Leafless shrubs with pendulous branches and blue-green shoots. The racemes of pea-like, purple-veined, pink flowers are produced in summer. Hardy but protect from cold winds. Height 2–3m.

Shorten the pendulous stems of young plants by one quarter to build up a framework of branches. Prune established shrubs in spring to thin out branches.

NYSSA (Tupelo)

Deciduous trees with dark green leaves that turn brilliant yellow, orange and red in autumn. Clusters of small, green flowers in summer are followed by blue fruit in autumn. Hardy. Height 10–20m.

Pruning is seldom necessary. Remove damaged or crossing branches in late winter while dormant. Succeeds best in a hot climate. In a cool climate grow as a bushy shrub. Thin congested branches to open up the centre.

OEMLERIA CERASIFORMIS (Oregon plum)

Deciduous shrub with glossy, dark green leaves, grey-green on the underside. Pendant racemes of small, fragrant, white, bell-shaped flowers are produced in early spring followed by plum-like, dark purple fruit. Hardy. Height 2.5m.

Prune in winter. Shorten the older branches by one third to a side shoot or healthy buds. Oemlerias are very prone to suckers which, if not removed, will quickly form a thicket.

OLEA EUROPAEA (Olive)

Evergreen tree with grey-green leaves, silvery green on the underside. Panicles of tiny, creamy-white, fragrant flowers are produced in summer followed by edible fruit. Hardy. Height 10m.

Pruning is seldom necessary but prune broken branches in winter when dormant.

▷ Ozothamnus rosmarinifolius: *prune in late summer, cutting bare stems back at the base.*

OLEARIA (Daisy bush)

Evergreen shrubs and small trees with bright or dark green, usually leathery, leaves. The panicles of single, daisy-like, white, yellow, pink or purple flowers are produced in spring or summer. Hardy but some species suffer frost damage to the new growth. Height 1.5–6 m.

Prune early-flowering species after flowering, shortening the flowered shoots back to healthy buds. Late-flowering species are pruned in early spring, or in late spring in cold areas, shortening the stems to balance the shape of the bush. They tolerate hard pruning and will produce strong shoots from stumps. Thin out congested plants in late spring.

OSMANTHUS

Evergreen shrubs and small trees with glossy, dark green or variegated leaves, often leathery. The clusters or panicles of small, tubular, white, orange or yellow flowers are often fragrant, appearing in winter and spring, summer or autumn and are followed by violet, purple or blue-black fruit. Hardy. Height 2–10m.

Prune late-flowering species in spring, shortening the flowered stems to keep the bush in shape. Early-flowering species are pruned immediately after flowering, shortening the flowered shoots back to the next pair of healthy buds. Prune hedges by trimming after flowering. They tolerate hard pruning. Rejuvenate by cutting the old branches to within 30–45cm of the base. Shoots will grow from dormant buds.

OSTEOMELES SCHWERINIAE

Deciduous or semi-evergreen shrub with bright green, pinnate leaves. The clusters of small, cup-shaped, white flowers are produced at the tips of stems in early summer followed by blue-black fruit. Hardy but succeeds best with shelter from cold winds. Height 3m.

Pruning is seldom required but crossing branches are removed after flowering. Long, arching branches may be shortened by one quarter to one third in early autumn to keep the plant in shape.

OSTRYA (Hop hornbeam)

Deciduous trees with heavily patterned leaves. The pendulous, male catkins are yellow, appearing in autumn and opening in early spring. Hop-like, white clusters are produced in summer, turning brown in autumn. Hardy. Height 15–20m.

Pruning is seldom necessary for mature plants. Damaged and crossing branches are removed in winter before the sap rises. Young plants are trained with a central leader. Prune out those stems that form narrow angles with the main trunk.

OXYDENDRUM ARBOREUM (Sorrel tree)

Deciduous shrub or tree with glossy, dark green leaves that turn brilliant yellow, red and purple in early autumn. Large panicles of small, urn-shaped, white flowers appear in late summer and early autumn. Hardy. Height 10–12m.

Pruning is seldom necessary. Thin congested branches in late winter or early spring. Old, bare-legged plants tolerate hard pruning, producing shoots from dormant buds on stumps.

OZOTHAMNUS

Evergreen shrubs with leathery, dark green, often aromatic, leaves. The terminal white or cream flowers are sometimes fragrant. Hardy but succeeds best in a sheltered site. Height 45cm–3m.

Prune after flowering, removing the flowered stems back to a sturdy side shoot. They tolerate hard pruning. Remove old branches as close as possible to the base.

PACHYSTEGIA INSIGNIS (Marlborough rock daisy)

Evergreen shrub with glossy, dark green leaves. Daisy-like white flowers appear in summer. Hardy but succeeds best when sheltered from cold winds. Height 80cm.

Prune in late winter to remove crossing branches. Shorten old branches to healthy side shoots.

PAEONIA (Peony)

Deciduous shrubs, sub-shrubs and herbaceous perennials. The tree peonies have mid- to dark green or bluish-green leaves and single or double, cup-shaped, white or yellow flowers, often with orange, pink or red marks and sometimes followed by large, pod-like fruit. Hardy but the flowers and leaves may be damaged by frost. Height 1.5–2.5m.

Pruning is seldom necessary but damaged or crossing branches are pruned in late winter, shortening them back to healthy buds lower down the stems. Remove spindly stems at the base.

PARAHEBE

Evergreen and semi-evergreen shrubs and sub-shrubs with mid- to dark or blue-green, sometimes leathery, leaves and racemes of small, saucer-shaped, white, pink or blue flowers in summer. Hardy but succeeds best in a sheltered site. Height 15–60cm.

Prune to lightly trim the plant after flowering, shortening the flowered stems by 2–5cm.

PARKINSONIA ACULEATA
(Jerusalem thorn)

This is the most commonly grown species. Deciduous tree or large shrub with spiny, green stems and pinnate, mid-green leaves that fold up at night. The racemes of small, cup-shaped, bright yellow flowers have light red stamens and appear in summer. Not hardy. Height 8m.

Pruning is not normally necessary but thin, spindly and congested branches should be removed in winter, pruning back to a strong side shoot. It dislikes hard pruning.

PARROTIA PERSICA (Persian ironwood)

Deciduous tree with peeling bark and glossy, rich green leaves that turn yellow, orange and deep red in autumn. The clusters of tiny, deep red flowers appear in late winter or early spring. Hardy but flower buds may be damaged by frost. Height 7m.

Pruning is tricky as there are two forms of the single species *P. persica*. Shrub-like forms never produce a leader and the branches tend to become horizontal. Don't be tempted to shorten the side shoots as this leads to a congested centre with branches criss-crossing one another. Remove damaged branches from late autumn to early spring. Don't leave a stump as it is prone to dieback. Tree-like forms have a central leader and, when young, the head of the tree can be lifted to show off the peeling bark. Remove the lower side shoots to 2m high. It dislikes head pruning.

PARTHENOCISSUS (Virginia creeper)

Deciduous climbers, either twining or using suckers at the tips of tendrils. The bright or dark green leaves turn bright red or red-purple in autumn. The clusters of inconspicuous, green flowers appear in summer followed by black or deep blue berries. Hardy. Height 10–20m.

Prune new plants in spring, nipping back the shoots to encourage side shoots from low down. Prune mature plants in late autumn after leaf-fall to keep within bounds. Growth is vigorous so cut well back from windows and roof eaves. They tolerate hard pruning, producing new growths from old stems.

PASSIFLORA (Passion flower)

Evergreen climbers with mid-green to bright, glossy, green leaves. The usually single, saucer-shaped flowers appear in the upper leaf axils during spring and summer or summer and autumn. They are multi-coloured with coloured stamens, sepals and stamens. Flowers are white, pink, red, mauve or purple, often followed by edible, yellow or orange fruit.

△ Passiflora caerulea *should be pruned every spring to prevent it becoming a tangled mess.*

Mostly hardy but some species need to be protected from frost. Height 2–15m.

Prune in early spring (late spring in frosty areas) to keep the plant within its allocated space. Side shoots may be shortened to within 3 or 4 buds of the main framework, building up a spur system. They tolerate hard pruning. Rejuvenate by pruning to within 45–60cm of the base in spring.

PAULOWNIA (Foxglove tree)

Deciduous trees with large, hairy leaves. Upright panicles of pink or purple, fragrant flowers are produced in spring from overwintering, felted buds. Hardy, but young plants and flower buds may be damaged by frost. Height 7–12m.

Prune in late spring or early summer. Form a clear 2m-high stem on young plants by removing buds rather than side shoots. Remove dead branches from mature trees in early summer. Cut to a strong side shoot or branch without leaving a stump. Prone to dieback (see page 16), so remove any diseased branches as soon as you spot them.

Rejuvenate by cutting to leave 45cm-long stumps to re-grow. Prune back to the new growths. Coppiced trees will, in a season, produce 2m-high upright shoots with enormous leaves.

PERIPLOCA GRAECA (Silk vine)
This is the commonly grown species, a deciduous climber with glossy leaves. The clusters of star-shaped, greenish-yellow flowers appear in summer and are purple-brown on the inside with an unpleasant smell. Hardy. Height 7m.

Prune in early spring before the leaves appear. Shorten long shoots by one quarter to one third to keep the plant within its allocated space. Cut out old, bare, non-flowering shoots at the base.

PEROVSKIA
Deciduous sub-shrubs with grey-green, aromatic foliage, and terminal panicles of small, blue flowers in late summer and autumn. Hardy. Height 1.2m.

Prune in early spring, shortening the stems to within 2cm of the permanent framework of branches. Perovskias tolerate hard pruning. When it is necessary to rejuvenate older plants, cut all the stems close to the base.

PERSEA (Avocado pear)
Practically evergreen trees with large, dull, dark green leaves, and small, greenish-yellow flowers. There are two growth periods per year, with clusters of

▷ *Perovskia 'Blue Spire': I like to cut all the stems back to the base every second year. This encourages new growths from the base – they will flower better than the old and prevent the plant getting 'bare-legged'.*

flowers often forming at the tips of the branches, which are brittle and easily damaged. Not hardy. Height 14–20m.

Prune after fruiting. Prune to remove damaged, dead or crossing branches. Shorten long stems back to sturdy side shoots. Cut the fruit and 1cm of stalk off the tree using secateurs. Perseas tolerate hard pruning.

PHELLODENDRON
Deciduous trees with aromatic leaves usually turning yellow in autumn. The clusters of small, cup-shaped, green flowers appear in summer with the male and female flowers on separate plants. Where both are grown, female flowers are followed by small, blue-black fruit. Hardy but new growth may be damaged by frost. Height 10–12m.

Prune in late winter to remove damaged or crossing branches. Cut above a side shoot. If the leading shoot is damaged the tree will probably become bushy rather than produce another upright shoot. They dislike hard pruning. Stumps are prone to dieback.

PHILADELPHUS
(Bride's blossom, Mock orange)
Deciduous shrubs with mid-green or variegated leaves. Flowers may be borne singly or in panicles or racemes as single or double blooms. They are white, bowl-shaped and fragrant, occasionally blotched with maroon, and are produced in summer. Hardy. Height 1.5–4m.

Prune in late summer immediately after flowering, shortening the flowered stems by two thirds to a sturdy side

shoot. Remove one in four of the branches at the base each year to encourage strong new growths. Plants tolerate hard pruning. To rejuvenate, prune, in winter, all the old branches at ground level and shorten by half the younger wood.

PHILESIA MAGELLANICA

Evergreen shrub with dark green leaves, blue-green on the underside. The single, trumpet-shaped, waxy, deep red flowers are produced at the leaf axils in summer and autumn. Hardy. Height 1m.

Prune in late spring, shortening flowered stems back by one quarter to a strong side shoot. Thin out congested branches after flowering. Don't leave stumps. Prone to suckers which, if not removed, will quickly form a thicket.

PHILLYREA

Evergreen shrubs with dark green or yellowish-green leaves. The greenish-white or white, fragrant flowers are produced in late spring and early summer followed by small, blue-black fruit. Hardy but prefers a sheltered site. Height 3–7m.

Prune in late winter, reducing long shoots to keep the plant in shape. Thin congested growths after flowering, cutting them out at the base. Don't leave stumps, which are vulnerable to disease.

PHLOMIS

Evergreen shrubs with light or grey-green leaves, woolly on the underside. The whorls of white, yellow or lilac, often hooded, flowers are produced in summer on erect stems. Hardy. Height 30–90cm.

Prune after flowering, reducing the flowered shoots back to a strong side shoot. Thin out congested plants, removing at the base any thin, spindly and old stems. They tolerate hard pruning. To rejuvenate, prune one third of the branches to the base each spring.

PHOTINIA

Deciduous and evergreen shrubs and trees. Evergreens have glossy, dark green leaves, often red when young. The panicles of small, white flowers appear in spring followed by red fruits in autumn. Hardy. Height 5–10m.

Prune deciduous shrubs such as *P. villosa* in winter when dormant, removing thin and congested branches back to sturdy side shoots. Prune evergreen species such as *P. × fraseri* in late spring. To produce more young red leaves, shorten side shoots by 20cm, cutting above an outward-pointing bud. Clip newly planted hedging back by a quarter to encourage strong side shoots from the base. Clip established hedges 3 times a year. Photinia tolerate hard pruning, growing away from 30–40cm stumps.

PHYGELIUS

Evergreen shrubs with dark green leaves. The panicles of tubular yellow, orange or pale or deep red flowers are produced in summer and autumn. Hardy but prefer a sheltered, sunny position. Height 60cm–1.5m.

Prune in late spring. Shorten flowered stems back to a strong side shoot. Deadhead to encourage more flowers. Cut old, bare stems as close to the base as possible. Rejuvenate by cutting all the growths to the base in late spring.

PHYLLODOCE

Evergreen shrubs with leathery, bright or dark green leaves. The terminal racemes or clusters of bell- or pitcher-shaped, pale green, white, pink or purple-pink flowers are produced in early spring or spring and summer. Hardy. Height 15–30cm.

Prune young plants by nipping out the growing tips to make them bushy. Prune mature plants after flowering, shortening the flowered stems to within 2cm of the old wood.

× PHYLLOTHAMNUS ERECTUS

Evergreen shrub with small, glossy, dark green leaves. The terminal clusters of funnel-shaped, rose-pink flowers are produced in late spring and early summer. Hardy but prefers shelter from cold winds. Height 30cm.

Prune after flowering, shortening the flowered shoots back to within 2cm of the old wood.

PHYSOCARPUS OPULIFOLIUS
(Ninebark)

Deciduous shrub with peeling bark. This is the usual species grown in gardens. Clusters of small, cup-shaped, pink-tinged white flowers are produced in early summer, followed by bladder-like red fruit. Hardy. Height 3m.

Prune in late winter or after flowering. Cut flowered shoots back by one third to a strong side shoot. Remove a quarter of the old shoots at the base in late winter.

PICEA (Spruce)

Evergreen conifers with needle-like, mid- to dark green, blue or yellow leaves. The green or yellow female cones ripen to brown or purple by the end of the year. Hardy although some species prefer a sheltered site. Height 50cm–35m.

Pruning is seldom necessary with mature trees. Dwarf sport cultivars may revert to the original habit of growth, so cut out such shoots before they smother the weaker cultivar.

PICRASMA QUASSIOIDES (Quassia)

Deciduous tree with sharply toothed, glossy, green, pinnate leaves turning yellow and red in autumn. The panicles of small, green flowers appear in early summer. Hardy. Height 7m.

Pruning is seldom necessary but remove the 3 Ds (see page 20) in late winter or in spring in cold areas. Prune back to a strong side shoot or healthy bud.

PIERIS

Evergreen shrubs and small trees whose leaves are often creamy-white, pink, red or bronze when young. Panicles of white or pink flowers appear in early and mid-spring. Hardy, but young growths may be damaged by frost. Height 10cm–5m.

Prune in late spring after flowering. Remove congested branches back to low side shoots. Prune off frost-damaged leaves. They tolerate hard pruning. Cut the oldest branches back to 25cm and thin out the new growths.

PILEOSTEGIA VIBURNOIDES

Evergreen climber with leathery leaves and panicles of star-like, creamy-white flowers in late summer and autumn. Hardy. Height 5m. Prune in early spring to keep within its allotted space. Cut old, bare and non-flowering stems as close as possible to the base. Shorten long growths back to a pair of strong buds.

PIMELEA

Evergreen shrubs with glossy leaves. Tubular rose-pink flowers appear in late spring and in summer. Not fully hardy, but will succeed in a sheltered, sunny position. Height 30cm–2m.

Prune after flowering, shortening the flowered stems to a strong side shoot. To encourage strong shoots to fill a gap in the branches, prune hard to a bud pointing in the direction of the gap.

PINUS (Pine)

Evergreen conifers with bundles of long, needle-like, light, dark, yellow or bluish-green leaves. Hardy. Height 4–30m.

Pruning is seldom necessary. If there are double leaders on a young pine, remove the weaker. Remove broken branches close to the main trunk.

▷ Pieris formosa forrestii: *very old plants may be rejuvenated over 2 to 3 years.*

PIPTANTHUS

Deciduous and semi-evergreen shrubs with palmate, glossy, dark or bluish-green leaves and racemes of pea-like, yellow flowers in late spring and early summer. Hardy but subject to late frost damage. Height 2m.

Prune in late spring to remove frost-damaged shoots. After flowering prune out the oldest shoots close to ground level. They tolerate hard pruning, reducing all the shoots back to within 30cm of the base.

PISTACIA (Pistachio)

Deciduous and evergreen trees and shrubs with pinnate, mid- to dark green leaves and panicles of small, green or red flowers in spring and early summer. Not fully hardy. Height 1–15m.

Pruning is seldom necessary. Shorten long, straggly shoots in late winter. Wounds are slow to heal and are prone to fungal diseases such as coral spot (see page 16).

PITTOSPORUM

Evergreen trees and shrubs with glossy, often leathery leaves. The flowers are white, greenish-yellow, red or purple and borne in clusters, panicles or singly. They are often fragrant, appearing in summer and followed by capsules containing black seed. Hardy, but some species are prone to frost damage. Height 3–10m.

Prune in mid- to late spring after growth commences. Little pruning is necessary. Hedges are pruned in late spring and again in summer. Pittosporum tolerate hard pruning, producing shoots from dormant buds even on stumps of large branches.

PLATANUS (Plane)

Deciduous trees with flaking bark and large, bright green, palmate leaves turning golden-brown in autumn. The inconspicuous flowers are followed in autumn by pendant, brown fruit clusters. Hardy although unripened shoots may be damaged by frost. Height 20–30m.

Pruning of mature trees is seldom necessary. Dead or damaged branches are removed in late winter or early spring. Young trees are pruned in spring to retain a central leader. Where double leading shoots are produced, remove the weaker shoot. Remove any upright shoots produced on side branches.

PLATYCARYA STROBILACEA

Deciduous large shrub or small tree with mid-green, pinnate leaves turning yellow in autumn. The greenish-yellow catkins appear in late summer followed by cone-shaped racemes of small, brown fruit that persist until the following spring. Hardy although young shoots may be damaged by late frost. Height 13m.

Prune in summer. The sap rises early and winter or spring pruning will result in heavy bleeding of sap. Broken and crossing branches should be pruned back to a side branch. The stems have soft pith and are easily damaged, so treat gently and protect from strong winds.

PLUMBAGO (Leadwort)

Evergreen shrubs and climbers with mid-green to dark, matt, green leaves. The long-tubed, white, blue or red flowers appear in late summer or winter. Not hardy. Height 2–4m.

Prune shrubs after flowering to retain a neat shape. Thin out congested branches in early spring. Prune climbers in late winter or early spring, cutting all the side shoots to within 2 or 3 buds of the main framework. Weak or spindly shoots are removed as close to the base as possible. Plumbago tolerate hard pruning and old stems will resprout after being cut to within 30cm of the base.

PLUMERIA (Frangipani)

Deciduous and semi-evergreen shrubs with succulent stems, fleshy branches and bright green leaves. The terminal clusters or panicles of fragrant, white, rose-pink, bronze or red flowers have waxy petals with a yellow centre and are produced in summer and autumn. Not hardy. Height 4–6m.

Prune in early spring to keep the plant in shape by shortening long, straggly shoots back to a strong side shoot or healthy bud. It dislikes hard pruning.

PODOCARPUS

Evergreen conifers with light, dark, bronzed or blue-green, linear leaves. The catkin-like, cone-shaped flowers appear in summer with male and female ones on separate plants. They are followed by red, red-purple or green fruit in autumn. Hardy but succeed best in a sheltered site. Height 2–15m.

Prune in late winter to retain the plant's shape, cutting back to a strong side shoot. No other pruning is necessary.

POLYGALA (Milkwort)

Evergreen shrubs with leathery, mid- to dark green leaves. The racemes of greenish-white, yellow, blue or purple, pea-like flowers are produced in late spring and early summer or in autumn. Some species such as *P. chamaebuxus* are hardy. Height 15cm–2m.

Seldom requires pruning. If necessary, cut back long, straggly shoots in late winter to retain the shape of the plant.

▷ Plumbago capensis: *in spring prune back all the side shoots to build up a strong flowering spur system.*

PONCIRUS TRIFOLIATA
(Japanese bitter orange)
Deciduous shrub with stiff, bright green shoots and long, sharp spines. The palmate leaves are dark green. The single, fragrant, white flowers appear in spring and early summer followed by inedible, green fruit turning to orange. Hardy. Height 4m.

Prune young plants to encourage bushiness by shortening the shoots by one quarter. Mature plants seldom require pruning but shorten long stems in late winter to keep the plant in shape. Lightly trim in summer if grown as a hedge.

POPULUS (Poplar)
Deciduous trees with mid-green to dark, matt or glossy green or variegated, often aromatic, leaves. The catkins of flowers appear in spring. Hardy. Height 10–30m.

Prune in late summer or early autumn to remove broken, diseased or crossing branches. Prone to canker, which should be pruned out as soon as it is seen (see page 16).

Prune the variegated *P. × jackii* 'Aurora' every year in autumn to encourage the attractive cream, pink and green leaves. Remove unwanted suckers by pulling them away from the roots. Some species such as *P. nigra* don't tolerate hard pruning.

POTENTILLA
Perennials and deciduous shrubs. The shrubs have pinnate, grey-green to dark green leaves. The saucer-shaped, white, yellow, pink, orange or red flowers are produced from late spring to late summer. Hardy. Height 60cm–2m.

Prune in early spring, shortening the branches that flowered back to within 5–7cm of the older wood. Long stems may be trimmed back in autumn to retain the shape of the plant. They tolerate hard pruning but old plants are best removed.

PROSTANTHERA (Mint bush)
Evergreen shrubs and small trees with glossy or matt, grey-green or mid-green, aromatic leaves and racemes or panicles of bell-shaped, white, yellow, blue or purple flowers in spring or summer. Hardy but some species are prone to frost damage. Height 60cm–4m.

Prune after flowering, shortening the flowered shoots by one third. They dislike hard pruning and won't recover if pruned into the older wood.

PROTEA (*illustrated on page 174*)
Evergreen shrubs with silvery or mid- to deep green leaves. Solitary and terminal cone-like clusters or flat heads of small flowers surrounded by white, green, pink or purple, petal-like bracts. Not fully hardy. Height 1–4m.

Pruning is seldom required. Where necessary, prune in early spring to keep the plant within its allotted space.

PRUNUS (Ornamental flowering cherry)
Deciduous trees and shrubs with mid- to dark green leaves that often colour well in autumn. The single or double, white, yellow or pink flowers are often fragrant, appearing in spring. Hardy. Height 2–12m.

Pruning is seldom necessary, but dead, diseased and crossing branches should be removed in summer, when there is least risk of diseases such as silver leaf (see page 16) entering the wounds.

▽ Prunus serrula: *remove dead and crossing branches in summer.*

PRUNUS ARMENIACA
(Apricot)
Deciduous tree with mid-green leaves and white or pink flowers in spring followed by edible, orange-red or yellow fruit. Hardy although flowers may be damaged by late frosts. Height 6–8m.

Prune young plants as the leaves are appearing. Mature trees should be pruned in summer to reduce the risk of diseases such as silver leaf. Apricots fruit on 2-year-old wood and older. Some fruit may form at the base of 1-year-old shoots. Thin the shoots to leave them 15–20cm apart. Shorten side shoots back to 5 or 6 leaves. After fruiting is finished shorten these shoots to 3 leaves. Where they have formed side shoots these are reduced to a single leaf. The unwanted shoots are pruned back to 5 or 6 leaves to carry fruit the following year.

Prune out old, unproductive branches without leaving a stump and train a young shoot into the space to replace it.

PRUNUS AVIUM HYBRIDS
(Sweet cherry)
Deciduous trees with bright green leaves and clusters of white flowers in spring followed by edible, yellow, dark red or deep purple fruit. Hardy although flowers may be damaged by late frost. Height 8m.

As with other stone fruit such as plums and peaches, pruning is carried out on mature trees in summer to limit the risk of an attack of silver leaf disease through the wounds. Remove dead, diseased or broken branches as soon as they are seen. When harvesting, cut the fruit stalks as pulling may damage the stem bark.

Prune young trees at bud-burst, removing crossing shoots and those that will spoil the shape. Where double leaders have formed remove the weakest shoot and any shoot that is forming a narrow angle. Trained trees such as fans are pruned as for *P. armeniaca.*

PRUNUS CERASUS HYBRIDS
(Acid cherry)
Deciduous trees with mid-green leaves and clusters of white flowers in spring followed by edible, red or purple fruit in late autumn. Hardy although flowers may be damaged by late frosts. Height 5m.

Acid cherries produce their fruit on growths made the previous year and, unlike sweet cherries that fruit on older wood, you are pruning to build up a constant supply of young growths. Pruning times are as for *P. avium* with formative pruning as the buds burst in spring and in summer for mature trees. Remove dead, diseased and broken branches as soon as they are seen.

When pruning a young tree to a bud pointing in the direction you wish the shoot to grow, remember to choose a thin, pointed growth bud (which will produce a shoot) rather than a fat bud that is going to form fruit.

Each year, after fruit has been harvested, shorten one quarter of the fruited branches back to a suitable side shoot. Remove crossing branches, keeping the centre of the tree open. Where there are strong shoots towards the ends of the branches, leave those branches to crop for one more year.

PRUNUS DOMESTICA (Plum)
Deciduous trees with bright green leaves and clusters of white flowers in spring followed by edible, yellow, red, violet or purple fruit in autumn. Hardy although flowers may be damaged by late frost. Height 3–6m.

Young trees are pruned in spring and mature trees in summer. No pruning is carried out in winter to avoid the risk of spores of silver leaf disease entering the pruning wounds. The aim of formative pruning is to produce a bush with well-spaced branches and an uncluttered centre. The leader is removed to encourage side branches to form and these are shortened by half to a growth bud pointing in the direction you want the shoot to grow. Pruning to upward-pointing buds will result in stronger branches. Horizontal branches are prone to break under the weight of a heavy crop of fruit. Remove weak, spindly shoots close to the main framework of branches.

Fan-shaped trees are pruned as for *P. armeniaca*.

PRUNUS LAUROCERASUS (Laurel)

Evergreen shrub with large, glossy, dark green leaves and fragrant racemes of white flowers in spring followed by red fruit turning black. Hardy. Height 7m.

Prune in summer after flowering has finished. Cutting hedges with clippers results in some of the large leaves being partially cut and then turning brown, so trim lightly with secateurs to avoid this.

PRUNUS PERSICA

(Peach and nectarine)

Deciduous trees with pink flowers in spring followed by edible, orange-red or red fruit. Hardy although flowers may be damaged by frost. Height 2–3m.

Formative pruning is carried out in spring. For bush trees purchase a feathered maiden and select 3 or 4 well-spaced side branches. Reduce their length by two thirds, cutting above an outward-pointing bud. Remove the low side shoots. Cut back the leader to just above the topmost side shoot.

Mature trees are pruned in early summer, removing any crossing branches and those cluttering up the centre. Shorten the side shoots by one half. Remove old branches that carry little fruit back to the main framework in summer. Peaches tend to produce too many fruits, so it is worth thinning the small fruits in late spring, leaving them 15–20cm apart.

Shape fan-shaped trees from the first year after planting. Select 2 low, side shoots and remove the leader and other side shoots back to just above the highest one. Shorten the 2 remaining side shoots and tie in the new growth at a 45° angle to the horizontal. In year 2, train the side shoots in on canes tied to horizontal wires to form the fan shape. Remove inward-pointing shoots close to the main branches without leaving a stump. Completely remove vigorous vertical shoots.

PSEUDOPANAX

Evergreen shrubs and trees with variously shaped, bright, dark green or bronze-green, usually spine-tipped, leaves. The small, purple-green or yellow-green flowers are produced in winter or early summer followed by purple-black fruit. Not fully hardy. Height 4–14m.

Pruning is not normally necessary. Where branches need to be removed prune in late winter and wear protective gloves against the spines.

PSEUDOWINTERA

Evergreen trees and shrubs with aromatic, leathery, green or yellow-green leaves splashed with pink. The small, cup-shaped, greenish-yellow flowers appear in spring followed by red berries ripening to black. Not fully hardy, although *P. colorata* will succeed in a sheltered site. Height 1–3m.

Pruning is seldom necessary but tolerates hard pruning and will re-shoot from stumps. *P. colorata* tends to form a bushy shrub and benefits from thinning out congested branches.

PSIDIUM GUAJAVA (Guava)

Evergreen shrub or small tree with white flowers followed by edible, pear-shaped fruit. The flowers and fruit are produced as frequently as three times per year. Not hardy. Height 3–9m.

Prune after the main fruiting period. Shorten the tips of the leading branches and side shoots by 5–10cm to encourage flowering shoots. Keep the centre of the tree open, removing crossing and congested branches. Remove suckers as they appear.

PTELEA TRIFOLIATA (Hop tree)

Deciduous shrub with aromatic bark and palmate, dark green, fragrant leaves. The star-shaped, greenish-white flowers appear in summer followed in autumn by pale green fruit. Hardy. Height 8m.

Prune in early spring to keep the tree in shape. When necessary it will tolerate hard pruning but cut above a side shoot without leaving a stump.

PTEROCARYA (Wing nut)

Deciduous trees with large, glossy, dark green, pinnate leaves that turn yellow in autumn. The inconspicuous catkins of male and female flowers are produced in spring, followed in summer by long, pendant spikes of winged green fruit. Hardy but leaves may be damaged by late frosts. Height 20–30m.

Prune in late winter to remove broken or crossing branches. Remove one of the branches where there is a narrow angle. Remove suckers without leaving a stump to re-grow.

PTEROCELTIS TATARINOWII

Deciduous tree with flaking bark and bright green leaves. The green male and female flowers are produced in spring from the leaf axils followed by small, round, winged, pale green fruit. Hardy. Height 10m.

Pruning is seldom necessary but remove damaged or crossing branches in late winter before the sap starts to flow.

◁ Punica granatum: *prune to keep the centre of the plant free of branches.*

PTEROSTYRAX HISPIDA

(Epaulette tree)

This is the species most commonly grown. Deciduous tree with aromatic bark and pale green leaves. The bell-shaped, white flowers are fragrant, appearing in panicles in early summer followed in autumn by ribbed fruit covered in yellow bristles. Hardy. Height 15m.

Pruning is seldom necessary but in early spring remove crossing or low branches on specimen trees.

PUERARIA MONTANA VAR.

LOBATA (Japanese arrowroot)

This is the species most commonly grown. Deciduous, vigorous climber with a large, fleshy tuber and palmate, mid-green leaves. The erect racemes of small, pea-like, fragrant, purple flowers are produced in autumn. Hardy but frost may damage early leaves. Height 20m.

Prune in spring, cutting old, bare, unproductive stems at the base. When you can reach them, cut back flowered shoots to within 5cm of the main framework of branches.

PUNICA GRANATUM (Pomegranate)

Deciduous shrub or tree with spiny stems and glossy green leaves that have red veins when young. Clusters of funnel-shaped, bright red flowers in summer are followed by edible, yellow-brown fruit. Not fully hardy. Long, hot summers are required for fruit to form. Height 5m.

Prune in late winter when dormant. Young trees are pruned by shortening the leader shoots by one third to encourage side shoots that will form a well-branched framework. Mature trees are renewed by removing the oldest stems each winter and filling the gaps by training in new shoots. Remove any suckers without leaving a stump.

PYRACANTHA (Firethorn)

Evergreen shrubs with spiny stems and glossy, dark green leaves. The clusters of small, hawthorn-like, white flowers appear in spring followed in late summer and autumn by yellow, orange or red berries. Hardy. Height 2–5m.

Prune in mid-spring to keep the plant within bounds. Shorten back long growths by one third. Wall-trained shrubs are pruned a second time in late summer, shortening the side shoots to expose the berries. Hedges are pruned in late spring without cutting back to the flowers. A light clipping in summer will tidy the hedge and expose the berries.

PYRUS CALLERYANA

(Ornamental flowering pear)

Deciduous tree with spiny stems and glossy, dark green leaves that turn red in late autumn and early winter. The racemes of white flowers are produced in early spring followed by small, brown, inedible fruit. Hardy. Height 12m.

Prune in winter to retain the conical shape and remove diseased, dead or crossing branches. Prone to canker (see page 16), so keep cuts to a minimum.

For fruiting pears, see pages 134–157.

QUERCUS (Oak)

Evergreen and deciduous trees whose leaves often turn brilliant yellow, orange and red in autumn. The tiny, male catkins and racemes of female flowers appear in late spring and early summer. The female flowers are followed by brown nuts (acorns) in scaly cups. Hardy. Height 30m.

Pruning is seldom necessary but remove broken, diseased and crossing branches in winter when the tree is dormant. Remove the lower side shoots of young plants to raise the head. Where two branches are competing as leader, remove the weaker shoot. *Q. ilex* (holm oak), which is evergreen, is pruned in late summer.

REHDERODENDRON

Deciduous trees and shrubs. *R. macrocarpum* is the most commonly grown tree with glossy, dark green leaves. The racemes of cup-shaped, fragrant, creamy-white flowers are produced in late spring at the same time as the leaves. The flowers are followed, in autumn, by ribbed, red fruit. Hardy but the leaves may be damaged by late frost. Height 8m.

Pruning is seldom necessary. It dislikes hard pruning. If branches have to be removed, prune in winter. Don't leave stumps as they will suffer from dieback.

RHAMNUS

Evergreen and deciduous trees and shrubs, often with spiny stems. The glossy, dark green or variegated leaves are often conspicuously veined. The tiny clusters or racemes of white, greenish-white or yellowish-white flowers are often fragrant. Hardy. Height 3–5m.

Prune in late winter to remove damaged branches or to thin out congested branches. Prune evergreen hedges in spring, reducing the previous year's growth by one half. Prune out reverted shoots on variegated *R. alaternus* var. *angustifolia* 'Argenteovariegata'.

RHODODENDRON
Evergreen and deciduous trees and shrubs with large, mid- to dark green, sometimes aromatic, leaves, often felted on the underside. The trusses of tubular, funnel- or saucer-shaped, mostly fragrant, flowers are produced in winter, spring and early summer. Hardy although some flowers and emerging leaves may be damaged by late frosts. Height 60cm–12m.

Remove the dead flowers immediately after flowering: if you allow them to produce seed it will be at the expense of next year's flower buds. Break off the old flower cluster gently, taking care not to damage the new buds on either side of the flower truss.

Remove straggly shoots in summer to maintain the shape of the plant. Most rhododendrons tolerate hard pruning to stumps. Once the dormant shoots appear, shorten the stump to just above a shoot.

RHODOTYPOS SCANDENS
Deciduous shrub with deeply veined, mid-green leaves. The 4-petalled, white flowers are produced singly at the shoot tips in late spring and early summer followed by glossy, black berries. Hardy. Height 1.5m.

Prune out flowered branches after flowering, shortening the arching stems to within 15–20cm of the ground.

RHUS (Sumach)
Deciduous and evergreen shrubs and trees with pinnate or palmate, mid- to dark green leaves that often colour to yellow, orange or red in autumn. The panicles of inconspicuous flowers appear in spring and summer, often followed by red fruit or pink-purple fruit clusters. Hardy. Height 1–12m.

Remove damaged or crossing branches in early spring. Thin out congested branches, removing them at the base. Remove suckers by pulling them away from the roots as soon as they are seen.

RIBES (Flowering currant)
Deciduous, occasionally evergreen, and sometimes spiny shrubs with mid- to dark green leaves and cup-, bell- or tubular-shaped, yellow, pink or red, often fragrant, flowers in winter or spring. Hardy. Height 60cm–3m.

Prune hedges by clipping after flowering. Prune flowered shoots back in early summer to strong side shoots or a healthy bud. They tolerate hard pruning. To rejuvenate, cut one third of the branches close to the base.

For fruiting currants, see pages 170–3.

ROBINIA
Deciduous trees and shrubs, often with thorny stems and pinnate, bright or dark green or yellow leaves. The pendant racemes of pea-like, white or pale to dark pink flowers appear in late spring and early summer. Hardy. Height 2–15m.

◁ Pyracantha *hedges should be pruned in late spring using secateurs. Avoid cutting the flowering shoots.*

◁ Salix alba *var.* vitellina *'Chermisina'*: *prune to within 2cm of the base in early spring to encourage lots of young stems with good bark colour.*

Prune in late summer or early autumn to avoid bleeding. Branches are brittle, so treat with care. Prune broken or crossing branches in summer to a sturdy side shoot. Don't leave stumps of branches beyond the new growth. Remove suckers as they appear.

ROMNEYA COULTERI (Tree poppy)

Deciduous sub-shrub with glaucous, grey-green leaves and cup-shaped, white flowers with yellow stamens in summer. Hardy but succeeds best in a sheltered position. Height 2.5m.

It is usually cut back to the ground in winter by frost. In mild areas prune in early spring, cutting all the stems back to within 2cm of the permanent framework of branches.

ROSA (Rose)

See pages 110–133.

ROSMARINUS (Rosemary)

Evergreen shrubs with leathery, dark green, aromatic leaves and tubular, white or pale to dark blue flowers in spring and early summer and again in autumn. Hardy. Height 40cm–1.5m.

Prune in early summer immediately after the main flowering period. To rejuvenate, reduce the length of all the branches by one half. Shorten bare branches in summer. Trim hedges after flowering and again in late summer.

RUBUS

Deciduous and evergreen shrubs and climbers, frequently with spiny stems and sometimes glossy leaves, often white-felted on the underside. The racemes or panicles of white, pink, red or purple flowers appear in summer. Hardy. Height 2–5m.

Prune in summer after flowering. To rejuvenate, cut all the stems to the ground in spring. Don't leave stumps. Where suckers are formed they will quickly become a thicket of stems.

For fruiting members of the *Rubus* genus, such as raspberries, loganberries and gooseberries, see pages 166–171.

RUTA (Rue)

Deciduous and evergreen shrubs with aromatic, blue-green leaves and yellow flowers in summer. Hardy. Height 1m.

Prune in early spring, reducing all the stems by two thirds. This will encourage

the attractive new leaves rather than the dull flowers. Thin out congested shoots and thin, spindly growth at ground level or back to the main framework of branches. Rejuvenate old plants by hard pruning to within 15–20cm of the base.

SALIX (Willow)

Deciduous trees and shrubs, often with coloured bark. The male and female catkins appear in late winter and spring. Hardy. Height 1–25m.

Prune from late autumn to spring to remove diseased and crossing branches. Dead branches are removed in summer without leaving a stump. Those species grown for their young, coloured bark are pruned in early spring before growth starts, shortening all the growths back to within 2cm of the base or the trunk.

S. caprea 'Kilmarnock' (Kilmarnock willow) is pruned in spring, thinning congested branches to leave a spaced 'umbrella' of stems. Shorten the remaining pendulous shoots by one half, pruning to an outward-pointing bud.

SALVIA

Evergreen shrubs with mainly aromatic leaves – S.*officinalis* is the culinary herb sage. Pink, blue, magenta or purple flowers appear in summer and early autumn. Hardy, although some species, such as S. *microphylla*, need protection from frost and cold winds. Height 30cm–1m.

Prune in mid-spring, lightly trimming the branches to shorten them by one fifth. Trim again in summer to remove the flowers. To rejuvenate, prune hard in late spring back into the old wood. New shoots will appear within weeks.

SAMBUCUS (Elder)

Deciduous shrubs and trees with pinnate, mid- to dark green or variegated leaves and panicles or umbels of small white, ivory or pink flowers, followed by white, red or black fruit. Hardy. Height 3–6m.

Prune in winter or spring, thinning out congested stems. Reduce long shoots by one half, pruning to a strong side shoot. Those with coloured leaves are pruned to within 2 or 3 buds of the base in spring.

SANTOLINA

Evergreen shrubs with pinnate, aromatic, grey-green to bright green leaves and small, white, pale to bright yellow flowers in summer. Hardy. Height 50–75cm.

Prune in early spring, cutting all the shoots back to within 2cm of the old wood. Replace old shrubs rather than rejuvenate them.

SARCOCOCCA (Christmas box)

Evergreen shrubs prone to suckering with glossy, dark green leaves, often paler on the underside. The clusters of small, pink-tinged, white or green flowers are incredibly fragrant, appearing in winter and early spring, followed by glossy black or blue-black fruit. Hardy. Height 60cm–2m.

Prune in spring to keep the plant in shape by shortening stems back to a strong side shoot. The suckers will form a thicket if allowed to grow.

SASSAFRAS ALBIDUM

Deciduous tree prone to suckering with dark green, aromatic leaves that turn yellow or purple in autumn. The racemes of tiny, yellow flowers appear in spring. Female flowers produce small, dark blue fruit on red stalks. Hardy. Height 20m.

◁ *Sambucus nigra 'Black Beauty' should be pruned hard every spring for best leaf display.*

△ Solanum crispum 'Glasnevin': prune after flowering to keep within its allocated area.

Prune young specimen trees with double leaders to leave a single, upright, main branch. Cut out damaged or crossing branches are in winter before the sap rises. Remove suckers by pulling them off from the root.

SCHISANDRA
Deciduous and evergreen climbers with leathery, glossy leaves. The cup-shaped, white, yellow, pink or red flowers are produced from the leaf axils in spring and summer followed, on female plants, by fleshy, red fruit. Hardy. Height 3–10m.

Prune in early spring, shortening the side shoots to within 2–5cm of the main framework of branches. Remove old, bare, non-flowering stems as close to the base as possible.

SEMELE ANDROGYNA (Liana)
Evergreen climber with glossy, mid-green, leaf-like stems and tiny, star-shaped, cream flowers in late spring and early summer. Not hardy. Height 5m.

Prune in late winter to keep the plant within its allotted space. Shorten stems back to a sturdy side shoot. Thin out congested stems at the base.

SEQUOIA SEMPERVIRENS
(Coastal redwood)
Evergreen conifer with thick, soft, red-brown bark and horizontal or downward sweeping branches. The deep green leaves are sharply pointed and white on the underside. Hardy. Height 20–25m.

Pruning is not normally necessary.

SKIMMIA
Evergreen shrubs with leathery, aromatic leaves. Panicles of small, star-shaped, creamy-white, yellow or pink, fragrant flowers appear in winter or spring, and on female plants are followed by red or black fruit. Hardy. Height 50cm–2m.

Pruning is seldom necessary but strong-growing shoots may be shortened after flowering, pruning back to a strong side shoot. Older shoots may be cut back to within 16cm of ground level. It is not worth rejuvenating old plants.

SMILAX
Deciduous and evergreen climbers of which the deciduous, prickly-stemmed S. china is the best known Tiny, green-yellow flowers appear in spring, followed on female plants by bright red berries. Needs a sheltered site. Height 4m.

Prune after flowering to keep the plant within its allotted space. Plants tolerate hard pruning to encourage new shoots from the base. Thin out congested shoots in early summer.

SOLANDRA MAXIMA (Cup of gold)
Evergreen climber with rich, dark green leaves. The night-scented, funnel-shaped, solitary, deep yellow flowers have purple veins and are produced in summer. Not hardy. Height 10m.

Prune in late winter to keep the plant within bounds. Thin out congested shoots, pruning them at the base to encourage strong new shoots from low down on the plant.

SOLANUM
Evergreen and deciduous trees, shrubs and climbers with mid-green to dark, glossy green leaves and bell- or star-shaped white, blue or purple flowers in spring or autumn often followed by white, green, orange, red or black fruit. Mostly hardy although some species, such as S. jasminoides, need shelter from frost. Height 30cm–6m.

Prune shrubs in late spring to keep the plant in shape. Shorten each stem back to a sturdy side shoot. Climbers are pruned after flowering has finished by shortening all the flowered shoots back to within 3 or 4 buds of the permanent framework of branches.

SOLLYA HETEROPHYLLA
(Bluebell creeper)
Evergreen climber with bell-shaped, blue flowers in summer and autumn followed by edible, blue berries. Not hardy but may succeed in a sheltered site in full sun. Height 1.5m.

Prune in late winter, shortening all the side shoots to within 3 or 4 buds of the main framework. Thin out any congested shoots at the base in early spring.

SOPHORA
Deciduous and evergreen trees and shrubs with pinnate, dark green leaves. The panicles or racemes of pea-like white, yellow or deep blue and white flowers appear in spring or in late summer and autumn. Hardy although late spring frost may damage new growth. Height 2–10m.

Prune in summer, when the plants are less likely to bleed, to remove damaged or crossing branches. Don't leave stumps. It dislikes hard pruning.

SORBUS
(Mountain ash, Rowan, Whitebeam)
Deciduous and evergreen trees and shrubs with mid- to dark green leaves, many with good autumn colour, frequently pinnate, sometimes white on the underside. The clusters of small, white or pink flowers appear in spring and early summer followed by white, yellow, orange, red or brown fruit. Hardy. Height 1.5–15m.

Prune from autumn to late winter to remove crossing, congested or diseased branches. Remove dead branches in summer. If severely pruned it will form a thicket of shoots rather than a tree shape. Grafted trees are prone to suckers, which should be pulled off. Don't leave stumps, as they will encourage dieback.

SPARTIUM JUNCEUM
(Spanish broom)
Deciduous shrub with dark green stems and small, dark green leaves. The terminal racemes of pea-like, fragrant, yellow flowers are produced from summer to early autumn. Hardy. Height 3m.

Prune new plants in early spring, shortening the stems by one half to encourage side shoots and a bushy habit. Prune established plants in spring when the leaves appear by lightly trimming the tips of stems. Every three years shorten the one-year-old wood to within 2–5cm of the old wood. It tolerates hard pruning.

▷ Spartium junceum: *prune every spring to prevent the plant becoming straggly.*

SPATHODEA CAMPANULATA
(African tulip tree)
Evergreen tree with leathery, dark green, pinnate leaves. The racemes of bell-shaped, scarlet flowers are yellow-rimmed with an unpleasant odour and appear in spring and summer followed by large, woody, brown seed pods. Not hardy. Height 20m.

Prune in late winter or in autumn when flowering has finished. Remove damaged branches, pruning back to a sturdy side shoot.

SPIRAEA
Semi-evergreen and deciduous shrubs with pale to dark green or multi-coloured leaves. The small, white, yellow, pink or mauve flowers appear in spring or summer. Hardy. Height 1–4m.

Prune shrubs, such as S. *douglasii*, that flower on the current season's growth in early spring, cutting back to the permanent framework of branches. Thin out suckers to prevent the plant becoming a thicket.

For those that flower on the previous season's growth, such as S. 'Arguta', prune after flowering, reducing each flowered shoot back to a strong side shoot. Remove one quarter of the old branches at the base.

STACHYURUS
Deciduous and semi-evergreen shrubs with glossy, red-brown shoots and mid- to dark green or variegated leaves. The pendant racemes of bell-shaped, greenish-yellow or yellow flowers appear in late winter or early spring. Hardy. Height 1–3m.

△ Stephanotis floribunda *has fragrant flowers followed by attractive seed pods, each seed with its own silken 'parachute'.*

Prune in spring after flowering has finished, removing the flowered shoots at the base. Overlong branches are shortened by one third.

STEPHANANDRA

Deciduous shrubs with mid-green leaves turning yellow and orange in autumn. Panicles of greenish-white or greenish-yellow flowers are produced in summer. Hardy. Height 2–3m.

Prune after flowering, shortening the flowered shoots back to a sturdy side shoot. They tolerate hard pruning. Older plants can be rejuvenated gradually by removing one quarter of the old branches at ground level each winter.

STEPHANOTIS FLORIBUNDA

Evergreen climber with glossy, thick, deep green leaves. The waxy, white, fragrant flowers are produced from spring to late summer. Not hardy. Height 3–4m.

Prune in late winter or early spring to remove bare-stemmed or non-flowering shoots. Shorten overlong shoots to keep the plant within its allotted space. Rejuvenate by cutting back to within 15cm of the base.

STEWARTIA

Deciduous and evergreen trees with peeling bark and glossy, dark green leaves often colouring well in autumn. The rose-like, cup-shaped, often fragrant, white flowers have cream, yellow or purple stamens and are produced in mid- to late summer. Hardy although they succeed best when sheltered from cold winds. Height 6–22m.

Pruning is seldom necessary. Remove any damaged branches in late winter or early spring.

STYRAX (Snowbell)

Deciduous and evergreen shrubs and trees with mid- to dark green, often glossy, leaves. The pendant, bell- or cup-shaped, white flowers are fragrant, appearing in early summer. Hardy. Height 2–10m.

Pruning is not normally necessary. Lower branches tend to die due to lack of daylight and are removed in early spring, cutting at the branch collar. Remove badly placed branches in winter.

SYMPHORICARPOS (Snowberry)

Deciduous shrubs with dark green, occasionally blue-green leaves. The tiny, white or pink flowers appear in summer followed by white, pink, dark blue or purple fruit. Hardy. Height 1–3m.

Prune in winter or early spring to remove congested branches. Remove old branches at the base. They tolerate hard pruning.

SYRINGA (Lilac)

Deciduous trees and shrubs with mid- to dark green leaves. The panicles of small, tubular, white, pink, red, magenta or purple flowers are usually fragrant, appearing in spring and summer. Hardy but late frost may damage new growths. Height 1.5–6m.

Prune in late winter, shortening branches to strong side shoots. Thin out congested branches. Deadhead after flowering, taking care not to damage the new shoots that will flower the following year. *S. vulgaris* and its varieties tolerate hard pruning and will re-grow from 30–45cm-long stumps. Remove suckers by pulling them off.

TAMARIX (Tamarisk)

Deciduous shrubs and trees with needle-like, bright green leaves. The racemes of pale pink flowers are produced in late spring on the old shoots (*T. tetrandra*) or in late summer and autumn on new growths (*T. ramosissima*). Hardy. Height 3–5m.

Prune young plants to build up a bushy shrub. Prune early spring-flowering plants after flowering, shortening the stems by one half. Plants that flower in late summer should also be pruned after flowering, cutting the flowered stems back to within 5cm of the main stems. All tamarix tolerate hard pruning and may be rejuvenated by pruning to 30–60cm-high stumps. Thin out the new growths.

TAXODIUM DISTICHUM
(Swamp cypress)

Deciduous tree with linear, pale green leaves, turning brown in late autumn, on the deciduous shoots. The permanent shoots have scale-like leaves. Male cones are red, female are green, turning brown in autumn. Hardy. Height 20–35m.

Pruning is not usually necessary unless the brittle branches break (which they often do), leaving the tree misshapen. Remove stumps of branches back to the main trunk in winter. It tolerates hard pruning into the old wood.

TAXUS (Yew)

Evergreen, coniferous trees and shrubs with mid-green to dark, matt or glossy green, yellow or variegated, linear leaves, often paler green on the underside. Female plants produce green seeds surrounded by usually red arils. The small, male cones are yellow. Hardy. Height 1.5–15m.

Pruning is seldom necessary but they tolerate hard pruning. Old trees may be rejuvenated by cutting to 45–60cm stumps. Thin out the new growths. Hedges are clipped in summer and early autumn. They will re-grow from hard pruning.

TECOMA

Evergreen shrubs, trees and climbers with bright or dark green leaves. Funnel-shaped, yellow, orange or red flowers are produced in summer or from winter through to summer. Not hardy. Height 2–8m.

Prune early-flowering species such as *T. stans* after flowering has finished, reducing the flowered shoots by one third to a strong side shoot to help retain the plant's shape. Late-flowering species such as *T. capensis* are pruned in early spring to keep the plant within its allotted space.

TELOPEA (Waratah)

Evergreen trees and shrubs with leathery, dark green leaves, sometimes silvery-hairy on the underside. Tubular, red flowers are surrounded by coloured bracts in spring and early summer, followed by woody seed pods. Not hardy. Height 2–8m.

Prune after flowering to retain the shape. Thin out congested growths, removing them at the base of the plant.

TETRAPANAX PAPYRIFER

Evergreen shrub with scaly, mid-green leaves, paler on the underside. Umbels of white flowers appear in autumn, followed by black fruit. Hardy but succeeds best in a sheltered site. Height 5m.

Prune in early spring, shortening the stems to within 2–3 buds of the base. Prone to suckers and if these are not thinned it becomes a thicket-like shrub.

TEUCRIUM

Evergreen and deciduous shrubs with white-woolly or grey-green, aromatic leaves. Bell-shaped, yellow, pink, blue or purple flowers appear in summer. Hardy. Height 20–60cm.

Prune in spring as growth commences to remove frost-damaged tips and keep the plant in shape. They tolerate hard pruning so remove the older stems at the base without leaving a stump.

THUJA (Arborvitae)

Evergreen conifers with small, aromatic, variegated, yellow and pale to dark green leaves. The male and female cones are small. Hardy. Height 30cm–10m.

Pruning is seldom necessary. Dwarf specimens may be clipped to retain their shape. Hedges are clipped in summer and early autumn.

◁ Tamarix ramosissima *flowers in late summer. Prune in early spring, cutting back to the main framework of branches.*

THYMUS (Thyme)

Evergreen shrubs and sub-shrubs with small, aromatic, bright or dark green leaves. The clusters or racemes of white, pink or purple flowers are produced in summer. Hardy. Height 5–30cm.

Prune tall-growing varieties in spring, shortening the shoots back to within 2–3cm of the old wood. Light clipping after flowering keeps the plants bushy.

TIBOUCHINA (Glory bush)

Evergreen shrubs with mid- to dark green, hairy leaves. The panicles of saucer-shaped, reddish-purple or bluish-purple flowers are produced in summer. Not hardy. Height 3–5m.

Prune in late spring to retain the plant's shape. Shorten straggly stems to a sturdy side shoot or a healthy, outward-pointing bud. They dislike hard pruning.

TILIA (Lime)

Deciduous trees, some with colourful winter shoots. The bright, mid- to dark green leaves often turn bright green in autumn. The creamy-white or yellow flowers appear in summer and are surrounded by green or pale yellow bracts and followed by nut-like fruits. Hardy. Height 10–30m.

Prune in autumn and early winter before growth starts. Check young trees for narrow-angled branches and double leaders, removing the weakest shoot. *T. platyphyllos* produces strong branches that are unlikely to split apart at the crotch. Remove crossing and damaged branches, making sure that the wound is smooth. Remove suckers by pulling or continual cutting.

TORREYA (Nutmeg yew)

Evergreen conifers with spine-tipped, pale to dark green, yew-like leaves. The olive-green or purplish-green, female cones appear in autumn. Hardy. Height 15–25m.

Pruning is not normally necessary. Where they become too vigorous the branches may be reduced by one third to a strong, outward-pointing side shoot. They tolerate hard pruning.

TRACHELOSPERMUM

Evergreen climbers of which *T. jasminoides* is the most commonly grown with glossy, dark green leaves that turn bronze-red in winter. The fragrant, pure white flowers appear in summer. Hardy but benefits from a sunny, sheltered wall. Height 8m.

Prune young plants, shortening the shoots by one half to encourage a bushy plant. In early spring prune established plants to fit their allocated space. They flower on side shoots on the old wood. Old, bare and spindly stems are shortened by two thirds to encourage new, strong shoots to develop from the base of the plant.

ULEX (Gorse)

Evergreen shrubs with spine-tipped shoots and stiff, dark green leaves. The coconut-scented, pea-like, bright yellow flowers are produced throughout the year but mainly in spring. Hardy. Height 1.5–2.5m.

Prune young plants in late spring, shortening all the shoots by one third to encourage a bushy plant with plenty of side shoots. Prune mature plants in early summer every third year, shortening the flowered shoots back to within 5–7cm of the old wood. They tolerate hard pruning.

ULMUS (Elm)

Deciduous trees with mid- to dark green or yellow leaves. The tiny, bell-shaped, red flowers are produced in spring followed by winged, green fruit in late spring and summer. Hardy. Height 10–30m.

Prune in late winter before growth commences to remove crossing or damaged branches.

UMBELLULARIA CALIFORNICA (Headache tree)

Evergreen tree with leathery, bright green leaves that are pungent when crushed. Umbels of greenish-yellow flowers are produced in early spring, followed by purple berries. Hardy but prefers shelter from cold winds. Height 18m.

Pruning is seldom necessary but remove crossing or congested branches in spring.

VACCINIUM

(Bilberry, Blueberry, Cranberry)

Evergreen, semi-evergreen and deciduous shrubs with dark green, often leathery, leaves that frequently turn red or purple in autumn. The bell-shaped, creamy-white, white, green, pink or red flowers are produced in early summer, followed by red, blue or blue-black, edible berries. Hardy. Height 15cm–3m.

Prune deciduous species in winter or early spring before growth starts, shortening misplaced or crossing branches and removing congested branches back to outward-pointing side shoots. Branches older than 3 years that are not producing much fruit are removed as close to soil level as possible. Prune evergreens in spring, removing congested branches at the base.

VESTIA FOETIDA

Evergreen shrub with glossy, dark green leaves with an unpleasant odour when crushed. The clusters of pendant, pale yellow flowers are produced in spring and early summer. Hardy but succeeds best in a sheltered, frost-free site. Height 2m.

Prune after flowering, shortening overlong or straggly stems by one third.

▷ Tibouchina: *under glass growth is vigorous and restrictive pruning is necessary in spring.*

VIBURNUM

Evergreen, semi-evergreen and deciduous shrubs with glossy green leaves, commonly deeply veined. The often fragrant, tubular, pink-tinged, white or pink flowers are produced in winter, spring or early summer, usually followed by yellow, red, blue-black or black fruit in autumn. Hardy. Height 1–4m.

Prune after flowering has finished in early spring or in summer. Thin congested branches and remove old wood at the base. Most viburnums tolerate hard pruning and will re-grow from stumps.

VITEX

Deciduous shrubs with aromatic leaves and small tubular, sometimes fragrant, violet-blue, lilac-blue or white flowers in late summer and early autumn. Needs a sheltered site. Height 2–6m.

Prune in early spring, shortening all the stems to within 2–5cm of the permanent framework of branches. Thin out old branches, removing them at the base.

VITIS (Vine)

Deciduous climbers with flaking bark and green or purple leaves, many turning yellow, orange and red in autumn. Panicles of tiny green flowers are followed by green, yellow-red or purple-black, often edible, fruit. Hardy. Height 6–15m.

Prune to above a bud in early spring, reducing the young growths to fit within the allocated space. A second pruning in summer will keep the plant in check. Where more regulated training is required then prune all the side shoots to within 3 or 4 buds of the main framework of branches. Spurs will form to produce the bunches of fruit. Vines tolerate hard pruning.

See also pages 158–165.

▷ Wisteria floribunda *needs to be pruned in both summer and winter if you want a good show of flowers.*

WEIGELA

Deciduous shrubs with dark green, yellow-bronze or variegated leaves. The bell- or funnel-shaped, white, yellow, pink or red flowers are produced in mid-spring or summer. Hardy. Height 75cm–3m.

Prune young plants by shortening the stems by one third to form a bushy plant. Prune mature plants after flowering, shortening the flowered shoots by one third to one half to a sturdy side shoot or healthy bud. Remove the oldest stems at ground level. They tolerate hard pruning. To rejuvenate, prune half the shoots to ground level in spring and the rest the following spring. Thin out the new growths to prevent overcrowding.

WISTERIA

Deciduous climbers with pinnate, dark green leaves. The trailing racemes of pea-like, fragrant, white, pink, blue, violet or purple flowers are produced in early summer. Hardy but flowers may be damaged by late frosts. Height 3–9m.

Prune young plants back to a strong, healthy bud 60–75cm above ground level. Shorten side shoots and train in the leading shoot. In the second year shorten the leading shoot to 60cm above the top lateral and shorten side shoots to 15cm to build up spurs.

Prune established plants in summer about 7 weeks after flowering has finished, shortening all the side shoots to 4–6 leaves from the permanent framework of branches. Prune those same stems in winter, shortening them to 2 or 3 buds. This builds up a spur system of flower buds.

XANTHORHIZA SIMPLICISSIMA
(Yellowroot)

Deciduous shrub with bright green leaves turning deep red in autumn. The pendant racemes of brown-mauve flowers appear in spring. Hardy. Height 60cm.

Prune after flowering, shortening the flowered stems by one third to a strong side shoot or to a healthy bud close to the base of the plant.

YUCCA (Spanish dagger)

Evergreen shrubs with long, dark green or variegated leaves. They are sometimes margined with thin, curly, white threads and are sharply pointed, stiff and sword-like. The upright panicles of bell-like, creamy-white or purple-tinged, white flowers appear in mid- to late summer or autumn. Not hardy but will succeed in a sheltered, sunny site. Height 2–8m.

Pruning is seldom necessary. After flowering, remove the flowered stem using secateurs. Cut as close to the centre of the rosette of leaves as possible.

ZANTHOXYLUM

Deciduous and evergreen trees and shrubs with aromatic bark, occasionally spiny, and dark green, pinnate leaves dotted with small glands that turn yellow in autumn. The small, cup-shaped, green or yellowish-green flowers are produced in early summer, followed by red fruit with black seeds. Hardy. Height 2–6m.

Prune in spring to remove dead wood and congested branches. Don't leave stumps. They dislike hard pruning.

ZELKOVA

Deciduous trees with dark green leaves turning to yellow then orange-red and red in autumn. The small clusters of green flowers are produced in spring followed by small green fruit. Hardy. Height 1–30m.

Prune in late winter to remove dead or damaged branches. Young trees are shaped by shortening the stems to strong side shoots. They dislike hard pruning.

▷ Yucca flaccida *'Golden Sword': take care when pruning as the leaves of all yuccas are sharply pointed.*

ZENOBIA PULVERULENTA

Deciduous and semi-evergreen shrubs with glossy, dark or glaucous, blue-green leaves. The upright racemes of pendant, bell-shaped, white flowers are fragrant and produced in early summer. Hardy. Height 2m.

Prune in midsummer as the flowers finish, cutting out the weak growths and shortening the flowered stems to strong side shoots. Rejuvenate in spring by removing all the old wood as close as possible to the base.

Glossary of pruning terms

Adventitious buds Buds produced from the stem without any relationship to leaves or stems. They usually appear close to a wound where a branch has been cut.

Apical bud The bud at the tip of the stem, also referred to as the terminal bud.

Axil The angle between the leaf and the stem.

Bark ridge A raised line of bark on the upper side of a branch close to the main trunk.

Branch collar A swollen ring of bark on the underside of a branch close to the major branch or trunk.

Bud The embryo shoot that may become a flower or a new growth.

Callus Corky tissue produced naturally by a plant to cover a wound.

Canopy The total branches forming the head of the tree; the term is usually used when a tree is in leaf.

Central leader The central, vertical main stem of a plant.

Coppicing The regular cutting of a tree or shrub close to the ground to encourage vigorous new growths from the base.

Cordon A tree on which all the growth is confined to a single stem, allowing fruiting spurs to build up.

Crown The upper, branched part of the head of a tree, the highest part of the canopy.

Current year's growth The stems that have been produced during the present growing season. Many summer-flowering plants flower on this new growth.

Dead-head To remove a flower after it has finished flowering and before seed forms. This encourages further flowering and prevents self-seeding, which can turn some plants into weeds.

Deciduous Losing leaves in autumn, as opposed to evergreen.

Disbud To remove surplus growth or flower buds before they open – the remaining flowers will be larger.

Dormant Having temporarily stopped growing, such as during the winter.

Epicormic growth Shoots that arise from adventitious buds close to where a main branch has been cut. Also known as water shoots.

Espalier A trained tree whose main stem is vertical but which has tiers of branches trained horizontally to either side.

Evergreen Retaining leaves throughout the year, as opposed to deciduous.

Eye On a vine or rose, the name given to a growth bud before it opens.

Fan A plant with its branches trained against a wall or trellis like the struts of a fan.

Feathered tree A one-year-old ('maiden') plant with side growths (laterals).

Framework The main branches that make up the plant, giving it its shape.

Grafting A method of propagation in which a cultivar (scion) is joined as a bud or shoot to the root of another plant (rootstock). Common with roses and some fruit trees such as apples and pears.

Lateral A side growth that grows at an angle from the main stem.

Leader The shoot at the end of a branch that continues to grow and give direction to the branch.

Leg The short length of bare trunk at the base of a plant.

Maiden A one-year-old tree.

Node The point on a stem where a leaf stalk joins.

Pinch out To remove the growing tip of a shoot using your fingers.

Pleach To weave or tie the branches of trees together to make a wall, canopy or avenue.

Pollard To prune a standard shrub or tree regularly back to the main stem, in order to produce strong and/or attractive new growth.

Renewal pruning Pruning to encourage healthy young growths that will produce flower and fruit.

Rejuvenate To prune an old plant in such a way as to give it a new lease of life, whether by removing old crossing branches to give the plant more air and light, or cutting back to the ground to promote healthy young growth.

Ring-barking The removal of a thin strip of bark from the trunk of a fruit tree to reduce growth and encourage fruiting.

Rod The main stem of a vine.

Rootstock See under grafting.

Scion See under grafting.

Snag A short stump of branch left after pruning.

Spur A compact branch system on a tree or shrub with lots of flower buds. A combination of summer and winter pruning encourages a spur system.

Stool A plant that is cut down annually to ground level to encourage new growths.

Sucker A shoot that arises from the base of a tree, either from the root or from a rootstock below the graft. Some plants spread this way and can become a nuisance; in others the suckers are ornamental.

Thinning The removal of branches to open up a plant, allowing light to the centre. Also refers to removing some flowers or young fruit to allow the remaining fruit to swell.

Truss A cluster of flowers or fruit.

Water shoot See epicormic growth.

Whip A young tree with an unbranched stem.

Whorl Three or more buds, leaves or shoots arising from a node.

Wind-rock Wind damage to the root system caused by the head of the plant blowing about.

Index

Page numbers in **bold** refer to pages with illustrations.

Acknowledgements

I would, as ever, like to thank everyone at Kyle Cathie for their continued faith and enthusiasm, particularly the sales team, who did so well with my previous book, *How to Propagate*, that we were able to consider a companion volume; to Kyle herself, whose idea this book was; to Caroline, who has now worked on eight books with me and may have the odd grey hair; and to Vicki, for holding the fort when Caroline was on yet another of her holidays. Thanks also to Isobel Gillan for the design and to Jane Struthers for cheerful and tactful tidying up of the text.

Finally, very special thanks to my good friends John and Anne Swithinbank, photographer and model respectively for all the step-by-step photography in this book. Their commitment and expertise have considerably lightened the load of author and editor alike.

Photographer's acknowledgements
Many thanks to the following for helping with photography and allowing us to photograph their gardens:

Kevin Croucher, Thornhayes Nurseries, Devon; Alan Davis, The Paddocks; Chris Bailes and David Squire, RHS Rosemoor; Stuart Henchie and Charles Shine, RBG Kew; Dick Bessant, Little Trill; Denise Evans, Pen-y-Fai; Hestercombe Gardens, Somerset; Forde Abbey, Dorset; Burrow Farm Gardens, Devon; Antony House NT, Cornwall; Caerhays Garden NT, Cornwall; Sudeley Castle Gardens, Gloucestershire; Perrie Hale Forest Nursery, Devon; Palm Traders, Devon

Photographic credits
JS: John Swithinbank, JB: Jonathan Buckley
MM: Marianne Majerus, PG: Photolibrary Group
SG: Simon Griffiths, SC: Sarah Cuttle

page 2 PG; 4 JB; 6, 7 JS; 8 (top) JB/design Beth Chatto, (bottom) JB/design Sue & Wol Staines, 9 (top) JB; 9 (bottom), 10, 11 JS; 12 MM; 13 PG; 14, 15, 16 JS; 17, 18, 19 PG; 20, 21, 22, 24 JS; 26 (top left) PG; 26 (step-by-steps), 27 JS; 28 JB; 29, 30 JS; 31 JB; 32, 33 PG; 34, 35 JS; 36 JB; 37 JS; 38 (top left) PG; 38 (step-by-steps), 39, 40 JS; 41 JB/design Christopher Lloyd; 42, 43 JS; 44 (top left) PG; 44 (step-by-steps), 45 (step-by-steps) JS; 45 (top right) MM/design Beth Chatto; 46 (top left) PG; 46 (step-by-steps), 47 JS; 48 (top left) SG; 48 (step-by-steps), 49 JS; 50 JB; 51 PG; 53, 54, 55, 56, 57 JS; 58–59, 60 PG; 61 JS; 62 PG; 64, 65, 66 JS; 67 MM/design George Carter; 68, 69 JS; 70, 71, 72, 73 PG; 74, 75, 76, 77, 78 (top) JS; 78 (bottom) PG; 79, 80, 81 JS; 82 MM; 83, 84, 85, 86 JS; 87 PG; 88 (top) PG; 88 (bottom) MM; 89 PG; 90 (top) JB; 90 (bottom) PG; 91 JS; 92, 93 PG; 94 (top left) MM; 94 (step-by-steps), 95 JS; 96, 97, 98 (top) PG; 98 (bottom) MM; 99 JS; 100 (top) PG; 100 (bottom) MM/design Jilayne Rickards; 101 JS; 102 MM, 103 MM/design Brian Cross (Lakemount Garden, Co. Cork), 104 MM; 105 JS; 106 MM; 107, 108 JS; 109 MM; 110 SC; 111 MM; 112, 113 (top left and centre) JS; 113 (bottom) MM; 114, 115, JS; 116 PG; 117 JS; 118, 119 PG; 120 SC; 121 JS; 122 SC; 123 JS; 124, 125 PG; 126 SC; 127 JS; 128 SC; 129 PG; 130, 131 MM; 132 (left) JS; 132 (right) MM; 133 SC; 134 JS; 136 MM; 138, 139, 140, 141, 142, 143 (step-by-steps) JS; 143 (top right) MM; 144 (top left) JB; 144 (step-by-steps) 145 JS; 146 PG; 147 JS; 148 (top left) PG; 148 (step-by-steps), 149 JS; 150 JB; 151 PG; 152 (top left) JB/design Sue & Wol Staines; 152 (step-by-steps), 153, 154, 155, 156, 157 JS; 158, 159 MM; 160, 161, 162 JS; 163 MM; 164, 165 JS; 166,167 JB; 168 (top left) PG; 168 (step-by-steps), 169, 170, 171, 172 (top left) JS; 172 (bottom) MM; 173 JS; 174, 175 PG; 177 JB/design Christopher Lloyd; 178 PG; 179 SG; 180 JS; 181, 183 (left) SG; 183 (right) JB/design Christopher Lloyd, 184 PG; 185, 186, 187 PG; 189, 190 JB/design Christopher Lloyd; 191 JS; 192 JB/design Christopher Lloyd; 193 SG; 194, 195 PG; 196 SG; 197 JB/design Christopher Lloyd; 198 PG; 200 JB/design Sue & Wol Staines; 201, 202 PG; 204 JB; 205, 206 PG; 207 SG; 208, 209, 210 PG; 211 SG; 212 JB/Hilliers Arboretum; 213 PG; 214 JB/design Alan Gray & Graham Robeson; 216 PG; 217 JB; 218 PG; 219 (left) JB/design Veronica Cross; 219 (right) PG; 220 JB/David & Mavis Seeney; 221 JB; 222 JB/Powis Castle; 225 JB/design Christopher Lloyd, 226 JB/design Paul Kelly; 228 SG; 229 PG; 230 JB/Mhairi Clutson, 231 JB; 233, 235, 236, 238, 239 PG; 240 MM/design Beth Chatto, 241 JB/design Christopher Lloyd; 242 PG; 243 JB/design Christopher Lloyd; 244, 245, 247 PG; 248 JB/design Judy Pearce; 249 PG